D0264849

The Art of Strategic Planning for Information Technology

Second Edition

Bernard H. Boar

Wiley Computer Publishing

John Wiley & Sons, Inc.

NEW YORK · CHICHESTER · WEINHEIM · BRISBANE · SINGAPORE · TORONTO

Publisher: Robert Ipsen
Editor: Theresa Hudson
Developmental Editor: Kathryn A. Malm
Managing Editor: Angela Smith
Text Design & Composition: Publishers' Design and Production Services, Inc.

Designations used by companies to distinguish their products are often claimed as trademarks. In all instances where John Wiley & Sons, Inc., is aware of a claim, the product names appear in initial capital or ALL CAPITAL LETTERS. Readers, however, should contact the appropriate companies for more complete information regarding trademarks and registration.

This book is printed on acid-free paper. ∞

Published by John Wiley & Sons, Inc.

Published simultaneously in Canada.

This publication is designed to provide accurate and authoritative information in regard to the subject matter covered. It is sold with the understanding that the publisher is not engaged in professional services. If professional advice or other expert assistance is required, the services of a competent professional person should be sought.

Library of Congress Cataloging-in-Publication Data:

Boar, Bernard H.
    The art of strategic planning for information technology / Bernard H. Boar. — 2nd ed.
        p.   cm.
    Includes index.
    ISBN 0-471-37655-8 (cloth : alk. paper)
    1. Strategic planning—Data processing.   2. Information technology—Management
Management information systems.   I. Title.
    HD30.28.B63   2001
    658.4′012—dc21   00-063310

Printed in the United States of America.

10 9 8 7 6 5 4 3

Contents

Foreword

The struggle of business has always been and remains the struggle for advantage. Those who build, compound, and sustain competitive advantage win; those who do not, lose. Competition is all about advantage. It really is that simple, yet at the same time, so complicated.

There is much confusion and misunderstanding in the information technology (IT) community. Many do not understand the purpose of the technologies that they deploy daily; they proceed in a fog. They do not understand why the IT industry is a $1.5 trillion-plus worldwide industry growing at over 10 percent per year. Some think the purpose is to "save money," some think it is to "help in making better and faster decisions," and others think it is to simply improve productivity. This understanding is very near-sighted and shallow; they have entirely missed the deeper point.

The purpose of IT is competitiveness. The purpose of IT is to provide a robust resource for the building, compounding, and sustaining of competitive advantage for the enterprise. Cost reduction, expedited decision making, and improved productivity, while of course important, are but specific instances of this greater purpose. In the new millennium, the purpose of IT is to be the foundation of competitive advantage for the business. The purpose of IT is to enable the business to engage in *IT fighting*: the uses of IT as the primary resource and weapon system to build, compound, and sustain competitive advantage.

At RCG Information Technology, we fully understand this mission and collaborate daily with our clients to fulfill this purpose. To compete and succeed, one cannot be confused about the purpose of such a valuable resource. We are in the business of developing, provisioning, operating, and selling competitiveness. Regardless of the industry and the technology set, we understand the critical importance that the superior deployment of IT means to their success, and we position our services to enable the realization of IT-based advantage.

The strategic planning methods presented in this book contribute significantly to our success. By applying concepts such as core competencies, critical success factors, Five Forces, driving force, strategic intent, scenario analysis, benchmarking value chain analysis, and product maps to our strategic planning efforts, we are better able to master the possibilities of technology and position chosen technologies for maximum leverage.

The business model of the new millennium is in significant transition. The "command-and-control" model of management, the "order chain," is dying and being replaced by a team model in which professionals are engaged, enrolled, and challenged to innovate. The resulting business structure more resembles an orchestra of skilled musicians than a traditional hierarchical military command structure.

But even an orchestra needs a score. Strategic plans provide the required score to enable our staff to craft ever more powerful solutions for our customers while maintaining harmony across the multitude of efforts. Agile employees working in an empowered environment require an anchor. The strategic plan provides that point of common reference; "super glue" for direction and purpose.

We are witnessing the emergence of a winner-take-all economy. The distance between the gold and silver and bronze medallist is widening. The rise of the digital enterprise makes the strategic management of IT for competitive advantage an urgent necessity. We all need ways to both understand the ascent of IT in strategic importance and to think and act strategically. Though information technologies over the last two decades have unquestionably gotten cheaper (on a unit cost basis), faster, and more functional, the resulting systems, from a user perspective, have not correspondingly gotten better. This will not suffice. We need better strategy. We must make strategy actionable.

We strongly urge you to study and apply the methods presented in this book. We are confident of continued future success and believe it is neither an accident nor simply good fortune; rather, it is the result of the stimulating, challenging, and exciting insights derived from careful planning. Though not at your command, the future is also not a totally impenetrable mystery. Sun Tzu, the master of strategy, said, "Much strategy prevails over little strategy, so those with no strategy cannot but be defeated." We concur completely; how else could it be? How else could it be in a world of intense IT fighting?

Thomas J. O'Brien

Vincent J. Raineri

Thomas J. O'Brien
Senior Vice President
RCG Information Technology

Vincent J. Raineri
Vice President—Enterprise Solutions
RCG Information Technology

Acknowledgments

The material presented in this book is the culmination of many years of learning, teaching, and participating in the development of information technology (IT) strategy. The contents build on a wide range of generic and IT-specific strategy practices that have been tailored for the IT domain. Much of the value-added in this book comes from integration and relevance—integration in taking individually authored techniques and creating a comprehensive model that "glues" them together in a coherent manner with well-defined interfaces; relevance in adopting the techniques to the nuances and subtleties of the IT planning challenge.

I would like to acknowledge the many people with whom I have participated in strategy work over the years. Whether during my many years at AT&T, NCR, working with consulting clients, or now at RCG Information Technology, I have had the pleasure and privilege to work with many outstanding people. I would like to thank them all for the opportunities that working with them provided to me. I learned as much, if not more than I gave, and had the excitement of working with people with vision, foresight, and commitment

I would like to especially thank Thomas O'Brien, Executive Vice President of RCG Information Technology, and Vincent Raineri, Solutions Vice President of RCG Information Technology. Tom and Vinny provide a uniquely rich environment to teach, learn, and execute strategy. They do more than talk strategy—they live strategy. Their analysis, thinking, and actions flow with strategic acumen. It is a privilege to work with such gifted people. Their mastery of strategy is such that our firm is well prepared to confront and win in the highly dynamic IT marketplace.

I have also included in this book many quotes from classics of strategy: *The Art of War* by Sun Tzu, *The Prince* by Machiavelli, and *Strategy* by B. H. Liddell Hart. I have supplemented these conventional sources with material from unconventional strategy sources such as *The Divine Comedy* by Dante and Greek mythology. Let's be candid; strategy can be a dry subject. I hope that the use of these nontraditional sources to make points and create allusions makes the text more interesting, informative, and, most of all, more instructive. It also demonstrates the important point that great strategy requires renaissance people, lateral thinkers. Insight is transferable between disciplines. The wider the scope of interests and knowledge brought to strategy formulation, the wiser the output.

Strategic learning, from whatever source, yields benefits in two dimensions: the obvious and the subtle. The obvious benefit is to achieve the requisite state of competency to intelligently participate in the strategic planning process. The more interesting and substantive benefit is that it prepares one to transmute presented advice into distinct advantage. To maximize the value of any advice, the one who seeks it must be wiser and shrewder than the one who gives it. Machiavelli explained this paradox as follows:

A prince must always seek advice. He should be a constant questioner, and he must listen patiently to the truth regarding what he has inquired about. Many believe that a prince who gives the impression of being shrewd does so not because he is shrewd by nature but because he has good advice; but this is certainly not so. *A prince who is not himself wise cannot be well advised.* When seeking advice of more than one person, a prince who is not himself wise will never get unanimity in his councils or be able to reconcile their views. Each councilor will consult his own interest; the prince will not know how to correct or understand him. So the conclusion is that good advice, whomever it comes from, depends on the shrewdness of the prince who seeks it (in interpreting it) and not on the shrewdness of the prince on good advice (in seeking it).

The maximum utility of advice is therefore not a function of the raw ideas of the advice giver, but the wisdom of the receiver to interpret, synthesize, build on, integrate, and customize it to his or her deeper and unique appreciation of his or her circumstances. Another can never truly know what you know or the manner in which you know it. Advantage must therefore always spring from within, not from without. Before seeking advice, we must prepare ourselves so that we can process the advice to achieve the highest return. Strategy, like any important and complicated discipline, must be studied and mastered to achieve the desired superior results.

CHAPTER 1

Strategic Planning for Information Technology

The struggle of business, as it always has been and always will be, is the insatiable struggle for advantage. The company with more advantages wins; the one with fewer advantages loses. It is so simple in concept yet so complex in execution. It is exaggerated, but only slightly so, to state that it's *all* about advantage. Advantage is the factor that separates the winners from the losers, the successes from the failures, the acquiring from the acquired, and the survivors from the rest. Those who "get it," "get it" that what they get is the primacy of competitive advantage.

What they also "get" is the realization that, in the hyper-competitive information age, business advantage equates to the superior and novel use of information technology. As illustrated in Figure 1.1, we are witnessing the rise of the digital enterprise wherein companies become part of electronic intermediated value chains. Businesses become digital partners in the new information-age economy. As businesses become members of e-business communities, they are discovering that they express their business strategies increasingly through information technology. Information technology (IT) has emerged as the new conduit for competitive advantage.

Information technology is the asset/capability base on which an enterprise constructs its business information systems. IT may be more rigorously defined as follows:

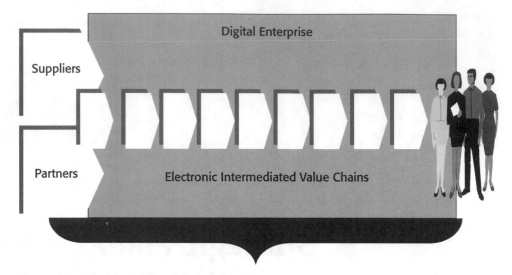

Figure 1.1   The rise of the digital enterprise.

Information technology is the preparation, collection, transport, retrieval, storage, access, presentation, and transformation of information in all its forms (voice, graphics, text, video, and image). Information movement can take place between humans, humans and machines, and/or between machines. Information management ensures the proper selection, deployment, administration, operation, maintenance, and evolution of the IT assets consistent with organizational goals and objectives.

Figure 1.2 illustrates this definition. IT is the relationship (mapping) of information form (text voice, video, image, and graphics) against information function (preparation, processing, storage, and transmission).

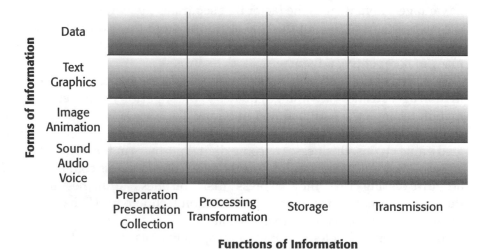

Figure 1.2   The information technology model.

What we are witnessing is the advent of the information age wherein information (digital) technologies do the following:

- Become the critical mechanism to lower costs, compress time to market, provide value-added, and interact with customer and suppliers
- Provide the functionality (software) that is increasingly the actual product that customers receive
- Become increasingly the vehicle of customer satisfaction and value-added innovation
- Become the primary vehicle for creating new advantages and parrying the advantages of competitors

Progressively, more and more of user satisfaction, product functionality, product quality, customer service, image, reputation, and branding are information technology-centric.

Why is this so? Why has information technology become so critically important? To answer these questions, we must understand business models and how information technology drives them. We must comprehend information technology as the information-age source of advantage.

Business Models and Information Technology

In the mid-1980s, I experienced a dramatic change in my career. Up until that time I had worked in various IT jobs such as software developer, project leader, technical group manager, and internal IT consultant. In 1984, however, I was given the assignment of leading a project team to develop an IT strategy for our business unit. Having never developed a formal strategy before, I threw myself into the books and attended subject seminars. I had three immediate reactions to these experiences:

1. "Strategy" was a very broad subject area with an incredible amount of methodologies and practices.
2. There were many conflicting opinions on how to develop and document a strategy.
3. The more I read and learned, the more it became evident that what "strategy," and its derivatives stratagem, strategic, and strategically, actually meant was extremely ambiguous or defined uniquely by each presenter.

As I read and learned more, I came to the conclusion that "strategy" was one of the most abused words in the business lexicon. It was used broadly, implied importance, demanded respect, and gained immediate attention but, at the same time, was left to the reader, audience, or practitioner to figure out exactly what it meant in the situational context. Was strategy a plan, an approach, a tactic, a path, an action, a hypothesis, a move, or a what?

It took time and considerable reflection, but I eventually settled on a definition that I felt comfortable with and that captured the essence of strategy:

> *The eternal struggle of business is the struggle for advantage. The one with more advantages wins; the one with fewer advantages loses. Strategy is the ceaseless pursuit of advantage.*

When someone uses the word strategy, or its derivatives, what he or she is saying to me is that, if we follow the proposal, we will build new advantages, elongate existing advantages, and/or reduce our disadvantages. Strategy is the never-ending quest for advantage, the most cherished asset of any business. The objective of IT strategy was therefore to define a set of actions that would enable the creation of business advantage.

Perhaps I was a bit naive, but I thought I had conquered the meaning of the most used and abused word in business. I was right and wrong at the same time. I was right in that I had developed an insightful meaning, but I was wrong in terms of viewing strategy as the most abused word. Perhaps it was the most abused word of the 1980s and early 1990s, but it has since been dethroned by the phrase "business model."

It is increasingly rare to read an article or attend a seminar today where the phrase "business model" is not mentioned. This is especially true with any discussion of the Internet or e-commerce. The phrase "business model" is now pandered about with more frequency and bullying than strategy achieved at its zenith. Seminar presenters talk about "the importance of an e-business having the right business model" or "how the Web start-up has a new and exciting business model." Industry analysts communicate that "e-commerce will disrupt existing business models" and that "company x has revolutionized its market by virtue of its e-centric business model." The magazine article talks about "company y reinventing itself through its new business model" or "the information age demands new adaptive and e-based business models" or "a new e-business model has disrupted the status quo of a stale industry." The phrase "business model" is everywhere and has surpassed strategy in attention and importance.

We know everything about business models except what they are. They excite, they revolutionize, they dislocate, they disrupt, and they reinvent companies and industries. But what is exactly meant by the phrase?

It is automatically assumed that the reader knows what business models means, in general, and what the presenter means in the immediate context. Nobody asks the question, "What does business model mean?", as it would profess ignorance of the core word of the information-age intelligentsia. One definer said, "A business model is what a business does and how it makes money." Is that enough of a definition, or is there more to it? Just like the word "strategy," don't we need a more insightful understanding of something as important to the Internet age as "business models"?

The remainder of this section will develop a rich definition of what a business model is and how IT enables it. We will show that a business model has many components and that IT is critical to Internet-age business models because IT has become the predominant means through which changes to business models are realized. Business models, going forward, will increasingly be made operational through information technology.

Business Models

A business model is the composite and coordinated answer to four broad questions that distinguish a business:

- What forces are driving the marketplace and industry in which the business is competing?
- How has the business defined itself?
- What are the competitive advantages that enable the business to prevail in a competitive marketplace?
- How does the business make money?

Figure 1.3 illustrates these questions (and their subquestions).

Business Definition

- Who and where are our customers/consumers and what compelling needs do we satisfy?
- What are our distribution channels and why are they the best?
- How do we promote our products/services and touch/service
- What are our products/services and how do we price them?
- How do we leverage our core competencies?
- How does our culture maximize performance?
- How do we optimize our critical processes?
- How do we work with our value chain?
- How are we organized to compete?
- How does our internal economy promote collaboration?

Advantage	SCA	TCA	CDA	Parity
Cost				
Focus				
Differentiation				
Execution				
Knowledge				
Maneuverability				

How do we make money?
- •
- •
- •

Business Drivers
- •
- •
- •

Figure 1.3 Business model.

A business model is the specific combination of answers to these questions, at any given time, that the business selects. There is an infinite set of answers to these questions. The choice of business models is therefore inexhaustible, and business success can be understood as the business that wins is one that has the business model, at a given time, that best meets customer requirements.

Much of the current rage with business models focuses almost exclusively on the impact of the Internet and e-commerce. The "hyped" implication is that they are the only things that change business models. Although they are certainly having a profound impact on business models, they are drivers and means of realization, but not the sole cause of change. Altering the organizational culture or structure, as much as electronic bonding with suppliers or interactively servicing customers over the Web, can equally change a business model. We will now focus our attention on analyzing the attributes of a business model in more detail by answering the four questions that distinguish a business.

Driving Forces in the Marketplace

A business model is a response, an aligned response we hope, to the marketplace. External events, forces, trends, opportunities, movements, new customer requirements, or any other type of change can create asymmetry between an existing business model and the marketplace. Business models relate to market forces in two ways:

- The "as-is" business model should be aligned with a set of prior forces to which the business has responded or future forces it anticipates.

- A "to-be built" business model should be in the process of creation to respond creatively to new and emerging forces.

Business models are always in motion and need to evolve to respond to the marketplace. Figure 1.4 illustrates the time-lapse nature of business models (the numbers on the list that follows correspond to the circled numbers in the figure):

1. There is an "as-is" business model that represents the current combination of decisions under which the company operates and creates value for customers.

2. There is a "vision" business model that represents a long-term strategic intent for the business.

3. In response to new and emergent marketplace forces, a new business model, a "to-be-built" business model, is designed and implemented.

4. With the successful implementation of the "to-be-built" business model, the "as-is" business model becomes an "as-was" business model.

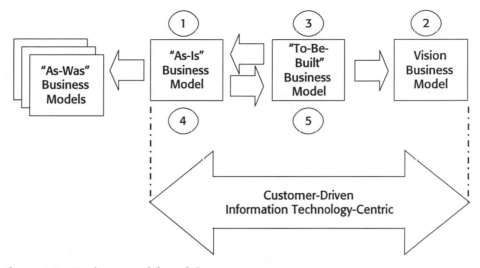

Figure 1.4   Business models and time.

5. With the successful implementation of the "to-be-built" business model, the "to-be-built" business model becomes the "as-is" business model.

This process is continuous and illustrates the constant change to which a business model must adapt.

Some major business drivers that are currently provoking change include the following:

- Globalization of markets
- Information technology in the forms of the Internet, e-commerce, broadband communications, increasing microprocessor power at decreasing costs, convergence of information forms (data, image, sound, and video), and mechatronics (adding intelligence to all kinds of mechanic devices)
- Deregulation of formally monopolized industries
- Decline in market barriers to entry
- Dis-intermediation of traditional marketplace intermediaries and re-intermediation with new electronic intermediates that create market-spaces (electronic marketplaces)
- Dramatic increase in customer power and churn due to commoditization of products and services and customer access to increased competitive information
- Emergence of one-to-one marketing, in which each customer is treated as a distinct market segment

- Intensification of competitive rivalry due to the decline in sustainable competitive advantages and their replacement with temporary competitive advantages

A well-designed and implemented business model can be understood as being a response to some historical and anticipated set of business drivers or a business model in creation in response to new and emergent business drivers.

Business Definition

Major decisions distinguish a business from any other. A business can choose who are its customers, what products and at what price points it will sell them, how it will organize itself, and so forth. The answers to these questions and others *define* the business. Because the answers to the questions are inexhaustible, the definitions of businesses are boundless. The goal, of course, is to define yourself in a manner that is symmetric with business drivers and customer needs.

The key defining questions are as follows:

- Who and where are our customers/consumers, and what compelling needs or wants do we satisfy?
- What are our distribution channels, and why are they the best?
- How do we promote our products/services and touch/service our customers (customer relationship management, or CRM)?
- What are our products/services, and how do we price them?
- How do we exploit technology to our advantage?
- How do we leverage our core competencies?
- How does our culture maximize performance?
- How do we optimize our critical processes?
- How do we work with our value chain (suppliers, partners, regulators, etc.)?
- How are we organized to compete?
- How does our internal business economy promote desired behaviors such as shared objectives and horizontal cooperation between organizational units?

Even though the answers to some of the questions stand on their own merit, most overlap and require synergy between answers and coordinated implementation actions to create a new model. The answers to each question, both individually and in unison, should be thought of as a set of controls with numerous possible settings. How you set and reset the controls, how you tinker with them, defines your business.

Competitive Advantages

A business attracts and retains customers by virtue of its portfolio of advantages. Its advantages define the value proposition that it offers to customers. Although there are endless ways to build advantage, all advantages can be classified into six generic categories:

Cost advantage. Results in being able to provide products/services more cheaply.

Differentiation advantage. Creates a product/service that offers some highly desirable and distinct feature/functionality.

Focus advantage. More tightly meets the explicit needs of a particular customer.

Execution advantage. Permits your operational processes to execute in a superior manner.

Knowledge advantage. The unique knowledge you possess enables you to deliver products and services that excite customers.

Maneuverability advantage. Permits you to adapt to changing requirements more quickly than others. Being maneuverable permits you to constantly refresh the other types of advantage. It is the only advantage that your competitors can never take from you.

Advantage comes in four flavors:

- Sustainable competitive advantage
- Temporary competitive advantage
- Competitive disadvantage
- Competitive parity

What distinguishes them from each other is durability. Having struggled to create a *sustainable advantage*, it will last a long time, be cherished by the organization, be predictable to competitors, and be difficult for competitors to replicate. *Temporary advantages*, as the name implies, are short-lived attractions. They create an advantage for a short period of time and can be rapidly duplicated or surpassed by competitors. *Competitive disadvantages* are advantages that your competitor has over you and, again, can be sustainable or temporary. Finally, *competitive parity* represents critical market issues on which you and your competitors have the same capability.

Two things occur concurrently when you are developing your business model. The advantages you choose, together with the business drivers, scope your business definition. Conversely, advantage emerges from your business definition as pushed by business drivers. Competitive advantage (or disadvantage or parity) is therefore the result of your business definition. By the control setting combination you choose, you create advantage, disadvantage, or parity. The advantage portfolio you choose will ultimately determine your attractiveness to consumers.

Money

The advent of the Internet has created new and novel ways to make profit. In its simplest case, Company X makes money by the difference between what it charges for products and services and the unit costs of offering the product or service. With the Internet, some companies now make money by providing marketplaces where auctions take place at which they get a percent of each sale. Other companies make money by matching perishable inventory with price-conscious consumers. Some companies make money by making a small margin on each item but turning their inventory multiple times per year. Other companies make money by selling products at a loss but selling customer demographics to other companies. Still others make money by providing personal courier services.

How the company makes money is the bottom line of the business model. It must react to business drivers, orchestrate the necessary portfolio of competitive advantages, and prescribe the business definition. In fact, defining a business model is the synergy between how the company makes money, the business definition, and the competitive advantage. They cannot be developed independently or sequentially but need to be interactively melded to derive a winning combination.

If we return to Figure 1.3, we can see that while the term "business model" is used rather loosely in the media, it is the distinctive joining of four things: business drivers, business definition, competitive advantage, and how the company makes money. It is the combination, synergy, and sum of all these control settings, the choices made, that identify the business model. What makes these times so exciting is that the choices are growing, and it is information technology that is expanding the range of choices. More and more, business models equate to the innovative and exploitative use of information technology.

Information Technology and Business Models

In the new millennium, information technology has become strategic because it has become the means to advantage, that is, more and more, changing your business model means the exploitative use of information technology. It is through information technology that advantage is created, the business definition is revised, and/or how money is made. Information technology has become the primary vehicle through which business models express themselves.

In the age of the Internet, to change your business model literally means to change your information systems. Business migrates to the marketspace—a marketplace created, defined, nurtured, and exploited through information technology. The marketspace is a virtual realm where the following occur:

- Products and services exist in digital form and are delivered through information-based distribution channels.

- Speed, innovation, community, interactivity, and personalization are IT-centric.

- Mass customization, one-to-one marketing, and customer participation are derived through information technology. Products and services become information-rich, and information technology becomes the touch point for customer interaction. It is therefore not surprising that the Internet and e-commerce are getting so much media attention. The Internet provides the infrastructure, and e-commerce provides the applications to accomplish all of the preceding goals.

Businesses are learning that in this new era they must engage in "IT fighting" (see Figure 1.5), the use of information technology systems to confront the marketspace. Figure 1.5 should be understood as follows:

- The information age converts the traditional marketplace to the marketspace.

- Hyper-competition converts the marketspace to the battlespace—a fiercely competitive marketspace.

- To compete in the battlespace, the business will need highly maneuverable information systems.

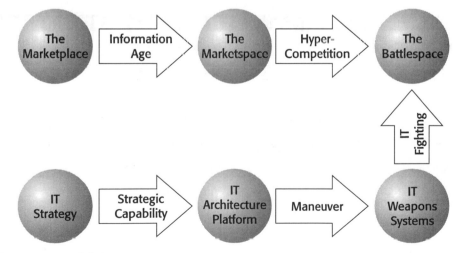

Figure 1.5   IT fighting.

- With information-based weapon systems, the business can engage the battlespace through IT fighting—the use of IT systems to attract/retain customers and deter competitors.

- Information-based IT weapon systems are built on a highly adaptive IT architecture platform.

- The root of your IT architecture, the root of information-age advantage, is built on a foundation of a powerful IT strategy.

As shown in Table 1.1, there is a dramatic change in the nature of advantage that is enabled by IT fighting.

As always, companies win by virtue of advantage. What we are witnessing is the "Dawn of IT Fighting" where advantage will be expressed through the power and agility of information technology. IT is no longer just an expense; it is the vehicle to touch customers, add value to products, parry competitors, and improve productivity. The measure of IT is no longer minimum cost per unit but maximum advantage per unit.

IT has become strategic because superior business models have become IT-centric. IT has become the tool through which the settings of the business model are adjusted. It is exaggerated, but only slightly so, that business models and IT are merging and becoming one. Business models are always a work in progress, and information technology is the brush with which you paint the canvas. In this way, the configurations of response to the marketplace, marketspace, and battlespace become infinite.

Table 1.1   IT Fighting: The Uses of IT Weapon Systems to Build and Sustain Competitive Advantage

INDUSTRIAL-AGE ADVANTAGE	IT FIGHTING ADVANTAGE
Mass production	Mass customization
Mass marketing	One-to-one marketing
Customer research	Customer participation
Optimization of physical value chains	Optimization of information chain
Physical collaboration with suppliers	Information collaboration with suppliers
Excellent customer service	Customer self-service
Physical location	Virtual globalization
Prompt delivery of physical products to door	Online delivery of virtual products
Knowledgeable sales help	Software agents

Hyper-Competition, the Information Age, and Strategic Paradox

The information age migrates the traditional brick-and-mortar marketplace to the virtual marketspace, as shown in Figure 1.5, and a new phenomenon called *hyper-competition* mutates the marketspace to the intensely competitive and cut-throat battlespace. What is hyper-competition? How does it relate to the information age and IT strategy?

As we have asserted, the objective of strategy is to take actions that build, sustain, and compound advantage. Acquiring and retaining customers and parrying competitors are functions of your advantages.

Advantage has three important attributes:

- Persistence
- Size
- Type

Advantage has persistence; the advantages may be sustainable or temporary. Sustainable advantages are durable. Once you have struggled to create them, they deliver something highly valued by the customer and are not readily duplicable by competitors. Temporary advantages deliver value to customers but have a short life span. Competitors find ways to mimic or leapfrog the advantage. Competing through a portfolio of temporary advantages requires the capability to continuously create a stream of overlapping and staggered advantages.

Advantages come in different sizes. Size is the distance between your advantage and your competitor's. The greater the distance, the more compelling is your product to your customers. Advantages can be sustainable but of such small size that they do not hold customers or deter competitors. Advantage is therefore a relative, as opposed to an absolute, concept.

Even though there are limitless ways to build advantage, all advantages can be classified into the six generic types introduced in the previous section: cost, differentiation, execution, focus, knowledge, and maneuverability. Consequently, business strategy must focus on the following:

- Building new advantages that increase customer satisfaction and create distance from competitors
- Maintaining existing advantages that increase customer satisfaction and create distance from competitors
- Compressing or eliminating the advantages of competitors

Creating an ever-evolving portfolio of advantages that mixes the suitable types and sizes of advantage with the appropriate persistence does this. The collage of advantage that a company can create is endless, but it will always be classifiable by the categories of persistence, size, and type.

While creating, compounding, and sustaining advantage have always been a struggle, the struggle is becoming exponentially more arduous. No matter how much diligence and creativity is applied or how hard people work, the advantages that are created seem to disappear without achieving any sustainability. No sooner is an advantage created than it is countered by a crafty competitor. Why is this happening now? Why are executives in industry after industry feeling that creating advantage is becoming an exhausting treadmill? The answer is *hyper-competition*.

Hyper-Competition

Many industries have entered into a state of competition called *hyper-competition*.[1] Hyper-competition is a state of intense and often lethal competition within an industry. It has some very alarming characteristics:

Advantage. It is increasingly difficult, if not impossible, to create and maintain sustainable competitive advantages. The war of advantage migrates to creating an endless stream of overlapping and staggered temporary advantages from trying to defend a set of sustainable advantages.

Innovation. There is rapid and dislocating innovation in the industry. All forms of know-how are subject to rapid devaluation and continually have to be refreshed.

Competitive escalation. Competitors continually raise the ante to play the game. A state of market equilibrium is neither achieved nor desired by winner-takes-all competitors.

Customer power. Customers become extraordinarily demanding and have ever-heightened expectations. These demands are made actionable by effortless substitution between suppliers' products and services.

Value proposition. There is a continuing market redefinition of what is valued by consumers. Competitors constantly search for new combinations of basic products and add-on features that will entice customers.

End of chivalry. There is no respect for the status quo by competitors. Barriers to entry are viewed as challenges to circumvent.

End of customer loyalty. Markets are characterized by excessive churn. Customer loyalty is fleeting and often needs to be bought.

Market disruption as the rule. Competitors take actions to disrupt markets rather than protect markets. The objective of competitive strategy shifts from protecting what one has to taking what one doesn't have. Explicit actions are designed and executed to devalue the opponent's advantages and renew one's own advantages before a competitor decreases the value of your advantages.

Hyper-competition is caused by the concurrence of a number of market factors:

Shift of market power to customers. Customers perceive a wide selection of choices and become accustomed to shopping across multiple alternatives.

Rapid decline in barriers to market entry. Ways are discovered to circumvent barriers to entry by creative and ambitious competitors. With ingenuity, it is often discovered that a seemingly impenetrable barrier to entry can be breached.

Accelerating technology/know-how change. The half-life of competencies is dramatically shortened by rapid innovation. The game of advantage through know-how is constantly restarting, with all the players starting over again.

Rise of multiple deep-pocket players. Multiple companies enter an industry with the financial resources to fight it out. One big company can no longer bully all the others into submission and make them stay in their places.

Deregulation. Government and regulatory authorities disassemble legal barriers to entry. Often, the deregulation not only disbands legal barriers to entry but also aggressively encourages intense competition.

Inability to sustain advantage. The durability of advantages dramatically declines. Dramatic innovation, shifts in technological know-how, and creativity in redefining the product value proposition conspire to reduce the resiliency of any advantage.

Globalization. Time and space barriers to market entry are overcome. Geographic strongholds become easily breached, and foreign competitors can effectively invade markets—often with deep pockets, no respect for the status quo, and rich resources.

Figure 1.6 illustrates the various states of competition that may exist within an industry as a continuum in which hyper-competition is the virulent state of competition that precedes profitless perfect competition. The four anchor states of competition are as follows:

1. **Low competition.** This is a state of competition enjoyed by monopolies. There is little or no competition, and because of the legally endorsed monopoly, the monopolist enjoys almost perfect advantage.

2. **Moderate competition.** There are competitors, but the competitors tacitly cooperate to divide the market pie; they avoid intense rivalry, they

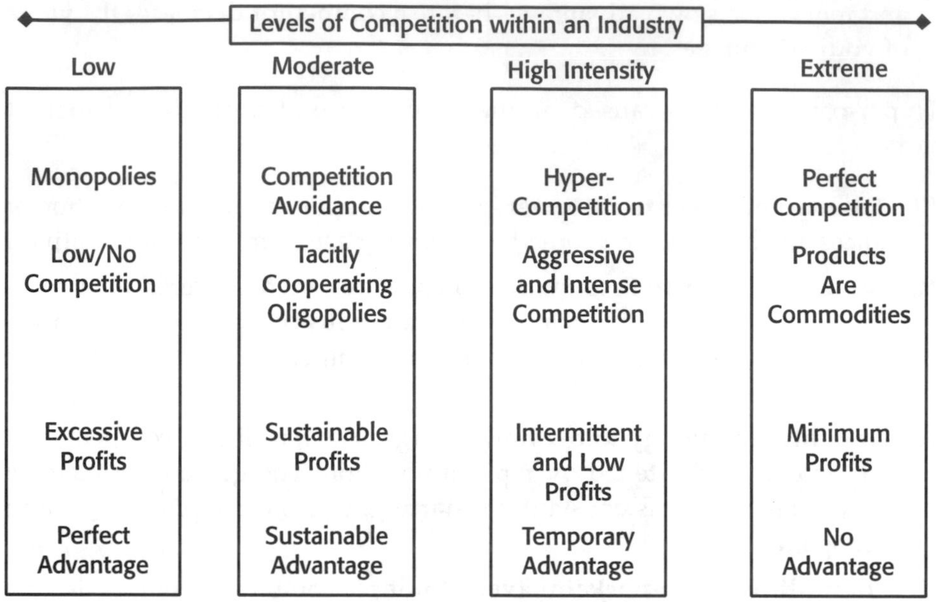

Levels of Competition within an Industry			
Low	Moderate	High Intensity	Extreme
Monopolies	Competition Avoidance	Hyper-Competition	Perfect Competition
Low/No Competition	Tacitly Cooperating Oligopolies	Aggressive and Intense Competition	Products Are Commodities
Excessive Profits	Sustainable Profits	Intermittent and Low Profits	Minimum Profits
Perfect Advantage	Sustainable Advantage	Temporary Advantage	No Advantage

Figure 1.6   Levels of competition within an industry.

avoid direct rivalry, and competition is quite civil. Competitors respect each other's advantages and barriers to entry and tend to defend rather than to attack.

3. **High-intensity competition.** There is aggressive, no-holds-barred, and intensive competition. Rather than defend, competition escalates to a war of movement with each competitor constantly moving to improve its competitive position. Advantages are not sustainable, and successful competitors become competent at creating and managing an endless stream of short-lived advantages.

4. **Extreme competition.** Products and services are completely commoditized. Attempts at differentiation are instantly matched by the competition. There is little advantage, and consumers enjoy ultimate *value*, that is, the absolute maximum product at the absolute minimum cost.

One of the most important points to take away from Figure 1.6 is the change in the nature of advantage in each state. Most of us, who have spent their careers in stable states of moderate competition, understand strategy as the creation and maintenance of sustainable advantage. As highlighted in Figure 1.7, the mode of advantage dramatically shifts in a hyper-competitive environment from sustainable advantage to temporary advantage.

This shift occurs for all the reasons we have previously discussed and means that the tools that are used to build advantage must be designed to enable speed, flexibility, the elimination of friction, and agility. What matters most are not your current advantages, which are rapidly aging, but your advantages

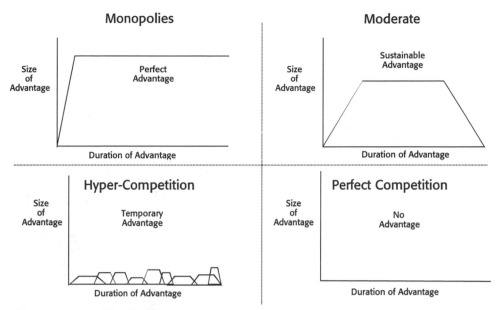

Figure 1.7   Models of advantage.

that are on the drawing boards and that will replace them. What matters most is not preserving what is but creating very rapidly what will be, and doing this over and over again.

Hyper-competition destroys sustainable competitive advantage (SCA). As shown in Figure 1.8, sustainable competitive advantage can be understood as

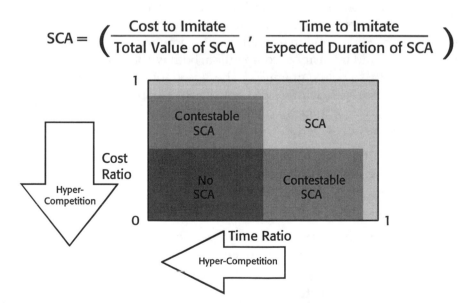

Figure 1.8   Hyper-competition destroys sustainable competitive advantage.

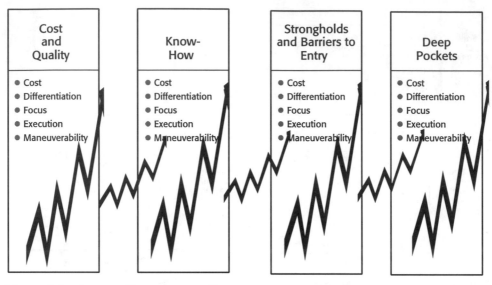

Figure 1.9 Arenas of hyper-competition.

a function of the variables of time and cost. The longer it takes to replicate an advantage or the more money it costs to replicate an advantage, the more sustainable is the advantage. By its nature, hyper-competition either reduces the time and cost of replicating an advantage or permits bypassing an advantage altogether. Consequently, advantages are not sustainable, and competition shifts to creating a stream of overlapping temporary advantages.

Hyper-competition takes place in four primary arenas of competition (see Figure 1.9). While competition takes place within these same arenas within a state of moderate competition as well, what is important to appreciate is the rapid escalation and intensity of competition, both within and between arenas, that occurs with hyper-competition. The speed of competitive interaction increases and escalates within an arena, and as opportunities depreciate within an arena, competitors rapidly jump to other arenas to continue the fray.

The four arenas of competition are these:

Cost and quality. Competition focuses on the price and value proposition mix to be presented to the customer.

Know-how. Competition focuses on competencies and creating the skills that are required to create future value for the customer.

Strongholds and barriers to entry. Competition focuses on creating advantages that block competitors from entering the market.

Deep pockets. Competition focuses on the use of financial resources to fund and endure the competitive war.

Ultimately, competitors have no choice but to become hyper-competitive or to exit the marketplace. Either you learn to compete as a hyper-competitor, or those who have leave you behind in the marketplace. You are left behind because the hyper-competitors keep redefining value for the customer. This makes your stable value proposition a dated artifact.

Hyper-competitors demonstrate very aggressive market behaviors. Typical hyper-competitive behaviors are as follows:

- A hyper-competitor quickly and purposely brings assets to a chosen point of opportunity that offers disproportionate returns for the effort.

- Hyper-competitors create menaces for their opponents. They make their opponents turn their attention from their planned agenda to the hyper-competitor's agenda.

- The hyper-competitor creates friction for the opponent. It destabilizes the opponent's business by making it respond to the hyper-competitor and, in so doing, forces the opponent to alter plans, processes, initiatives, and alliances.

- The hyper-competitor continually raises the tempo and occurrences of the marketplace maneuvers in all the arenas of competition. Unable to respond and being confronted with an increasingly deteriorating situation, the opponent's internal processes begin to collapse under the strain and stress of rapid and unpredictable change.

- The hyper-competitor deliberately creates imbalances and destabilizes the market. There is no respect for the status quo.

- The hyper-competitor wins by being the marketplace puppeteer. It creates a dynamic set of actions, built on opportunism, to excite customers.

- The hyper-competitor continually redefines the value proposition offered to the customer. By aggressive redefinition of value propositions, established and long-standing competitor advantages are devalued.

- The hyper-competitor shows no respect for the competitors' advantages. It views every advantage as having an innate disadvantage component.

- The hyper-competitor robs opponents of the ability to make choices. If it can keep them busy chasing it, they don't have time or energy to develop plans of their own making.

- The hyper-competitor improvises to take advantage of opportunistic situations as they unfold. Opportunities emerge, as opposed to being planned.

- The hyper-competitor lures opponents out of their strongholds to fight on more favorable turf. This nullifies stronghold and barrier-to-entry advantages.

- The hyper-competitor is an experimenter. It tests opponents to learn where they are strong and where they are weak.

- The hyper-competitor uses deception, speed, and surprise to paralyze opponents into inaction. Shocked and numbed by the speed and surprise of the hyper-competitor's actions, the hyper-competitor gets a long grace period before the opponent regroups and mounts a counter-offensive to its actions.

- The hyper-competitor competes against time. Through rapid innovation, the hyper-competitor contracts the anticipated duration of return that competitors expected on their advantages and mangles their business model.

- The hyper-competitor focuses on satisfying the customer while its makes its opponents focus on the hyper-competitor.

The competitive attitude of a hyper-competitor is best captured in the classical dictum of Sun Tzu to "Go forth where they do not expect it, attack where they are unprepared."[2]

Hyper-competitors see competition as a war of movement where market success goes to those who can move with purpose and alacrity. Even when wrong, speed and dexterity permit rapid corrections. As illustrated in Figure 1.10, the battle shifts from a slow industrial-age war of attrition to an information-age war of disruption and maneuver. One cannot make peace with a hyper-competitor that wants it all and doesn't accept peaceful coexistence.

Examples of Hyper-Competitive Markets

If hyper-competition is a framework for understanding and analyzing dynamic competitive markets, then there is no shortage of proof-of-concept case studies. A marketplace would be considered hyper-competitive if only three or four of the drivers were present. In many industries, all of the drivers are present, and their intensity is increasing daily. Table 1.2 provides a succinct list of marketplace actions classified according to their hyper-competitive drivers and arenas of competition.

All industries are built on fundamental assumptions. As long as these assumptions hold, the players can continue business as usual. When the assumptions become obsolete, the result is a period of chaos and change until, and if, a new order is established. The modern telecommunications industry, for example, was built on four critical assumptions:

1. The infrastructure is scare and expensive and can therefore be rationed to offer premium services.

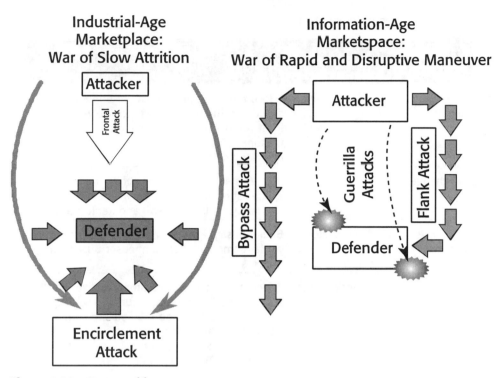

Figure 1.10 From attrition to maneuver.

2. The network will carry primarily voice traffic.
3. Circuit switch calling is the technology of choice.
4. The Telephone Company is in control.[3]

All of these assumptions are now under attack, becoming obsolete, and creating fertile ground for hyper-competition. The collapse of assumptions that guaranteed stability is also occurring in other industries and contributing to emerging hyper-competition. The Internet is disrupting traditional sales, marketing, product delivery, and service in innumerable industries because, for the first time, mass markets can be directly addressable on an individual basis and digital products permit mass customization.

How does a company formulate strategy in a hyper-competitive market? What do you do when confronted with competitors who don't play nicely? What do you do when confronted with the end of sustainable advantage? Surprisingly, at least part of the answer to how you formulate winning strategies in hyper-competitive markets is rooted in paradox.

Table 1.2   Examples of Hyper-Competition

HYPER-COMPETITION DRIVER	AREA OF COMPETITION	EXAMPLE
Shift of marketplace power to customer	Cost and quality	Telecommunications industry: Bundled services including long distance, cellular, local, Internet access, paging, messaging, personal 800 service, security, and direct broadcast satellite
Technological change	Know-how	Real estate industry: Competing Internet real estate listing and referral services such as HomeAdvisor by Microsoft and Realtor.com
Shift of marketplace power to customer	Cost and quality	Beer industry: Price, advertising, and promotion warfare among Miller, Annheuser Busch, and Coors
Globalization	Deep pockets	Telecommunications industry: Effective 1/1/98, World Trade Organization countries no longer have to prove that their markets are competitive before they can offer services in the United States. This opens U.S. market for NTT, France Telecom, Royal Dutch PTT, British Telecomm, etc.
Shift of marketplace power to customer	Cost and quality	Travel reservations: Dis-intermediation of traditional travel brokers through electronic services
Decline in barriers to entry	Strongholds and barriers to entry	Banking industry: Online brokers such as Ameritrade, E*Trade, Schwab, and Fidelity are offering banking services such as credit cards, mortgage applications, and insurance
Deep-pocketed players	Deep pockets	Soft drink industry: Commercials that go for the jugular and court cases by Pepsi against Coke in asserting that Coke is illegally freezing it out of selling to independent food distributors
Shift of marketplace power to customer	Cost and quality	Telecommunciations industry: Customers have numerous and easily substitutable options: long distance picked carrier, prepaid cards, dial-around access, 800 access
Deregulation	Strongholds and barriers to entry	Electric power industry: Creation of chaotic wholesale electricity exchange markets
Technological change	Know-how	Traditional brokerage industry: Discount electronic brokerages and Web-based information services challenging traditional brokerage suppliers
Shift of marketplace power to customer	Cost and quality	Pharmaceutical industry: Advent of life-style-enhancing drugs such as Viagra

Strategic Paradox

In conducting our daily lives, purposeful opposition to our routine efforts does not exist. No one has the explicit goal to deliberately thwart our actions. We use what is called linear logic to solve our problems. Linear logic consists of using common sense, deductive/inductive reasoning, and concern for economies of time, cost, and effort to solve problems. One is routinely criticized for taking a circuitous route when a more direct one is available. Daily life applauds the logical, the economic, and the rich application of common sense.

Hyper-competitive business strategy, to the contrary, is executed against a background of intense conflict and intelligent counter-measures. Able and motivated competitors, purposefully and energetically, attempt to foil your ambition. Because of this excessive state of conflict, many strategic actions demonstrate a surprising and counter-intuitive paradoxical logic.

Two types of strategic paradox[4] are routinely encountered in hyper-competitive business situations:

Coming together of opposites. A linear logic action or state evolves into a reversal of itself ("A" becomes "not A") or "you can have too much of a good thing." An example of this is that an advantage, unrefreshed, becomes a disadvantage. This paradox occurs because conflict causes an inevitable reversal due to the complacency of the winner and the hunger of the loser. While the current winners gloat in their success, this same success lulls them into a false sense of permanent security while it paradoxically stimulates the current losers to tax their ingenuity to overcome it.

Reversal of opposites. To accomplish your objectives, do the reverse of what linear logic would dictate. So, "If you wish peace, prepare for war," to accomplish "A," do the set of actions to accomplish "not A," or your primary competitor should be yourself. This occurs because the nature of conflict reverses normal linear logic. While taking a long, dangerous, and circuitous route is bad logic under daily circumstances, in a state of conflict (i.e., war), this bad logic is good logic exactly because it is bad logic (it is less likely to be defended). The logic of conflict is often in total opposition to the logic of daily life. Conflict causes strategic paradox to occur, bad logic becomes good logic, exactly because it is bad logic, and the able strategist must learn to think and act paradoxically. Paradoxically, IT strategists often have to recommend, to an unbelieving and astonished audience, that they should take actions that are directly contrary to routine business sense.

An example of reversal-of-opposites thinking is illustrated by the *Kano Methodology*. The Kano Methodology is an analytical method used to stimulate

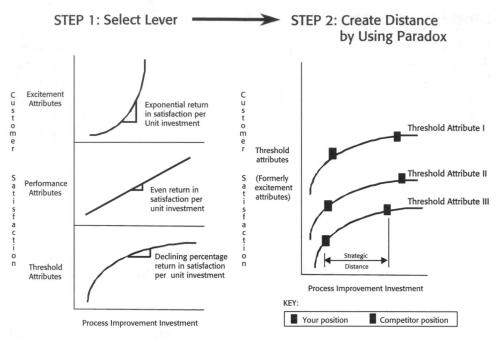

Figure 1.11 Kano Methodology.

strategic thinking. As illustrated in Figure 1.11, the logic of Kano suggests that candidate strategic actions be divided into three types:

Threshold actions. For every dollar invested in this type of action, customer satisfaction increases but gradually reaches a point where less than a dollar of satisfaction is achieved for each dollar of investment. It therefore doesn't make sense to invest beyond the break-even point.

Performance actions. For every dollar invested in this type of action, there is a constant positive increase in customer satisfaction in excess of your investment. It pays to continue to invest in these actions.

Excitement actions. For every additional dollar invested in this type of action, there is an exponential increase in customer satisfaction. These are prized actions and are the best actions to invest in.

Although this is solid linear thinking, the true brilliance of the methodology occurs next through paradoxical thinking. What is suggested is that after one has developed the excitement capability, it should be presented to the customer as a threshold attribute, that is, paradoxically, the truly exceptional is most exceptional when it is the ordinary. What this does is position your capability as the minimum ante to play the game. A customer may be willing to forgo the exceptional, but every customer will minimally expect and demand the ordinary. Because you can do it and your competitors can't, you create strategic distance between yourself and your competitors. While they struggle to do the exceptional as the norm, you raise the tempo of the game and work on converting another excitement attribute to threshold status and ad infinitum. The great insight of the Kano Methodology is not the linear thinking of threshold to performance to excitement attributes, but the recognition that maximum value and market disruption occur when excitement capabilities are presented, paradoxically, as the ordinary (reversal of opposites).

This kind of thinking is common among hyper-competitors. Hyper-competitors act as their own worse competitors. They replace their own advantages before their competitors can. They understand that when they position an excitement attribute as a threshold attribute they totally disrupt the status quo. With one sweeping move, they turn their opponent's threshold and performance attributes into dissatisfier attributes and radically redefine value in the marketplace.

Most important and paradoxical of all, however, is their view of a competitor's advantages. While traditional strategy and common sense tell you to avoid strength, paradoxical logic teaches that "a competitor's greatest weakness lies in its greatest strength." By understanding its strengths, you understand what it will defend, leverage, and not discard under any circumstances. When the hyper-competitor develops a superior alternative, it is safe from being copied because the opponent is committed to what has made it great rather than what will make it great. As the opponent lovingly hold onto its advantage, the hyper-competitor, with immunity, changes the rules of the game and develops a superior alternative. In the ultimate paradox, the hyper-competitor is able to engage in strategic judo and turn the opponent's great strength into an even greater weakness.

Strategic paradox also explains the often difficult-to-accept logic of replacing sustainable advantages with temporary advantages. Hyper-turbulent conflict results in the following self-contradiction: The most sustainable advantage is a series of overlapping, staggered, and contemporaneous temporary advantages. Hyper-competition causes paradox to apply to advantage, and the phenomena of reversal of opposites causes sustainable and temporary advantages to dramatically swap roles. The ability to create a ceaseless stream of temporary advantages becomes sustainable advantage, and classic sustainable advantage becomes reversed into temporary advantage (it cannot be sustained). As initially difficult as this is to accept, it is perfect strategic logic under the framework of strategic paradox.

An analogy can be helpful in making you feel comfortable with accepting the uncommon sense of strategic paradox as a means to successful strategy formulation in hyper-competitive markets. In Einstein's famous theory of relativity, objects behave as we all expect and have experienced, as long as the objects move at velocities that are small compared to the speed of light. As an object's velocity approaches the speed of light, however, weird and bizarre things, in complete contradiction to our normal experiences, happen. For example, as an object approaches the speed of light from the frame of reference of the viewer to the object, the following happen:

- The object shrinks in length.
- The mass of the object increases.
- Time dilates and slows down.

The values of these variables, to our logical disbelief and astonishment, are not constant but a function of frame of reference and speed. While this clashes with common sense and our normal logical reasoning, it is the scientific accepted theory of motion at speed-of-light velocities.

The same would seem to be true with regard to linear logic and strategy formulation. What is logical or illogical is not a constant but a function, not of speed, but of intensity of marketplace conflict. Because in our daily lives we routinely experience mild conflict, if any, the common-sense rules of linear logic hold, and we act with conventional rationality. In intense conflict situations—for example, hyper-competitive environments—however, the rules of logic change and become seemingly bizarre.

Logical behavior is therefore a function of intensity of conflict. Logical actions are to conflict as behaviors of objects in motion are to speed. Though our common sense fails us, it fails us only because our normal personal and business experiences have been in the low-intensity portion of the conflict experience curve. Objects moving near the speed of light do not really act bizarrely; they act exactly as they should at that speed. Similarly, strategic paradox is not really paradox at all. In intense conflict, the nonconflict common-sense illogical is the high-conflict logical. So the strategic reversal of opposite paradox of "position your excitement attributes as threshold attributes" is not a paradox at all. It is the correct linear logic for the domain of high-intensity hyper-competitive environments.

The Information Age and Strategic Paradox

The dramatic changes in information technology over the last decade have been some of the primary drivers of hyper-competition (technology change) and have led to the labeling of our era as the "information age." The information age is proving itself to be a period of extraordinarily intense competition. New forms of information technology have led to the collapse of traditional industrial-age barriers to entry such as economies of scale, access to distribution systems, mass advertising, location, and competency access. The nature of digital products enables mass customization and micro-marketing, while the ability to perform comparative shopping electronically drives prices to commodity levels. Suddenly, everything becomes a generic product.

Consumers, for the first time in history, can have almost perfect knowledge of what is being offered, at what price, and with what value proposition. The result is the creation of a highly competitive and swift marketspace that prizes speed, nimbleness, aggressiveness, entrepreneurship, and niching—a marketspace that rewards maneuver as opposed to attrition fighters. It is therefore not surprising that companies that compete in the marketspace will be subject to strategic paradox (due to the hyper-competition). Information-age companies will have to clearly understand the paradoxes of the information age, deduce their implications, and adapt to them appropriately. The business logic of the more staid industrial age will not suffice in the extremely cut-throat information age.

This chaotic information-age environment will result in a shift to the nurturing of temporary competitive advantages at the expense and decline of sustainable competitive advantages. Rather than making huge investments, with the associated risk of imitation, and expecting to create an advantage that provides extended benefits, companies will covet styles and systems that enable the rapid creation of sequential and overlapping temporary advantages. Companies will prize speed, surprise, opportunism, niching, prototyping, and modularity to enable dynamic reusability. The tempo of competition will accelerate as there are no longer any safe fortresses and the marketspace becomes an ever more frenzied war of movement.

Given this unruly, competitive, and combative environment, the aware strategist must be sensitive to the following five information-age strategic paradoxes and take them into account in formulating how to engage the battlespace. The first four paradoxes occur at the information-age level. The last one is a paradox specific to IT.

> **Information-age strategic paradox I.** As the world get smaller, small companies get bigger and big companies get smaller.
>
> *Explanation:* As products and services become digitized and the primary distribution channels shift to electronic commerce, the world shrinks and many industrial-age advantages of large companies erode. Small companies have access to the same consumer reach technologies and value chain enhancement technologies as large companies but, in addition, often have the advantage of being nonbureaucratic, nimble, fast, specific customer (market fragment) focused, and entrepreneurial. Everyone, large or small, shares the same storefront location in cyberspace. The competitive playing field is leveled by broad availability of convergent technologies and the ability to precisely choose whom to serve and how to serve them. As traditional time and space constraints on markets are dislodged by global electronic markets, large companies find themselves confronting

thousands of small companies fighting for every niche who exploit one-to-one marketing and customized services to overcome the large companies' mass advertising and scale advantages. Of course, a little niching here and a little niching there and before you know it, there is nothing left.

Information-age strategic paradox II. To create advantage, you must quickly destroy your advantages.

Explanation: The strategic paradox of the coming together of opposites is at work here. In a world of hyper-competition, it is better to eat your young than have others do it. The pace of information-age change will rapidly convert advantages into disadvantages. It will be necessary to ride learning curves and continually roll out new temporary advantages even though they destroy your own incumbent temporary advantages. What you may expect to see, paradoxically, is companies announcing new releases and features of products that appear to make their own products prematurely obsolete for no apparent reason. Quite the opposite, however, is what is really happening. What they are doing is not permitting the coming together of opposites to occur. An advantage terminated before its time is much better than an advantage held on to beyond its utility. Because nobody can control the marketplace nor have intimate knowledge of competitor plans and announcements, the result is to err, of necessity, on the side of rapid self-obsolescence.

Information-age strategic paradox III. To make money, you don't need money.

Explanation: The greatest barrier to entry of all industrial-age barriers to entry was the scarcity and cost of capital. This resulted in the common maxim: To make money, you need money. The basis of wealth in the industrial age was capital (land and labor). In the information age, the basis of wealth is ideas. The wide availability of global electronic markets makes it relatively inexpensive to start a business and gradually scale it as it grows. So smarts, not capital, will drive who makes money. More than in other eras, the information age will reward entrepreneurship, risk taking, and foresight.

Information-age strategic paradox IV. To remain innovative, don't listen to your customers too carefully.

Explanation: Established customers have huge financial, skills, and emotional investments in existing technologies. They most often state new requirements only in terms of the evolutionary development of those technologies. Current customers tend to want to sustain investments in existing technologies rather than underwrite research and experimentation in innovative but disruptive technologies that date their own skills and investments. As a consequence, if you listen and follow your customers' requirements too closely, you will meet their stated needs through incremental improvements to what is while starving research and development in innovative technologies that will eventually substitute for them. Paradoxically, when entrepreneurial companies, unbounded by these customers, do innovate, your conservative customers, who limited your fields of investment, will abandon you for the superior and now demonstrable substitute.

Information-age strategic paradox V. To use IT efficiently, you must use it in excess.

Explanation: The most striking strategic paradox of IT in the information age is that the cost-concerned IT strategist does not seek to use just enough means but an excess of means to accomplish his or her ends. "Excess" means more than analytically justified by circumstances; it does not mean, however, wasteful or prodigious. IT achieves, paradoxically, its greatest value for the business when it is used in excess.

It is typical to observe project teams engage in extensive and exhaustive cost-justification exercises (net present value, return on investment, cost/benefit justification, pay-back period, etc.) to convince cost-conscious decision makers to approve each IT expenditure. Their actions are understandable with linear logic but are inappropriate because of the reversal of opposites. When the battle shifts to information-age hyper-competitive environments, IT becomes subject to strategic paradox and must be managed as such to achieve optimum results.

Consider a military commander who needs to engage his enemy. If he uses linear logic and deploys just enough resources, he will win but it will be an expensive (Pyrrhic) victory. If he applies a force far in excess of his opponent, he will achieve his ends with minor causalities. All the downstream costs of battle will be avoided (damaged weapons, confusion, wounded/killed soldiers, etc.) At the point of conflict, the efficient commander does not seek to use just enough, but applies means far in excess of the opponent. The commander does not use accounting logic that holds in nonconflict situations but applies paradoxical logic that rules at the point of battle.

Unquestionably, it is easier to accept this paradox with regard to the military situation than IT. This is because of the differences in the two situations between cause and effect. In the military situation, the cause and effect are tightly coupled in time and space. One can immediately see the results of the excess and correlate the success to that excess. With IT, the cause and effect are often dispersed across wide gaps of time and space. The use of excess IT will have the desired effect, but it may occur perhaps months later at a remote branch office. While it stretches and strains your business common sense, I believe that strategic paradox is an important dimension of the spirit of exploiting IT. Ultimately, experience will prove that those who use it in excess will achieve greater benefits than those who attempt to rigorously cost-justify, exactly parcel it out, or horde its deployment. They will learn that their approach is mathematically correct but strategically sterile. The logic of success in the hyper-competitive information age is the logic of a warrior; not an accountant.

A Remarkable Challenge

It would therefore seem that IT strategists are confronted with a remarkable challenge. They will not only have to think paradoxically and formulate actions in opposition to their normal thought processes, they will also have to convince an astounded and unbelieving management team that a seemingly paradoxical action is the right thing to do. Strategic performance will become a function of actions that most will view as not even good nonsense. What will drive strategic success will be the illogical.

Hyper-competition challenges conventional strategic thinking to renew itself. Paradoxical thinking is an intimate and fascinating part of that renewal. Paradoxical actions are perhaps the ultimate hyper-competitive behavior. As they lead you to success, your competitors will not only have their business plans disrupted by them but, constrained by conventional logical thinking, they will be unable to grasp the deeper rationale of your actions. This will serve only to further your window of opportunity as they respond inappropriately with conventional thinking. Their seemingly logical actions will ruin their strategic performance, and your seemingly illogical actions will enrich yours.

How well management teams accept and adopt the logic of paradox might well make the difference as hyper-competitive environments accelerate in intensity and conventional strategy formulation methods collapse under the demands of the hyper-competitive portion of the conflict curve. The root of all strategic performance, as always, originates in deep and far-reaching strategic thinking; in hyper-competitive markets, the laws of strategic paradox will increasingly curve and guide our actions. What we will learn is that in such hyper-competitive markets, the long way home is often the shortest.

Strategic Thinking

Strategic actions, linear or paradoxical, are the progeny of strategic thinking. Strategic thinking is quite different than the daily thinking that governs our routine lives. Figure 1.12 illustrates the three dimensions of strategic thinking:

Time. Strategists think across time. They think about a problem from the perspectives of the past, the present, and the future.

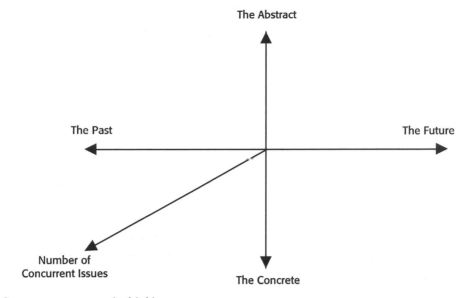

Figure 1.12   Strategic thinking.

Substance. Strategists think about problems in turns of both their concrete and their abstract natures.

Cardinality. Strategists think about multiple issues concurrently. Synthesis, not analytical decomposition, lies at the heart of strategic thinking

Most of the time, most of us, as illustrated in Figure 1.13, engage in mundane thinking to solve our daily problems. All we need to do to meet our needs is to think about one issue at a time, in the present, and in the concrete. Anything more sophisticated would be overkill. This thinking pattern that we use to solve our daily problems is also referred to as *point thinking* because all our problem-solving efforts converge on one point.

Figure 1.14 illustrates the strategic thinking bubble. A strategist uses the same dimensions as the mundane thinker but thinks dynamically within the thought bubble defined by those three dimensions. A strategist concurrently thinks about many issues in multiple dimensions at many levels of abstraction and detail over time (past, present, and future). Strategic thinking is a creative and dynamic synthesis, which is the exact opposite of point thinking.

Synthesis as opposed to analytical decomposition is a particularly critical part of strategic thinking. When you examine things in artificial isolation from their natural linkages, you lose the dynamics of the big picture. You simplify and hide from the complexity of the real-world relationships. Having lost the linkages by virtue of your analytical decomposition, it is often impossible to reintegrate them until implementation problems surface. Synthesis permits you to discover the whole that is greater than the sum of the parts.

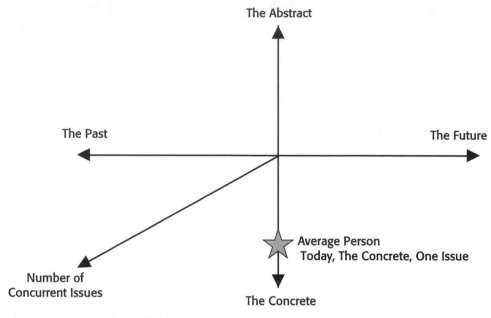

Figure 1.13 Mundane thinking.

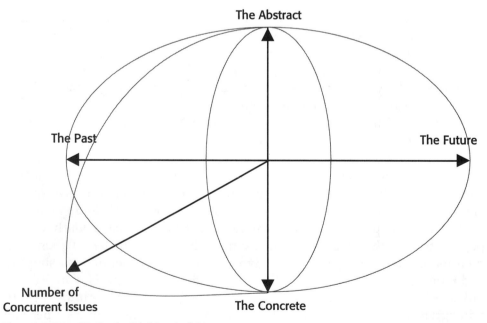

Figure 1.14 Strategic thinking bubble.

When an IT strategist looks at a problem, he or she will often think about it in terms of strategic ideas or themes. While new perspectives can always be developed, time and experience have demonstrated the power of looking at problems through certain enduring and tested strategic lenses. The following are a partial and representative list of powerful strategic ideas that are particularly relevant to strategic thinking for hyper-competitive markets:

Indirection. Opponents should not be confronted directly. The maximum gain at the minimum expense is achieved by deception, surprise, and chipping away at the edges of the opponent. Exhaust them before you confront them.

Speed. All matters require speed. Speed alone can compensate for numerous other shortcomings.

Strategic conflict. The opponent is to be contested strategically. Attack and ruin its strategy, do not engage its advantages.

Prescience. The leadership must have deep and far-reaching foresight. Leaders must see and know what others do not. The height of prescience is to see the formless and act on it.

Formlessness. The architecture of your advantages must be inscrutable. In this way, opponents do not know against what to attack and against what to defend.

Positioning. Forces must be preplaced in winning positions by design. In this way, the actual confrontation is anti-climactic as you have already won by your superior positions.

Commitment. All must share the same commitment to the objectives. Forces that do not share the same aims will lack the will and resolve to overcome the endless barriers to victory.

Maneuver. Maneuver means finding the best way to go. Forces must be able to maneuver to exploit gaps.

Coordination. The problem of coordination is the problem of managing the many as though they were one. The few can defeat the many if they act with one purpose. When perfect coordination is achieved, one cannot distinguish the will of the individual from the will of the many nor the will of the many from the will of the individual.

Psychological conflict. Victory and defeat first occur in the mind. Defeat your opponents psychologically so that even if they are intact, they lack the will to contest you.

Foreknowledge. All matters require competitive intelligence. Nothing is more important than understanding the plans of your opponents and the needs of your customers.

Learning. One must continually learn and adapt based on that learning. All progress includes making mistakes, but the same mistakes should not be made twice.

Surprise. To surprise means to do the unexpected. Surprise results in a positive reaction by customers and confusion and disorder by competitors.

Disruption. You must take actions that not only lead to your end but concurrently create friction and difficulties for your competitors. An excellent strategic action both creates new value for the customer and dislocates the value proposition of the competitors.

Asymmetric response. Matching what a competitor has done achieves parity and results in an exhausting war of attrition. The idea is different and better—not cheaper, faster, and the same.

Initiative. Commanding the initiative means taking actions before any others and defining the game. The one who commands the initiative controls the tempo and directions of the competition.

Friction. Friction is the counter-force that resists acting. Take actions that reduce your own friction and those of your customers and increase the friction of your competitors.

A strategic thinker does the following:

- Chooses a problem (or set of problems).
- Samples strategic ideas (singularly and simultaneously).
- Thinks about solving the problem(s) by applying the strategic ideas within the Figure 1.14 bubble. This demands intuitive, holistic, dynamic, and abstract thinking. It demands being able to synthesize as opposed to uni-dimensional analytical decomposition.

Because the combinations of strategic ideas are inexhaustible, strategic thinking is a very powerful way to develop insight about problems and solve them in novel, unanticipated, and creative ways. It is from this kind of thinking that advantage is born and nourished. For hyper-competitive markets, one must be able to think strategically about IT as a matter of course.

Information Technology Strategy Methodology

Against this background, it is urgent that IT organizations elevate their skills for building and executing a commanding IT strategy. IT strategy is no longer optional. It is the very ground of business survival. It is important to understand the notions of strategy, master the techniques and tools of the discipline, follow a structured methodology, and carefully manage its execution.

The IT strategic planning process (see Figure 1.15) provides an ordered set of steps designed to culminate in the development and execution of a comprehensive IT strategic business plan. The process is performed as follows:

- *Assessment* is the activity of developing a clear and thorough understanding of the business situation from both an internal and external perspective. Assessment culminates in the identification of "conclusions" that pinpoint critical issues requiring strategic attention. Two major substeps, positioning and situational analysis, are used to generate conclusions. *Positioning* provides a graphical way to understand the "position" or state of information technology in all relevant strategic areas (i.e., IT architecture, customer satisfaction, core competencies, etc.). *Situational analysis* is the use of various analytical methods to interpret the data about the organization and its environment. Assessment is both a data-intensive and analysis-intensive activity.

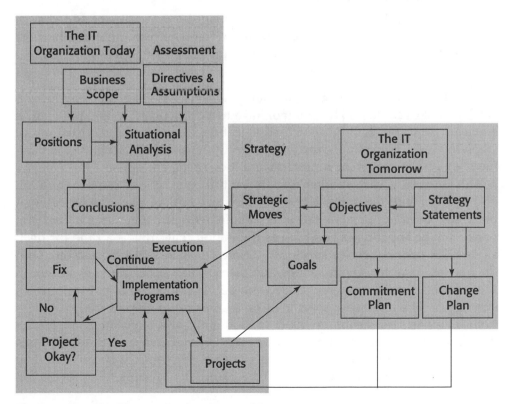

Figure 1.15   The IT strategic planning model.

- *Strategy* consists of identifying strategy statements for the business, the specific objectives to be achieved, and the strategic moves needed to realize the future state and objectives. *Objectives* are descriptive of what we wish to achieve. *Strategic moves* are prescriptive, identifying the actions to be undertaken. To support the realization of the objectives, a commitment plan to focus organizational attention on the objectives and a change management plan to anticipate and reduce resistance to change are also developed.

- *Execution* is the action of putting the plan into motion. It is the translation of intent into reality. Strategies are made operational through implementation programs that are partitioned into multiple projects. Projects achieve objectives and interim objectives called *goals*. A process monitoring and control step is used to do the following:

  - Adjust and tune the projects
  - Provide learning feedback from the project experiences
  - Observe the ever-changing environment for additional situations requiring strategic response

  Success of the execution step depends on the commitment and change management plans designed in the strategy step to minimize barriers and obstacles and ensure persistence in response to often-fleeting management attention.

Throughout the entire process, quality control actions are interwoven to catch mistakes as close to the point of introduction as possible, and procedural steps are undertaken to maximize organizational input and participation. All steps focus on understanding and achieving the strategic intent of the business, which represents the long-term ambition of the enterprise.

This process is very adaptable to the culture and style of the organization and evolves with the organization. To minimize bureaucracy, the process can be "time-boxed" to force its execution within a specific time period. This prevents "analysis paralysis" and forces the notion that "this is a time for decisions." The process results, specifically strategy, can be leveled consistent with the desired degree of centralization and distribution of decision power within the organization. For very centralized and tightly controlled organizations, the strategy can be extremely specific in detail. For more empowered organizations, emphasis can be put on the definition of the strategy statements for the organization and the specifics of how can be left to the entrepreneurial talents of the management team. The degree of specificity can also be mixed on an item-by-item basis to reflect varying importance. By leveling, the process can be used to control or empower.

While this is an extremely abbreviated explanation of the process, it does catch the essence of the process, which is to identify and clarify exactly where you are (assessment), specify what is to be done (strategy), and do it/monitor it (execution).

Benefits

This strategic planning approach offers the IT strategist a number of distinct benefits in addition to the customary benefits accrued through strategic planning. These supplemental benefits are completeness, integration, being analytically based, being participatory, and being quality focused.

Completeness

The model provides a comprehensive process for doing all the steps and substeps of assessment, strategy, and execution. Much of the strategy literature and course instruction emphasizes a specific step or technique to the exclusion or minimization of all the others. Focus provides necessary in-depth coverage of the subject area but leaves the aspiring IT strategist asking, "How did I get here?" or "What do I do next?" or "Where does this fit in?" This model has synthesized all the individual ideas and packaged them into an actionable, composite framework.

Integration

Just as the IT community is fractured into schools of technology zealots, the strategic planning community is also partitioned into ideological schools. This book integrates the multiple perspectives of the rationalist school of strategy. The rationalist school believes that strategy is primarily the product of rational, purposeful, and conscious analysis. Strategy must be developed in this deliberate manner because of the irreversibility of commitment, the effort of forcing organizational alignment, the time to build and nourish specific sustainable advantages, the effort of accruing the benefits of leverage, and the difficulties of managing organizational change.

The three schools of the rationalist approach differ in their assessment of the dominant factor for strategy formulation. The competition school emphasizes strong competitive position as the essence of strategy. The coordination school asserts the supremacy of winning through strong directional alignment. The resource school emphasizes winning through the development of superior resources (competencies, capabilities, etc.). All the schools agree in their acknowledgment that meeting the needs of the customer is the context for their approach.

This book is unbiased and includes methods from each school. The different approaches result in a variety of perspectives that all contribute to understanding the essence of the problem. This variety promotes clarity, stimulates debate, and broadens insight. The techniques presented were therefore chosen for their pragmatic utility, not their ideological adherence.

The rationalist school is not the only school of strategy. Some propose that strategy is the product of politics. Others propose that strategy is the by-product of the organization's experience; strategy emerges from the pragmatic test of what is working in practice. Others emphasize speed. The ready-fire-aim school or the trial-and-error school holds that success cannot be designed, so strategy consists of blanketing the organization with many experiments and then focusing on the identified winners. Some suggest that strategy often equates to no more than hustle.

Analytically Based

Strategy formulation is extremely difficult. While methods sometimes look superficially simple, the value of the outputs is proportional to the depth of analytical insight developed by the strategy team. Thinking holistically, abstractly, and with an open mind about a complicated business is a daunting challenge.

Although the problem is not eliminated by the extensive use of proven analytical methods, it is simplified. The methods help to focus the attention of the debate on proven critical items. By elevating the discussion to an abstract level without the clutter of the details, the essence of the problem can be studied. The use of models ensures that all relevant bases are touched and that multiple views of a problem are studied in order to generate a variety of insights. In later chapters, numerous analytical models will be introduced and explained. These models are invaluable for effectively and efficiently performing the analytical tasks. The use of models provides a robust toolbox from which the IT strategist can attack the dual problems of understanding *what is* and deciding *what to do*. A few points about analytical models follow:

- The utility of the models is preeminent during the assessment step. As one would expect, developing frameworks to model *what is* is simpler than developing formal frameworks to model *what should be*. As one moves from assessment to strategy, there is decreasing utility of analytical models and increasing utility of vision, intuition, feel, and business savvy as means of decision making.

- The analytical models "clip onto" the strategic planning model at the appropriate step (see Figure 1.15). The strategic planning model serves as an overall infrastructure on which analytical models are appended to perform specific steps. This makes the methodology easily extensible and flexible. As analytical models are developed or discarded, they can simply be clipped-on or removed from the framework as required.

- It will become obvious that it is impossible to use all the techniques in a given planning period. The techniques should be viewed as tools, which are selected based on problem appropriateness. Additionally, it will become clear that the time and effort in using some techniques could not be done within one planning period. Consequently, in a given period, the results of previously sponsored studies are included in the process, and new studies are sponsored for inclusion in future planning cycles.

To be used effectively, many of the tools would require an entire book of explanation or extensive classroom training. Consequently, the tools will be introduced and explained, but it is not intended that all the nuances and procedural details of usage will be developed to a point where from this book alone you can use the technique. You should review the references to obtain more detailed knowledge for specific tools you wish to use. All the models used in this book are generic strategic planning models. This provides added credibility to the assertion that IT is not "special and different" and can be managed strategically just the same as any other business function.

Participatory

The planning model encourages broad organizational participation. As will be explained in later chapters, there are numerous process points to encourage strategic planning participation from all levels of the organization. The model does not encourage the few to go off into an isolated corner and develop a plan for the many.

Quality Focused

While there is immense value in strategic planning and its benefits, there are also limitations. The critical limitation is always having to remember the difference between a method, however good, and an execution of that method. In the end, the results of the process are only as good as the intellectual investment of the participants in thinking deeply about the issues. What makes the difference is insight, not rote execution of analytical steps. The strategic planning process works best only for those who are prepared and committed to work extremely hard at thinking through the issues. Sun Tzu calls this "winning by intelligence." Recall that what the Greek army of Achilles, Ajax, and Ulysses couldn't achieve in 10 years of brutal combat in the Trojan War, they achieved in 1 evening by using a ruse.

Book Overview

The remainder of this book builds on the initial ideas introduced in this chapter and fully explains the strategic planning model and the application of that process to the IT discipline.

Chapter 2: Managing IT for Competitive Advantage

This chapter explains the necessity of adopting strategic planning practices. Adopting strategic planning methods is not an optional extra for the IT management team. This chapter provides a series of loosely linked essays that explain key IT issues in a profound manner and links them to competitive success in the hyper-competitive information age.

The essays are as follows:

- Understanding IT Architecture Strategically
- Understanding Data Warehousing Strategically
- Understanding E-Commerce Strategically
- Information Technology Substitution and Diffusion: A Primer for the IT Executive
- Commitment in Information Technology Strategy
- Breeder Strategy
- IT Strategy as Structure

Chapters 3 through 7 explain the strategic planning model. Chapters 3 through 5 explain the major steps of assessment, strategy, and execution, and Chapters 6 and 7 explain quality control and administration that apply equally to Chapters 3 through 5.

Chapter 3: Assessment

This chapter explains in detail how to perform the assessment step. It explains the notion of a business scope, directives and assumptions, positioning, situational analysis, and conclusions. Assessment is the first step of strategic planning, and its output, conclusions, feeds the next step, strategy.

Chapter 4: Strategy

This chapter explains the attributes of the strategy step. Strategy defines what is to be done. The plan consists of strategy statements, objectives and goals, strategic moves, a commitment plan, and a change-management plan. The strategy provides clear direction and purpose for the organization.

Chapter 5: Execution

This chapter explains the mechanics of executing the plan. Major activities include formulating implementation programs, dividing these programs into manageable projects, and monitoring the environment. Execution makes strategy happen. Its success is tightly tied to the preparation work done in previous steps to plan for the elimination of obstacles.

Chapter 6: Quality Control

This chapter explains quality control methods to be applied throughout the process. Quality control methods will be partitioned into three types:

- *Completeness checks* ensure that the plan is comprehensive and complete.
- *Logical checks* ensure that the plan logically flows and is logically whole.
- *Correctness checks* test the plan to ensure that it is the best possible plan for the organization.

Quality control is interleaved throughout the entire planning process.

Chapter 7: Administration

This chapter explains how to administer the entire process. Topics covered include roles and responsibilities, calendar scheduling, interfacing with other organizational processes (budgeting, objective setting, etc.), maximizing organizational participation, and data collection.

Chapter 8: Epilogue

This chapter provides some final thoughts on strategy.

Strategic planning is a difficult subject to teach because in order to understand the whole you must first understand the parts; but to understand the parts, you must first understand the whole. While the book is presented in a linear order by necessity, you may find it advantageous to read the book more than once. In this way, terms that are used to describe certain subjects before the subjects themselves are fully developed will take on richer meaning in the second reading.

Conclusion

Sun Tzu taught:

When your strategy is deep and far reaching, then you gain much so you can win even before you fight. When your strategic thinking is shallow and near-sighted, then you gain little and you lose before you even do battle. Much strategy prevails over little strategy so those with no strategy cannot help but be defeated. Therefore it is said that victorious warrior win first and then go to war while defeated warriors go to war seeking to win.

The strategic intent or vision of an IT strategy must therefore be as follows:

The strategic intent of our IT strategy is to enable the business to win in the marketplace every day, with every customer, and with every purchase. By repositioning IT assets, we will empower our employees so that they can routinely delight and excite our customers. Through our unique appreciation of the value of IT, we will elevate our IT to the point where it becomes a compelling and durable contributor to the sustainable and temporary competitive advantage of the business. In this way IT will enable the business to impress its attitude on the marketplace and prevail over its competitors who have already lost.

This is the type of strategic intent that will enable the business to command the battlespace and win respect for information technology within the business.

Notes

1. The seminal work on hyper-competition is *Hyper-Competition: Managing the Dynamics of Strategic Maneuvering* by Richard A. D'Aveni (The Free Press, 1994). Professor D'Aveni's book, supplemented by his executive education course at Dartmouth University on hyper-competition, provides the basis for the description of hyper-competition that is provided in this book.

2. *The Art of War* by Sun Tzu, translated by Thomas Clearly (Shambhala Dragon Editions, 1988). *The Art of War* is generally recognized as the premier treatise on the strategy of conflict. Sun Tzu is recognized as the greatest strategist who ever lived.

3. See "Rise of the Stupid Network" by David Isenberg at www.isen.com.

4. See *Strategy: The Logic of War and Peace* by E. Luttwak (Belknap Press, 1987) for a discussion of strategic paradox.

CHAPTER

2

Managing IT for
Competitive Advantage

The purpose of this chapter is to analyze some of the key IT issues that are driving the need for developing a deep and far-reaching IT strategy. If IT is going to be used to build and sustain competitive advantage, then strategic acumen becomes a fundamental competency for the IT community. To make the case for this, it is beneficial to analyze some of the major drivers that are pushing us in this direction.

This chapter consists of seven loosely coupled essays that will analyze key drivers of IT strategy in the new millennium. They analyze each issue from a strategic perspective, as opposed to the more common technical perspective. Each essay is self-contained, and the contents partially overlay because the same analytical framework can be used to explain multiple drivers.

The seven essays are as follows:

Understanding IT Architecture Strategically. As hyper-competition accelerates and the information age matures, companies are discovering that IT acumen in general and IT architecture in particular are becoming the foundation of competitive advantage. Almost every business is an information-intensive business, and IT is increasingly the vehicle for creating new customer value and parrying competitors. Though value creation and the ability to maneuver are IT architecture-driven, many companies have not designed an IT architecture environment that ensures them the agility and cost efficiencies that will enable them to successfully compete in a world that is both hyper-competitive and information-intensive. This essay explains the underlying strategic logic of IT architecture and the necessity of designing an adaptive and cost-efficient meta-architecture. The meta-architecture defines the overall schema under which daily architecture work is done and evolved. By reading this essay, you will understand the challenges and opportunities of redesigning the IT architecture environment to create strategic advantage for the enterprise.

Understanding Data Warehousing Strategically. The objective of this essay is to develop an insightful and broadened understanding of data warehousing. Data warehousing, along with IT architecture, electronic commerce (the Internet), and object-oriented programming, is one of the four subjects that dominate the IT industry debate. Though many superficial reasons are given for justifying data warehousing projects, the reality is that the deep strategic logic of data warehousing is not as well developed as the others. This essay explains the fundamental strategic logic of data warehousing. By reading this essay, you will develop a much deeper and far-reaching understanding of the rationale for data warehousing and will be able to maximize your return on data warehousing investments. You will get a fresh perspective of why data warehousing is so important to competitive advantage in the hyper-competitive information age, and you will develop new insights into the strategic value of data warehousing initiatives.

Understanding E-Commerce Strategically. E-commerce is rapidly becoming the dominant subject in both the IT and the business communities. In the rush to implement tactical e-commerce applications, the underlying strategic rationale is often being ignored to the detriment of long-term strategic returns from the e-commerce investments. By reading this essay, you will develop a more profound understanding of the underlying strategic logic for e-commerce and will be able to maximize the value of e-commerce assets. You will get a novel analysis of why e-commerce is so critical to competitive success.

Information Technology Substitution and Diffusion: A Primer for the IT Executive. Aggressive management of information technology (IT) portfolios is becoming critical for businesses that need to respond electronically to global hyper-competition. At the root of the ability to manage information technologies is the process used to select new technologies and replace existing technologies. Orderly technology introduction, however, has become increasingly more difficult due to the urgent requirement to promptly respond to user demands for functionality while making judgment calls on the timing of technology substitution

This essay analyzes technology substitution and diffusion theory and illustrates how it can be applied to information technology selection and portfolio evolution. By using "S" curves, the primary tool of technology substitution and diffusion theory, IT executives can develop far-reaching insight into the underlying dynamics of technology competition and make prudent choices as to the timing of technology substitution events. In this way, user needs for high-functioning information technology can be satisfied while turnover of information technology inventory is managed prudently.

Commitment in Information Technology Strategy. While most IT program/project managers routinely focus their attention on the technological issues of implementing new information technologies and systems, experienced and battered program/project managers have come to learn that the most difficult problems center on people issues. The building, sustaining, and compounding of organizational commitment by overcoming overt and benign intellectual, emotional, and political opposition to a program or project often sits at the foundation of success. The way to deal with this problem is to explicitly design commitment into program/project plans. Just as one defines objectives and actions for other parts of the program/project, one must design objectives and actions to achieve necessary levels of commitment by all roles and players. One does not leave the building and sustaining of commitment to chance— one analyzes the organizational roles and players and their probable level of commitment, and one designs explicit actions to bring and sustain commitment to the necessary level to minimize friction and achieve positive enrollment and participation. This essay will help you understand the nature of commitment and how to develop pragmatic ways to invigorate your program/projects with it.

Breeder Strategy. As hyper-competition accelerates and advantage becomes an ever more fleeting commodity, strategic acumen is becoming more important. Marketspace success is becoming closely tied to the ability to disperse strategic thinking and creativity throughout the organization. While this is highly desirable, it has also proven quite challenging. This article suggests an approach called *Breeder Strategy* that can be used to successfully diffuse strategy expertise across the enterprise.

IT Strategy as Organizational Structure. As competition accelerates and companies strive to become digital enterprises, the insightful design of the IT organization's structure grows in importance. IT organizational design must be done at two levels: the macro level that decides the placement and number of IT organizations across the enterprise and the micro level that decides the specific design of a given organization. In all cases, design must be executed to maximize speed, adaptability, and the elimination of friction in execution. It is recommended that most IT organizations will be optimized by adopting a center-of-competency model, coupled with the introduction of an internal market structure for IT products and services.

At the end of this chapter, the composite key implication of these essays is analyzed. We now turn our attention to each of the essays and the strategic knowledge that they share.

Understanding IT Architecture Strategically

We are living through an era that is called the information age. It has the following distinguishing characteristics:

- The dominant technologies of the era are the computer and high-speed communications. Computing intelligence is dispersed into anything and everything that can be improved by being smart. The computerization of anything and everything is called *mechatronics* (mechanical electronics). High-speed communications permit both people and computers to communicate vast amount of information at nominal costs.

- The icon of the era is the microprocessor. Inexpensive and programmable chips permit products to be customized and made dynamically and personally responsive to each user.

- The output of the era is knowledge. Making products information-rich results in products and services with a high attraction to consumers.

- The basis of wealth of the era is information. Information drives the creation of knowledge that drives agile strategic actions that create temporary competitive advantage for the business.

- The defining work is the knowledge worker. Greater than half the work force is involved with collecting, processing, and communicating information.

- The means of moving things is communications networks. Logistics is concerned with moving bits (electronic products) rather than atoms (physical products).

- The marketplace, where people gather to buy and sell products and services, shifts from the physical marketplace (a mall or shopping center) to the marketspace (an electronic marketplace in cyberspace).

- Information-based enhancements become the primary way to create new products and services and to embellish the value of existing products and services.

- People buy dynamic and variable nondiscrete combinations of information-based products. Value is created at the time of purchase through digitized customization.

- Customers are treated (marketed, sold, and serviced) as individuals; not as statistical averages. A broadly accessible information highway (the Internet) permits global and interactive access to multimedia information.

- The convergence of information forms yields entirely new ways of working and living. Time and space constraints on markets collapse, permitting people to live where they please, work with remote employers, and purchase products from local or distant providers as the situation warrants.

The information age means, more than anything else, radical shifts in the basis of wealth. In the industrial age, products were physical; in the information age, products become virtual. In the industrial age, the focus of effort was the automation of labor; in the information age, the focus of effort is the creation and exploitation of knowledge. In the industrial age, information flow was physical and paper-based; in the information age, information flow is virtual and digitized. This results in the movement from manufacturing as the basis of societal wealth to knowledge as the linchpin of wealth. It results in the entire global economy becoming merged and information-centric, that is, the new economy. It results in the creation of electronic enterprises and electronic marketspaces that have been liberated from the constraints of physical products, time, and distance.

In summary, the information age can be understood from five primary perspectives:

Technology. Continued innovation in information technologies results in information technology permeating all aspects of life. As the internal combustion engine permitted the automating of labor, the computer permits the informating of society.

Economics. The economy becomes information-centric. Wealth creation is closely tied to the ability to create new information-based products and amend existing products with information. Information technology permits entirely new ways of collaboration to create products and services with closer ties to all value chain participants.

Employment. The density of employment shifts to knowledge workers. Most people make their living creating, moving, analyzing, interpreting, or disseminating information.

Spatial. The networking of computers throughout the world results in a collapse of the traditional market constraints of time and space. The world becomes one global marketspace.

Cultural. Society becomes media-laden. Information is readily available in multimedia formats, customizable, and interactive. We expect information in forms that are readily accessible and convenient to our needs. The social capabilities of computers and communications permit new social structures to emerge.

The information age is driven by three concomitant technological changes:

The digitalization of information regardless of form. All forms of information, audio, data, image, and video, become a series of bits. With the digitalization of all forms of information, all information shares the same bit-based DNA and becomes interoperable, transportable, and subject to interactive manipulation by the consumer. This has the net effect of radically changing business value chains, dramatically altering products and services, and completing revising consumer expectations as they are presented with interactive multimedia.

The rapidly declining cost of computing. The physics of computing has had only one impact on its price/performance for the past 30 years, and the exact same impact is anticipated for the foreseeable future—its cost will continue to dramatically decline. This cost efficiency is critical because it enables computing to become ubiquitous and available with sufficient power at an enabling and attractive price point.

The availability of broadband communications. The emergence of broadband communications is critical because multimedia is both storage-intensive and time-sensitive. The availability of gigabit communications will enable information-age companies to improve both the efficiency and effectiveness of work as follows:

- Individual personal productivity will be enhanced through wireless communications, fax, and personal digital assistants.

- Rather than people moving to work, work will move to people through telecommuting and video-conferencing.

- Business organization structures can become more adaptive to include virtual structures, remote employees, and part-time employees.

- Information can be made widely available to all employees through intranets.

- Electronic commerce can be used to interoperate with all value chain partners (suppliers, distributors, customers, regulators, etc.).

Bringing appropriate interactive multimedia, hypertext, or hypermedia to each task can enable work processes. The daily generic work activities of problem solving, decision making, creativity, process management, information exchange, relating, and influencing can all be enriched by informating them.

The key strategic implications of the information age are as follows:

All information becomes digitized and is subject to interactive manipulation. The interface to the user becomes multimedia-rich and is as much entertainment as it is instructive or transactional.

The economy becomes digital. More and more, products and services take on electronic personas. Employment is dominated by knowledge work.

Information becomes available to all anywhere, anytime, and in any form. People are free of time and space barriers to information access.

Information exchange occurs on a global basis. The location of information and the people with whom you interact is virtual to you, and their location makes no difference. There is just one all-encompassing cyberspace.

The economy becomes very knowledge-centric. Creating and applying knowledge rather than making things creates value.

Business, shopping, leisure time, games, and socialization all take an electronic character. It is often easier, more efficient, and convenient to conduct daily affairs through electronic media than through physical presence.

People become more self-sufficient in satisfying their needs through electronic distribution channels. This is the phenomenon of dis-intermediation.

Products and services undergo mass customization. Information-age products undergo final assembly at the point of purchase in response to the exact desires of the consumer.

Computing becomes ubiquitous. Everything that can benefit from being made smart is made smart. Once made smart, it is necessary that it be connected to be able to relate its knowledge to others. Like the availability of electricity today, the universal presence of computers will be taken for granted.

Information becomes democratized. The first 30-year tyranny of text data comes to an end as image, video, audio, and animation are all equally accessible and often much more valuable.

Speed is of the essence. A digital society is a society where things happen quickly. A business must have the ability to respond ever more quickly to rapidly changing consumer tastes. In the industrial age, the large companies ate the small companies. In the information age, the fast and agile companies eat the slow and ponderous companies.

Software agents that search, negotiate, and buy for you replace or complement human agents. Thousands of offerings can be electronically evaluated for cost, quality, convenience, and other buying factors.

Traditional barriers to market entry, as well as the historical market constraints of time and space, collapse. It becomes a war of all against all as customers become free to choose from a global marketplace. Market power shifts to consumers as information access creates a near friction-free marketplace where consumers have unlimited ability to comparative shop.

Commerce becomes continuous. Business is conducted around the world around the clock, without respite. Neither your personal software agents nor the databases that they operate on ever need a vacation or time off.

The information age is built on information technology. The utility of information technology is built on its architecture. The technologies that are deployed are transient. The business functions that they deliver offer only temporary advantage. Architecture, however, has persistence as the organizing framework for both technology and the derivative business function that is delivered. Herein lies the root of the response to hyper-competition and the information age.

IT Architecture as the Basis of a Strategic Response to Hyper-Competition

The tempting response to hyper-competition is to retreat into your strongholds and try to keep the barbarians at the moat (i.e., build bigger and better barriers to entry). This will not prove successful. The hyper-competitors will find a way to bypass your fortress and leave your value proposition antiquated as customers abandon you. Paradoxically, your barrier to entry will motivate your opponents to tax their ingenuity to overcome it.

The only response that is viable is to transform your business into a *hyper-competitor*. This means the following:

- Replacing moderate competitive behaviors with hyper-competitive behaviors
- Replacing your devotion to sustainable advantages with an endless string of temporary advantages (see Figure 2.1)
- Make speed, agility, surprise, and the ability to maneuver and disrupt the cornerstones of your strategy
- Be able to compete against time, for time is of the essence

What it means most of all is that you must make a war of rapid and disruptive movements replace your traditional strategy of defending your strong-

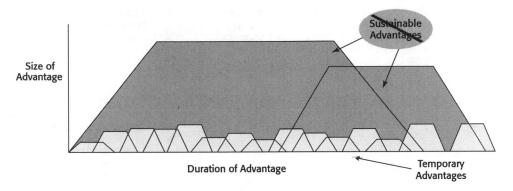

Figure 2.1   Temporary competitive advantage.

holds. There is no safe harbor in retreat. Either you surrender, or you become a hyper-competitive predator. Those are your only choices.

You make yourself into a hyper-competitor by mastering and exploiting information technology. Software is the fuel of information-age advantage. Software is the critical mechanism to lower costs, compress time to market, provide value-added, and interact with customers and suppliers. Software, or software functionality, is increasingly the actual product that customers receive. Software is increasingly the vehicle of customer satisfaction and value-added innovation. Software is the primary vehicle for creating new advantages and parrying the advantages of competitors. It is through software, its associated information technologies, and the foundation of IT architecture that you engage in hyper-competition. In the information age, you engage in hyper-competition, dislocate, disrupt, exploit, and surprise, through your information business systems.

John Zachman, the most noted industry expert on information technology architecture, has stated:

> We are now on the verge of IT architecture coming into its own. In the 21st century, IT architecture will be the determining factor—the factor that separates the winners from the losers, the successes from the failures, the acquiring from the acquired, the survivors from the rest.

Why is Mr. Zachman right?

As illustrated in Figure 2.2, Mr. Zachman is right because of the following:

- The business wins in the marketplace by virtue of a continuously evolving set of temporary advantages.

- In a hyper-competitive business environment, the ability to continuously create temporary advantages is based on the ability to maneuver.

- In the information age, the ability to maneuver is built on the information technology architecture.

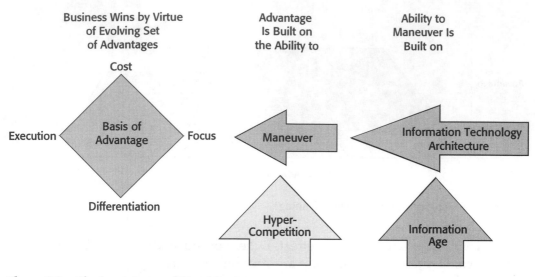

Figure 2.2 The importance of IT architecture.

The heart of the response to hyper-competition is to be able to maneuver, and the ability to maneuver in the information age is based on IT architecture. The all-compelling need to maneuver creates a solution junction between hyper-competition and the information age. IT architecture emerges as critically important to any business that is information-based, and, of course, that exactly describes almost every business.

The Strategic Logic of IT Architecture

To an information technology strategist, businesses are no more than massively parallel information processing factories. Numerous streams of information flow into a business, the information is massaged, new information is created, and numerous streams of information flow out of it. IT has historically existed to make these information flows happen with maximum efficiency and effectiveness to enable the noninformational business purpose. In the hyper-competitive information-age environment, these information flows become the mechanism of maneuverability.

Information flows within a business are exceedingly complex. We model that complexity by using a business diversity box (see Figure 2.3). Four dimensions define diversity:

Work site diversity. Defines the variable geography of where people work.

Work unit diversity. Defines the different types of work groups within which people work.

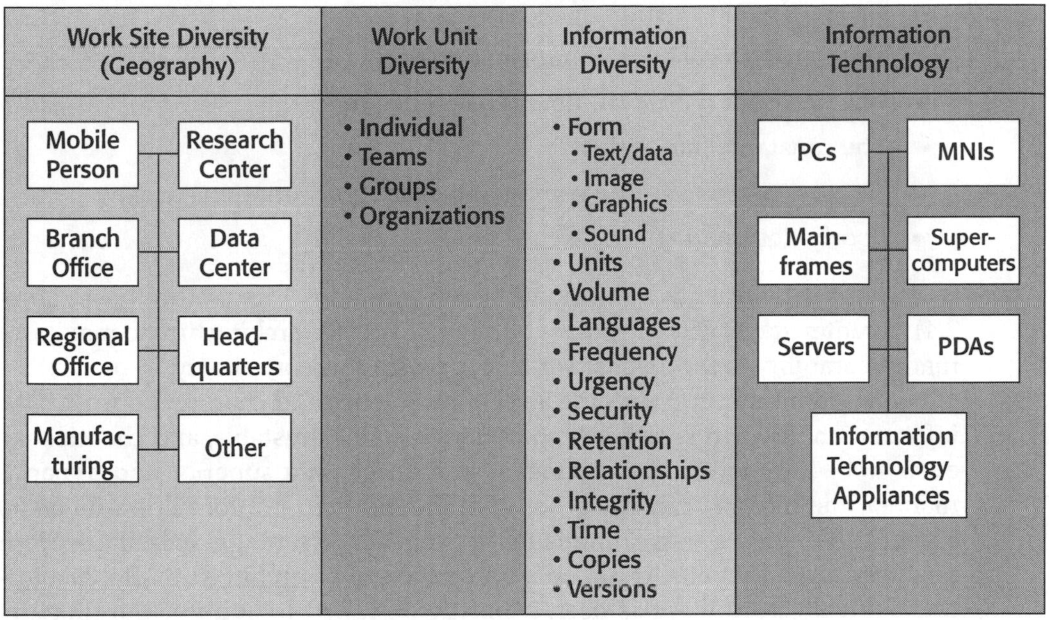

Work Site Diversity (Geography)		Work Unit Diversity	Information Diversity	Information Technology	
Mobile Person	Research Center	• Individual • Teams • Groups • Organizations	• Form • Text/data • Image • Graphics • Sound • Units • Volume • Languages • Frequency • Urgency • Security • Retention • Relationships • Integrity • Time • Copies • Versions	PCs	MNIs
Branch Office	Data Center			Main-frames	Super-computers
Regional Office	Head-quarters			Servers	PDAs
Manufac-turing	Other			Information Technology Appliances	

Figure 2.3 Business diversity box.

Information diversity. Defines the different forms of information with associated attributes that people require.

Information technology diversity. Defines the different types of information processing technologies that are used to create, present, move, store, and analyze information.

In a company of even small stature, the number of permutations and combinations of information flows across these four dimensions becomes astronomical. These flows, of course, do not remain constant. They are not still-life pictures but undergo continuous revision, as required, by the business dynamic. The ability to efficiently revise information flows is a function of the IT architecture.

What happens to this maze when we add the value chain? A business does not exist as an isolated entity. It participates with other trading partners in a value chain. As shown in Figure 2.4, each partner, supplier, regulator, distributor, financier, insurer, or consumer, first, has its own proprietary diversity box with all its private information flow complexities and, second, must interface diversity boxes across the value chain. The attempt to move information across the value chain with the information diversity boxes is difficult because of the following factors:

- The proprietary nature of each one
- The dynamic changes of information flow
- The uncertainty of what flows will be needed next
- The constant state of flux
- The continuous shifting combinations and permutations of flows
- Poorly designed IT architectures

The hyper-competitive information age promotes this picture (see Figure 2.4) to center stage. The purposeful design of your IT architecture to maximize maneuverability is the mechanism to cope with this complexity.

Hyper-competition excites the level of turbulence and change and makes the information flows in Figure 2.4 more unpredictable, unstable, and chaotic than ever. To be a hyper-competitor means to manage, in a superior and dynamic manner, the information flows both within and across information diversity boxes. What we are suggesting is that you create advantage by building your business diversity value chain on a foundation of IT architecture. By virtue of the IT architecture that has been explicitly designed to support information-based adaptive maneuverability, you are in a superior position to engage in hyper-competitive behavior. You exploit your IT architecture to make life miserable for your competitors while exciting your customers. You use it to deliberately disrupt the status quo to your advantage by doing the following:

- Changing information-based value propositions
- Manipulating the tempo and rhythm of change
- Rapidly attacking emerging but unexploited market niches
- Preempting competitor moves with your own announcements to which they must respond
- Performing acts of mass customization
- Being first to market
- Surprising your competitors with acts of collaboration that they cannot duplicate
- Attracting the best combination of value chain partners by virtue of your superior methods of value chain collaboration
- Rolling out a continuous stream of temporary advantages

Your disrupt the environment by being able to go forth where opponents don't expect it and attacking where they are unprepared. You fracture the cohesion of your opponents' processes and plans by creating a turbulent and deteriorating situation with which they cannot cope while concurrently satisfying your customers. Your prowess enables you to defeat your opponents

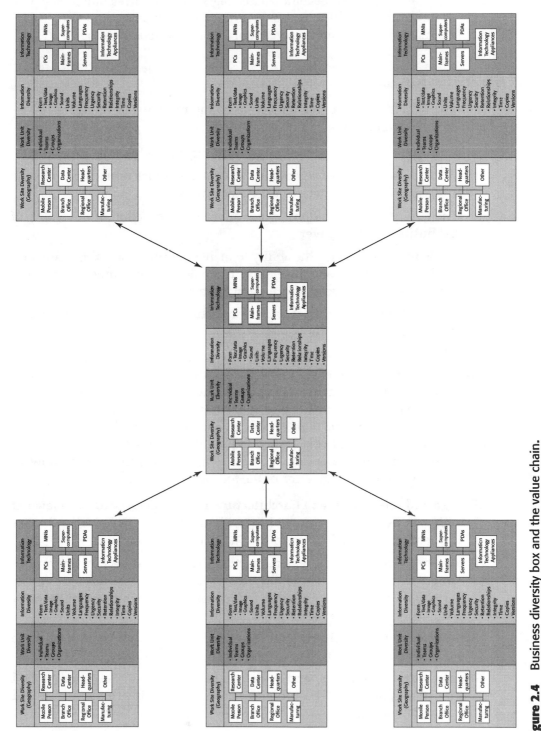

Figure 2.4 Business diversity box and the value chain.

psychologically. As they become discouraged and quarrelsome, they will begin to flail about and fall hopelessly further and further behind you. This is how IT architecture becomes the weaponry of a hyper-competitor.

Conclusion

The logic for focusing on IT architecture as the mechanism to create hyper-competitive advantage is as follows:

- Companies in all industries are confronting global hyper-competition.

- An endless stream of temporary advantages must replace sustainable advantage as the means to marketplace success.

- The ability to build temporary advantages is a function of the ability of the business to maneuver.

- In the information age, the ability to maneuver the business is a function of the malleability of information technology. What must be maneuvered, literally, are your information systems.

- The malleability of your information technology is built on your information technology architecture.

Figure 2.5 summarizes this argument. IT architecture is no longer just an enabler of business success; it is the very essence (weaponry) of competing in the hyper-competitive information age. It is the essence of competing because it is the mechanism for creating and re-creating a continuous stream of customer value. Your business will be able to maneuver if, and only if, your IT architecture has been explicitly crafted to permit friction-free change.

What is to be done? There must be a dramatic transformation in how IT architecture work is done in terms of the following:

Design and selection of an IT architecture. IT architecture must be elevated to the status of a core competency with appropriate technical and management resources allocated to such a critical function.

Extensibility of architecture. Architecture design must become more concerned with lifetime adaptability than with initial cost. Issues such as portability, scalability, modularity, openness, and reconfigurability must take precedent in making architectural decisions.

Standardization of architecture. Speed and resistance to friction must be enabled by encouraging reuse through subassembly standardization.

Architect training, skills, and tools. Architects must undergo prescribed education paths that ensure the necessary training that is matured through mentoring.

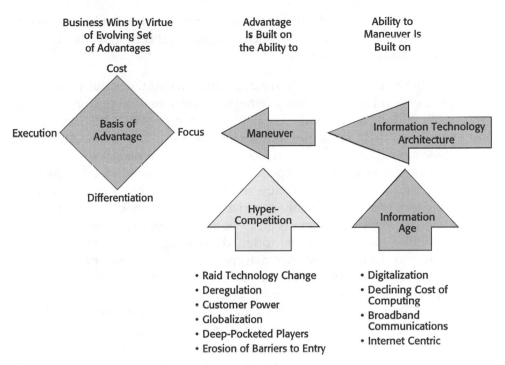

Figure 2.5   Strategic logic summary.

Definition of outputs of architecture work. As is true in engineering disciplines, IT architectures must be delivered in terms of formal blueprints that can be precisely understood by all affected stakeholders.

Ability for large audiences to understand architecture. Both nonarchitect management and technical personnel need to be educated on the importance of architecture and the methods of architecture.

Ability to assess changes to architecture rapidly. Architecture blueprints must be made Web accessible. Everyone who needs to know the current architecture of a system or work-in-progress architecture needs to have simple access to the information. Architecture blueprints are an important part of the corporate digital library.

Visibility and clarity of architecture. All architecture work must be delivered in a predictable manner using standardized notations. The meaning of architecture must reside in the architecture drawing, not in the private interpretation of that drawing by each individual.

Currency of architecture. Architecture drawings must always be current. There must always be an architecture-of-record set of architecture blueprints that define the architecture as it is.

Professionalism of architecture. IT architecture work must be elevated to the status of other professions such as legal, engineering, medical, and, of course, building architecture.

What must be done is to position architecture so that the business can use it to be a hyper-competitive predator. What must be done is to position IT architecture so that the business will prevail over its competitors who have already lost by virtue of their inferior architectural prowess. Your IT architecture must be the mechanism that enables you to move swiftly and decisively.

When one studies hyper-competition and the environmental turbulence routinely associated with it, one of the most interesting things one discovers is that turbulence is a very unevenly experienced phenomenon. Turbulence is an attribute of the recipient of an event, as opposed to being an attribute of the event. Whether something is disruptive, dislocating, process upsetting, friction causing, or in any other way detrimental to the orderly processes of a business is entirely dependent on the reaction of the business to the event, as opposed to the inherent nature of the event.

The same initiative by a hyper-competitor can generate entirely different reactions by its opponents. One opponent, rigid and inflexible in its architecture, is unable to respond, and tremendous organizational friction emerges as everyone blames each other for the failure. Another competitor, agile and flexible, takes the initiative in stride, responds promptly, and ruins the advantage period anticipated by the initiator. Turbulence or nonturbulence is something within you, not something done to you. An event or an environment is not turbulent to you as long as you have the ability to promptly meet the new demands it presents to you.

By virtue of your IT architecture, the actions of your hyper-competitors can be matched or surpassed, and you can reposition yourself from being hyper-competitor prey to being a hyper-competitive predator. As hyper-competition defines the competitive landscape into the new millennium, what will be the basis of advantage will be the agility of IT architecture. This is a most surprising and important insight that cannot be ignored and must be acted on. An insight that will ultimately *separate the winners from the losers, the successes from the failures, the acquiring from the acquired, and the survivors from the rest.*

Understanding Data Warehousing Strategically

Architecture enables one to maneuver. One of the most important things to be able to maneuver is your access to information. Data warehousing provides a strategy to extract knowledge from the operational data stores of the business. This next essay explains the strategic logic of data warehousing initiatives.

It is obvious to anyone who culls through the voluminous information technology (IT) literature, attends industry seminars, user group meetings, or expositions, reads the ever-accelerating new product announcements of IT vendors, or listens to the advice of industry gurus and analysts that four subjects overwhelmingly dominate IT industry attention as the new millennium unfolds:

IT processing architecture. This is embodied in the shift to Internet-centric computing from aging computing architecture.

Electronic commerce. This is exemplified in the explosive growth of novel communication services that enable ways of engaging in commerce, as personified by the Internet.

Application developer productivity. This is observed in the extreme interest in object-oriented technology in all its myriad forms, for example, object-oriented analysis, object-oriented design, object-oriented programming, and object-oriented distributed processing frameworks.

Knowledge management, decision making, and learning. This is illustrated in the intense interest in and implementation of data warehouses.

The fundamental strategic logic of the first three pervasive IT trends is clear, as shown in Table 2.1. They are, respectively, maneuverability, reach, and leverage (productivity).

Maneuverability is the strategic imperative that propels IT architecture. To cope with the extreme business turbulence of the new millennium and beyond, a company must be agile and fast. An agile architecture permits a business to respond quickly and forcefully to constantly changing times and circumstances in a cost-competitive manner.

Reach is the strategic imperative that supports the unparalleled interest and investments in the *Internet.* Electronic commerce provides entirely new ways to distribute and sell to consumers—ways that are faster, cheaper, more informative, customer-intimate, and customer-empowering, and that compress time and space. The history of free-market commerce is that suppliers irresistibly gravitate toward technologies that enable them to reach customers in more cost-effective and efficient ways. Customers naturally gravitate toward

Table 2.1 Four Key Subjects Dominate the IT Landscape

SUBJECT	TECHNOLOGY	STRATEGIC LOGIC
IT processing architecture	Distributed systems	Maneuverability
E-commerce	The Internet	Reach
Developer productivity	Object-oriented	Leverage
Knowledge and learning	Data warehousing	????

distribution channels that provide them with ease of use and convenience at a fair cost. Electronic commerce, the Internet, converges the interests of suppliers and consumers. The Internet replaces local and physical marketplaces with a global and virtual *marketspace*.

Leverage is the strategic imperative that motivates interest in object-oriented technology. Through the prospect of treating software as preengineered parts, new productivity levels can be achieved by shifting the unit of software development from a line of code to preassembled, reusable, and certified parts.

Data warehousing is the last of the four dominant trends, but its underlying strategic logic has not been well articulated. As shown in Table 2.2, numerous companies in multiple industries are committing to and achieving tremendous benefits from data warehousing. Typical reasons given are faster and better

Table 2.2   Various Industry Uses of Data Warehousing (Sample Industries)

LEADING-EDGE USES OF DATA WAREHOUSING	REPRESENTATIVE COMPANIES
Retail	
Analysis of scanner check-out data	Wal-Mart
Tracking, analysis, and tuning of sales promotions and coupons	Kmart
	Sears
Inventory analysis and redeployment	Osco/Savon Drugs
Price reduction modeling to "move" product	Casino Supermarkets
Negotiating leverage with suppliers	W. H. Smith Books
Frequent buyer program management	Otto Versand Mail Order
Profitability analysis	
Product selections for granular market segmentation	
Telecommunications	
Analysis of:	AT&T
• call volumes	Ameritech
• equipment sales	Belgacom
• customer profitability	British Telecom
• costs	Telestra Australia
• inventory	Telecom Ireland
Purchasing leverage with suppliers	Telecom Italia
Frequent buyer program management	
Banking and Finance	
Relationship banking	Bank of America
Cross-segment marketing	Citibank
Risk and credit analysis	BancOne
Merger and acquisition analysis	Merrill Lynch
Customer profiles	CBOE
Branch performance	CNA

decision making, push-down employee empowerment, leveraging of operational data, scenario analysis, customer intimacy, analysis of anything and everything, and process control. These are certainly good reasons, but are they adequate motivations to maximize the return on data warehousing? What is the underlying deep and compelling logic of data warehousing? How are we to understand data warehousing strategically so that we may fully optimize the investment?

This essay attempts to answer those questions. We will demonstrate that data warehousing is best appreciated as a realization of the deep and far-reaching strategic idea of a *rising-tide strategy*. The maximum return from data warehousing occurs when it is conceptualized, implemented, managed, and evolved within that context. Before doing that, however, it is beneficial to level, set, and review the data architecture origins of data warehousing.

A Data Architecture Perspective of Data Warehousing

The business processes of the enterprise are automated in the form of business applications that collectively compose the business systems portfolio. Companies have innumerable processes requiring IT capability. Typical applications include order realization, customer service, contract administration, product development, benefits administration, staffing, budget development and monitoring, and information sharing (e-mail, conferencing, team support, etc.). The list is seemingly endless.

As illustrated in Figure 2.6, the business practices can generally be partitioned into two broad classifications:

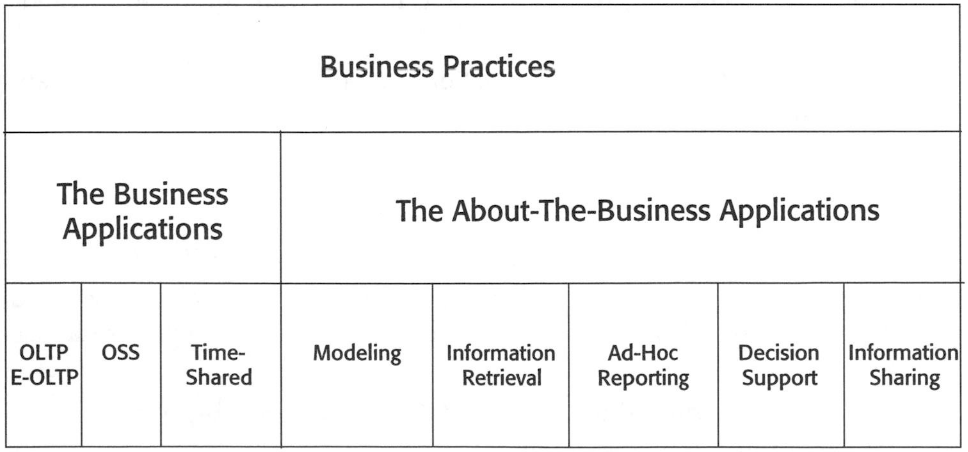

Business Practices							
The Business Applications			The About-The-Business Applications				
OLTP E-OLTP	OSS	Time-Shared	Modeling	Information Retrieval	Ad-Hoc Reporting	Decision Support	Information Sharing

Figure 2.6 The application portfolio.

The business applications. Those business applications that operationally "run" the business on a daily, weekly, monthly basis. When they cease to run, the business literally stops operating.

The about-the-business applications. Those applications that analyze the business. They aid both in interpreting what has occurred and in deciding prudent actions for the future. When they cease to run, there is no immediate, obvious business failure, but their utility is critical to the long-term competitiveness of the enterprise. Data warehousing embraces these types of applications.

The business applications are often called electronic online transaction processing systems (E-OLTP) or operations support systems (OSS) and have the following general attributes:

- "Heavy duty" production transaction record-keeping systems directly support the execution of a business practice.

- They may have to provide 24-hour by 7-day service and have carefully managed outage periods.

- Database integrity and availability are crucial. The database must be recoverable from a failure within a guaranteed restoration period.

- Performance is measurable in terms of transactions per (sub)second and/or user response time (X percent of the transactions must respond in less than Y (sub)seconds).

- Structured applications have both predefined transactions and predefined transaction flows. The execution paths are predictable.

- Database schemas are quite complex in terms of number of entities and number of inter-entity relationships. The inter-entity relationships impose multiple dependency, referential integrity, and validation requirements on the system.

- Elaborate editing of input transactions is required to ensure and maintain database quality.

- Security of access is important.

- Sophisticated dialogue management is required.

- User ergonomics to maximize productivity is a big concern.

- They are often large applications by the metrics of database size, total number of users, total number of concurrent users, and types of transactions.

- Extensive off-prime time batch updating and reporting must be completed within a tight batch window.

Business performance is the payoff advantage from these types of applications. Consequently, they will often contain exception monitoring subsystems used to advise management when an abnormal situation has occurred or an undesirable pattern is developing.

The about-the-business applications are called data warehouse applications (decision support, modeling, information retrieval, ad hoc reporting/analysis, what-if, data mining, etc.). This class of applications is oriented toward retrieval/analysis/report/information sharing. The data sources are often triggered extracts from E-OLTP or OSS applications or public information services. These applications have the following attributes:

- Static (low update) databases
- Periodic refresh of the database from the source E-OLTP or OSS applications
- Extended time accumulation of data
- Simple restore/recovery
- Facilities to enable the "canning" of repetitive user requests
- Flexible import/export facilities
- Enabled information sharing
- An analyst workbench that may include graphics tools, report writers, statistical modeling tools, spreadsheets, simulators, query languages, word processors, desktop publishing, project management software, artificial intelligent tools, data mining tools, information discovery tools, application development tools, and information exchange tools

Better knowledge about the business and the development of superior business strategies arethe payoffs from this class of applications.

Applications are often continuous in capability, and their functionality may not be discrete. Though an application will naturally migrate to one classification as its primary definer, it may have subsystems that are more aligned to the other type. Both the business applications and the about-the-business applications, with all the endless variations, are built on top of a data architecture and a processing architecture that jointly compose the IT architecture for the business.

Data Architecture Choices

Business applications are performed by programs that collect, create, modify, retrieve, and delete data and programs that use, analyze, summarize, extract, or in other ways manipulate data. Data is the common thread that ties together the extensive corporate application portfolio. Data, as it is transformed into information as it flows between users, can provide current advantage in the form of superior operational systems and future advantage in the form of superior analysis for planning. How the data asset is positioned is of vital long-term importance to the health of the enterprise.

Increasingly, corporations are recognizing that the purposeful management and leveraging of the corporate data asset must take on increased attention in the new millenium. In the 1970s, management attention was focused on hardware cost. During the 1980s, management's attention shifted to software as both a growing element of the IT cost structure and the source of advantageous applications. In the 1990s, management's attention focused on migrating aging host-centered applications to client/server architectures. In the new millennium, management will increasingly focus on data exploitation as the path to improved customer service, cooperation with suppliers, and the creation of new barriers for competitors.

Data engineering theory (data engineering is the discipline that studies how to model, analyze, and design data for maximum utility) indicates that there are four generic data environments on which to build business applications. For a variety of technical and architectural reasons they are not equally advantageous. Figure 2.7 illustrates the four options and can be explained as follows:

Dedicated file architecture. Each application has a set of privately designed files. The data structure is tightly embedded with the application, and the data files are owned by the application.

Closed database architecture. A database management system (DBMS) is used to provide technological advantage over file systems (exemplary advantages are views, security, atomicity, locking, recovery, etc.), but distinct, separate, and independent databases are still designed for each application. The DBMS is used as a private and powerful file system with the data remaining the proprietary property of the application. As is true with the dedicated file architecture, there is a high degree of data redundancy and frequently poor data administration. "Spaghetti-like" interfaces move data between the closed databases. Because these interfaces often have to convert, edit, and/or restructure data as it moves between proprietary definitions, they are often called "data scrubbers" or translators. Data scrubbers do not add value; they compensate for inadequate data administration.

Subject database architecture. Data is analyzed, modeled, structured, and stored, based on its own internal attributes, independent of any specific application. Data is administered as a sharable resource through a data administration function that owns the data for all potential users. Extensive sharing of data occurs through application-sensitive views. Subject databases run the day-to-day operations of the enterprise.

Data warehouse database architecture. Databases are constructed for quick searching, retrieval, ad hoc queries, and ease of use. The data is normally

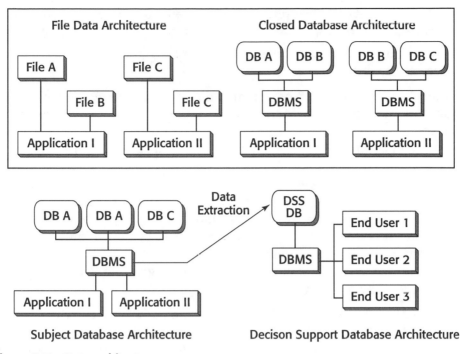

Figure 2.7 Data architecture.

a periodic extract from a subject database or public information service. To minimize the number of extracts and to ensure time/content consistent data, data is shared at the corporate, departmental, and local levels—not extracted per user. Data definitions are kept synchronized with the source databases to ensure the ability to interrelate data from multiple subject database extracts without the need to resort to data scrubbers. These databases are used to analyze the enterprise.

The recommended data architecture is a mixture of the subject database and data warehouse database environments. Subject databases support the business applications, and data warehouse databases enable the about-the-business applications. This dual database architecture is most advantageous for the following reasons:

- Data quality, accessibility and sharing are maximized.
- Unplanned data redundancy is eliminated.
- Interapplication interaction is simplified.
- Data standardization is ensured.
- Application life cycle productivity is maximized.

■ Development of new applications is accelerated through the reuse of in-place data resources.

■ Creation of centers of excellence in data management to protect the data asset is enabled.

Figure 2.8 illustrates what the optimum data architecture would look like. It merges the subject database and data warehouse database environments together.

Some data architects would prefer a single database environment where both OLTP and decision support needs are fulfilled concurrently against a single database and thereby eliminate duplication and extraction altogether. It is our assessment that the two user communities have fundamentally different and incompatible requirements that preclude this option. Table 2.3 summarizes the major points of conflict. These dichotomies present a formidable barrier to a single database environment.

When routine access of operational databases is given to decision support users, major problems can occur:

Performance. The unpredictable nature of the ad hoc queries disrupts the requirement of predictable response time for operational systems. Predictable and guaranteed performance cannot be engineered into the system design if the transactions are not predictable.

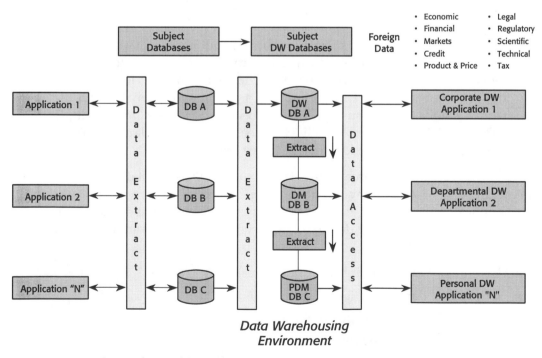

Figure 2.8   Optimum data architecture.

Table 2.3   Subject Database and Data Warehouse Database Dichotomies

OPERATIONAL ENVIRONMENT	DATA WAREHOUSE ENVIRONMENT
Subject Databases	Decision Support Databases
THE BUSINESS APPLICATIONS	**THE ABOUT-THE-BUSINESS APPLICATIONS**
Stores very detailed data	Short-running and engineered transactions
Stores entire subject database	Stores detailed and/or summarized data
Requires to-the-last-transaction accuracy	Stores only data of interest
Disciplined, highly structured, and planned transactions	Requires "as-of" accuracy
Optimized for performance, efficiency, and availability	Unstructured and ad hoc transactions
Maintains rigorous data structures	Optimized for flexibility and ease of use
Runs the business	Supports dynamic data structures
Emphasizes needs of all potential users	Analyzes the business
	Emphasizes needs of each user
	Potentially long running and dynamically defined transactions

Data retention. The decision support applications often require longer retention of data for cumulative analysis than the operational systems, which need it for only the active business practice cycle. The growth in the size of the database can negatively affect performance, integrity, and the ability to meet any recoverability time constraints.

Logical reasoning. Because the database is dynamically changing with each transaction, information queries are nonrepeatable, and chained queries do not necessarily operate on the same set of data. Deductive reasoning against a stable data store is not feasible. A temporal database that maintains a time view of the data could resolve this problem but creates a new set of issues unrelated to the pressing operational needs.

We may summarize our views on data architecture as follows:

- There are four generic ways to design and organize the corporation's data asset.

- They are not equal.

- A combination of the subject database and data warehouse database environments is most advantageous. This is called the dual database environment.

- A single database environment from which both operational and decision support requirements are met is desirable but plagued by many practical problems that make it infeasible.

Data warehousing is the modern term used to describe a mature and robust decision support database environment consistent with the model in Figure 2.8. It implies that decision support databases have been carefully selected and designed to provide maximum utility and that a powerful set of tools has been provided to users to maximize their ability to leverage and exploit the captured operational data.

While data warehouses today are primarily single, physical databases with staged replication to data marts, it should be anticipated that with the emergence of industrial-grade distributed database management technology, data warehouses will become logical databases that transcend physically distributed decision support databases.

Data Warehousing and Strategic Thinking

To understand data warehousing strategically, we should now appreciate that it is the consequence of strategic thinking, which means that it is the product (result) of some combination of strategic ideas. In this case, we must reverse-engineer strategic thinking. We know the result of the strategic thinking process, data warehousing, but what are the strategic ideas from which it emanated?

Data warehousing is an unusually rich strategic action. A strong case can be made that it is the product of numerous strategic ideas. If we argue, however, that data warehousing is the product of everything, we cloud our analysis. What are the key ideas that it realizes?

In Miyamoto Musashi's classical book on strategy, *The Five Rings*, he teaches that all weapons have a distinctive spirit. It is the challenge of a warrior to understand that spirit, master it, and become in harmony with it. In that way, there is perfect integration between the warrior and his weapon.

When I think about data warehousing's distinctive spirit, I think about *time*. More than any other strategic theme, I believe that what data warehousing does is permit one to compete across time. One competes across time as follows:

Past. One must learn from the past so that the best lessons can be learned and deployed and mistakes not repeated.

Present. One must be able to analyze current events quickly so that one can maneuver in real time to adapt to them.

Future. One must have prescience about the future so that opportunistic investments and actions can be taken now to position for an even better tomorrow. Foreknowledge is the source of extraordinary success.

The strategic ideas from which data warehousing emanates are the time-oriented ones:

Data warehousing permits one to compete *across* time.

Figure 2.9 Competing across time.

Learning. One must continually learn and adapt based on that learning. All progress includes making mistakes, but the same mistakes should not be made twice.

Maneuverability. This skill requires finding the best way to go. Forces must be able to maneuver to exploit gaps.

Prescience. The leadership must have deep and far-reaching foresight. Leaders must see and know what others do not. The height of prescience is to see the formless and act on it.

Foreknowledge. All matters require competitive intelligence. Nothing is more important than understanding the plans of your opponents and the needs of your customers.

These four strategic ideas are not just any set of strategic ideas; they are uniquely important because they overlay the time dimension of strategic thinking (see Figure 2.9). Time is one of the three fundamental dimensions of strategic thought, and data warehousing enables one to directly think in that dimension. Data warehousing is, therefore, not just another good result of strategic thinking; it is a very special result because it provides the tools to permit an organization, through the action of building data warehouses, to compete in the primary strategic dimension of time.

By giving your employees robust access to information about customers, markets, suppliers, and financial results, you enable them to strategically *learn* from the past, *adapt* in the present, and *position* for the future. To the nonstrategist, the mundane thinker, data warehousing is about spending (wasting?) money to let employees play with data. To the strategist, data warehousing is about winning the endless battle against time.

Data Warehousing as a Rising-Tide Strategy

There is a special name given to certain strategic actions. This name is a *rising-tide strategy*. As the tide comes in, it raises all the ships in the harbor. The tide does not discriminate; it raises the dinghy, the canoe, the yacht, the warship, and the ocean liner. The single action of the incoming tide raises all ships. All of them, by no action of their own, enjoy the effect of the rising tide.

A rising tide symbolizes the strategic notion of *leverage*. Leverage is what gives strategy muscle. Leverage means that you do one thing, but multiple benefits derive from it. Typical words used to describe leveraged events are reuse, sharing, economies of scale, economies of scope, cascading, cloning, duplicating, layering, amplifying, and multiplying. Mathematically, the value of leverage equals individual payoff times instances of payoff.

Data warehousing supports a rising-tide strategy. By the single action of making information readily available to employees, we can bring benefits to all the employees as they go about their daily work. Hundreds of times every day, employees solve problems, make decisions, control processes, develop insights, share information, relate to others, and attempt to influence others. All of these actions can be made more efficient and effective if better information is made available in a timely manner at the point of need. This is called *informating* your business. Data warehousing *informates* the business.

Rising-tide strategies are cherished strategies because of the *multiplier effect*. While it is excellent that data warehousing permits you to compete across time, what is remarkable about data warehousing is that it can permit all of your employees to compete across time. The single act of making information available creates distinct strategic leverage for the business. You have the ability to further increase your leverage by increasing the amount of data available and the number of employees to whom it is made accessible. Data warehousing is an awesomely powerful rising-tide strategy—a strategy that is most effective when the tide is kept as high as possible and raises as many ships as possible.

Data Warehousing and Strategic Paradox

Data warehousing needs to be understood in terms of reversal of opposites. As shown in Figure 2.10 and characterized in Table 2.4, we are moving from the industrial society to the knowledge society[3]. Knowledge becomes the premier weapon of advantage, and business-to-business conflict migrates from competing on industrial-age economies of scale to information technology fighting (IT fighting). Key strategic information technologies such as Internet-centric computing and data warehousing, therefore, become subject to strategic paradox in their implementations.

The strategic paradox of data warehousing is that the strategist concerned about cost does not seek to use just enough means but an excess[5] of means to

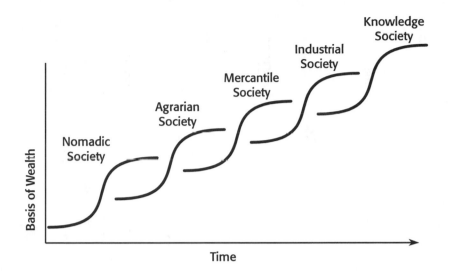

Figure 2.10   Basis of economic wealth.

accomplish his or her end. Data warehousing achieves, paradoxically, its greatest value for the business when it is used in excess.

It is typical to observe customer teams engage in extensive and exhaustive cost-justification exercises (net present value, return on investment, cost/benefit justification, payback period, etc.) to convince cost-conscious decision makers to approve data warehousing expenditures for a predetermined fixed set of uses. Their actions are based on linear logic, understandable but inappropriate because of the reversal of opposites. When the weaponry shifts to IT fighting, data warehousing becomes subject to strategic paradox and must be managed as such to achieve optimum results.

Consider a military commander who needs to engage his enemy. If he uses linear logic and deploys *just enough* resources, he will win, but it will be an expensive (Pyrrhic) victory. If he applies a force far in excess of his opponent, he will achieve his ends with minor casualties. All the downstream costs of battle will be avoided (damaged weapons, confusion, wounded/killed soldiers, etc.). So at the point of conflict, the efficient commander does not seek to use *just enough* but applies far in excess. He does not use accounting logic that holds in nonconflict situations but applies paradoxical logic, which rules at the point of battle.

In the information age, data warehousing is a key strategic weapon. As we have discussed, not only does it let you compete across time, it is a rising-tide strategy that can elevate the strategic acumen of all employees. The attempt to cost-justify such powerful weaponry in terms of net present value misses the

Table 2.4 Comparative Ages

ATTRIBUTE	AGE NOMADIC SOCIETY	AGRARIAN SOCIETY	MERCANTILE SOCIETY	INDUSTRIAL SOCIETY	KNOWLEDGE SOCIETY
Dominant Technology	Crude hunting tools	Manual farm equipment	Sailing ships	Machines	The computer
Icon	The hunting club	The plow	The great sailing boat	The gasoline engine	The microprocessor
Science	Superstition	Civil engineering	Marine engineering	Mechanical engineering	Computer science
Output	Slaughtered animals	Farm food	Trade	Mass consumer goods	Knowledge
Energy Source	Fire	Animals	Wind	Fossil fuels	The mind
Basis of Wealth	Hunting ability of tribe	Farm land	Sailing ships	Land, labor, and capital	Information
What Makes the Difference	Courage	Muscle	Fleets	Economies of scale	Intelligence
Defining Work	Hunter	Farmer	Merchant	Laborer	Knowledge worker
What Are You Doing?	Surviving	Eating	Trading	Automating	Informating
Organizational Form	Tribe	Feudalism	Trading house	Hierarchical corporation	Networks
Means of Logistics	People	Animals	Ships	Airlines, trains, ships, and trucks	Network
Where Is the Marketplace?	Person-to-person	Village square	Town stores	Shopping malls	Cyberspace (the marketspace)

whole point. When one invests in a national highway infrastructure, one does not cost-justify or attempt to anticipate each event of commerce that will transverse the highway. Rather, one has the strategic vision to understand that the strategic action is putting in place the enabling infrastructure and then permitting the marketplace to take care of the rest.

The same is true with data warehousing. Once the infrastructure is in place, you have raised the tide for all employees. Your initial justifications are constrained by the limits of your imagination. How the data warehouse will ultimately be beneficial will emerge as your employees use it to respond to the dynamics of the marketplace and as it is exploited by their creativity. As they respond by using the *excessive* data warehouse, they will experience the same phenomenon as the military commander. Though they will be spending in excess at the point of conflict, it will ultimately prove to be much cheaper because all the downstream business processes will be more efficient and effective. While cost consciousness is always in vogue and a specific set of business needs to be addressed is welcomed, the absence of a priori adequate tactical savings should not dissuade you from the deep and far-reaching strategic merits of an encompassing data warehousing initiative.

Unquestionably, it is easier to accept this paradox with regard to the military commander than data warehousing because of the differences between cause and effect in the two situations. In the military situation, the cause and effect are tightly coupled in time and space. One can immediately see the results of the excess and correlate the success to that excess. In the data warehousing situation, the cause and effect are often dispersed across wide gaps of time and space. The use of excess data warehousing will have the desired effect, but it will occur perhaps months later at a remote branch office.

The strategist must take solace in that he or she is engaged in deep and far-reaching strategy, not tactical, short-term decisions. Things that are readily cost-justifiable are things that are obvious and known to all. Strategic thinking is involved in seeing victory before it exists. How can anyone cost-justify the formless? While cost-conscious accounting methods are appropriate for sustaining wealth, strategic vision has always been the ingredient required to create it.

While it stretches and strains your business common sense, strategic paradox is an important dimension of the spirit of data warehousing. Ultimately, experience will prove that those who use it in excess will achieve greater benefits than those who attempt to rigorously cost-justify and constrain its deployment. They will learn that their approach is mathematically correct but strategically sterile. You do not want a rising tide; you want a permanent high tide of information with which you can win the battles for the past, the present, and the future.

Use data warehousing to position yourself so that you will surely win, prevailing over those who have already lost. Win through intelligence, not brute force. Cost-justification is supposed to be a tool of strategy, not the reverse. Strategic paradox alters the rules; understand and justify data warehousing strategically.

Data Warehousing and Maneuverability

Businesses must always be prepared to respond creatively to marketplace dynamics. The normal marketplace state is constant upheaval. It is therefore obvious that those companies that can navigate with greater alacrity, speed, and dexterity have a distinct advantage. In fact, with speed, dexterity, and alacrity as your allies, you can further exaggerate your advantage by deliberately promoting marketplace mayhem to the benefit of your customers and the detriment of your competitors.

Companies take two basic roles in engaging the marketplace:

Attrition fighter. Marketplace supremacy is achieved by taking a strong but fixed position and "slugging it out" for marketplace dominance. Through confrontational marketplace battles and by concentrating superior assets against inferior foes, you win by exhausting the opponent's will and ability to compete. The optimum situation is to win in a few decisive battles and, by virtue of your proven superior power, deter prospective competitors from stepping into your marketplace and challenging you. An attrition fighter, like a classical heavy-weight boxer, wins by brute superiority of assets and the ability to deliver a crushing and decisive knockout blow.

Maneuver fighter. Marketplace superiority is achieved by staying in a state of perpetual motion. A maneuver fighter continually looks for opportunistic gaps in the marketplace and swiftly moves assets to maximize the opportunity. The maneuver fighter attempts to continually disrupt the marketplace by changing the rules of competition. It is through the actions of movement that advantage is gained. Advantage is best understood as a succession of overlapping temporary advantages rather than a set of sustainable competitive advantages. The maneuver fighter expects that the maneuver process will cause friction and disruption in the ability of opponents to respond. At best, this will eventually lead to a collapse in the opponent's business systems. A maneuver fighter uses speed, flexibility, opportunism, and dexterity to chip away at the edges of the marketplace until the entire marketplace has been taken. In doing so, unlike the attrition fighter, the maneuver fighter makes a deliberate attempt to avoid expensive, time-consuming, and exhausting confrontations with competitors. You win by artfulness and indirection—not by brute force. The great heavy-weight fighter, Mohammed Ali, summed up the defining style of the maneuver fighter when he said "Float like a butterfly, sting like a bee."

There is now a global and fundamental marketplace transition occurring from national wars of attrition to global wars of maneuver, and successful companies must adapt to this shift.

Sun Tzu described the eternal character of maneuver warfare when he said:

Go forth where they do not expect it; attack where they are unprepared.

As advantageous as this is, it is not easy to do. It demands intelligence— both the sense of being smart and having knowledge about your competitors and customers. A maneuver fighter must continually zig and zag. The problem is to decide where and when to zig and zag. Done well, the maneuver fighter will delight customers and drive competitors crazy. Done poorly, the maneuver fighter will inadvertently zig or zag directly into the attrition fighter who will crush him or her.

Data warehousing is a prerequisite to a maneuver strategy. An infrastructure of knowledge must be available to engage in maneuver fighting. With a solid infrastructure of accessible information that can be manipulated as demanded by swirling times and circumstances, the maneuver fighter can make calculated judgments as to where and when to move. Without such knowledge, a maneuver fighter will make one guess too many and be cornered by the behemoth attrition competitor.

An instructive example of maneuver is happening in the retail industry. Historically, retailers engaged in *push* marketing, where they purchased large volumes of an item from a supplier and then attempted to convince their customers to buy it. Retailers are now moving to *pull* marketing wherein they attempt to understand exactly what customers want to buy and provide a desired product assortment at ideal value points. The former doesn't require much knowledge about one's customers, but the latter requires a great deal. The push retailer stands still and doesn't need much data; the pull retailer needs precise information to support continuous moving (zigging) and maneuvering (zagging) slightly ahead of customers.

The final way to understand data warehousing strategically is to understand it as the necessary foundation for changing your business from being a slow and ponderous attrition fighter to an agile and quick maneuver fighter. Attrition fighters stand still. If you're going to stand still, of what value is knowledge to you? To the contrary, and as illustrated in Figure 2.11, a maneuver fighter is a business in constant motion. Maneuver fighters win through intelligence, not brute force. In this way, by virtue of knowledge-enabled maneuvering, you act sooner rather than later, you learn rather than repeat, you anticipate rather than react, you know rather than guess, you change rather than atrophy, you exceed rather than satisfy, and ultimately, through the accumulation of *rathers*, you win rather than lose.

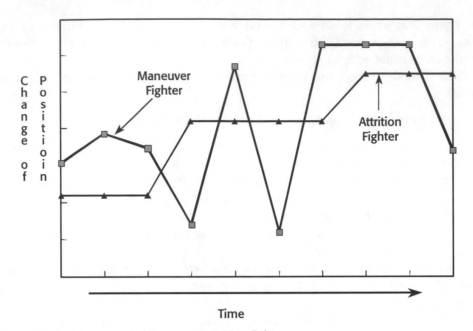

Figure 2.11   Maneuver fighter versus attrition fighter.

Conclusion

The strategic analysis of data warehousing is as follows:

- Strategy is about, and only about, building advantage. The business need to build, compound, and sustain advantage is the most fundamental and dominant business need, and it is insatiable.

- Advantage is built through deep and far-reaching strategic thinking.

- The strategic ideas that support data warehousing as a strategic initiative are learning, maneuverability, prescience, and foreknowledge. Data warehousing meets the fundamental business needs to compete in a superior manner across the elementary strategic dimension of time.

- Data warehousing is a rare instance of a rising-tide strategy. A rising-tide strategy occurs when an action yields tremendous leverage. Data warehousing raises the ability of all employees to serve their customers and out-think their competitors.

- Data warehousing achieves optimal results when one understands strategic paradox. When used as a weapon of conflict in the information age, data warehousing, paradoxically, achieves the greatest economies when it is applied in excess. One always wants the tide to be at high tide.

- Data warehousing is a mandatory prerequisite to engage in a maneuver market style, which will be the dominant form of marketplace warfare as we begin the next millennium. To continually and abruptly change business direction requires both judgment and knowledge. Hard-won experience provides the former, and data warehousing provides the latter.

Companies enter markets to win profits, not to engage in expensive and endless pitched battles with competitors. Data warehousing is of strategic value because it enables us to achieve the former while deftly avoiding the latter. This is the strategic spirit in which we should understand, implement, and manage data warehousing.

Understanding E-Commerce Strategically: The Dawn of IT Fighting

Complementing data warehousing in strategic importance to the business is e-commerce. The rise of the Internet has created radically new ways to touch customers, service customers, and deliver revolutionary products and services. This essay will provide a penetrating analysis of why e-commerce has become so vital to business success.

In an industry well known for exaggeration and hype, the phenomenal ascent of electronic commerce (e-commerce) to the forefront of industry attention has set a new standard for user interest and business opportunities. Driven by the unique ubiquity of the World Web Wide, the global Internet, and availability of universal browser interfaces, the growth and importance of e-commerce to the digital business of the new millennium cannot be over-hyped or exaggerated. Consider the following e-commerce forecasts:

- The size of the U.S. online population is expected to grow to more than 100 million in 2001 from under 20 million in 1996.

- U.S. online retail sales are expected to grow to $17 billion by 2001 from less than $1 billion in 1996.

- It is anticipated that by 2003, close to 10 percent of all business-to-business commerce will be conducted through e-commerce.

- It is forecast that U.S. business-to-business e-commerce revenue will grow by a factor of 10 to more than $300 billion by 2002.

It is no wonder that every business will need to become a high-performance e-business in the coming years or become no business at all.

What is e-commerce? As the word gets widely used, its definition continually morphs. Consider the following recent definitions from industry publications:

- E-commerce encompasses all business operations and transactions based on communication via electronic media.
- E-commerce is the buying and selling of goods and services on the Internet, especially the World Wide Web.
- E-commerce is the conduct of business on the Internet, not only buying and selling but also servicing customers and collaborating with business partners.
- E-commerce is Internet-based facilitation of trade between companies.
- E-commerce means conducting these business activities online and worldwide:
  - Company promotion
  - Product marketing
  - Negotiating and taking orders through virtual storefronts
  - Receiving payment
  - Interacting with customers for pre- and post-sales support

I would suggest that e-commerce is a very rich concept that needs to embrace all these ideas and would offer the following comprehensive definition:

E-commerce is the use of Internet-centric technologies to engage in business transactions with customers, suppliers, within the business itself, and/or any other business partners. E-commerce embraces the following:

- E-tailing (electronic retailing) or virtual storefronts on the World Wide Web (WWW)
- The gathering and use of customer demographic data through WWW contact
- Customer pre- and post-sales care, service, and inquiry
- Electronic data interchange, the business-to-business exchange of business transaction data
- The creation of the electronic or digital enterprise wherein internal business transactions, embracing the entire value chain, are intermediated through Internet-centered technologies

With the advent of e-commerce, competition and business opportunities migrate from physical marketplaces to the *marketspace*—a marketplace created, defined, nurtured, and exploited through information technology. The marketspace is a virtual realm where products and services exist in digital form, are delivered through information-based distribution channels, and that rewards speed, innovativeness, interactivity, and personalization.

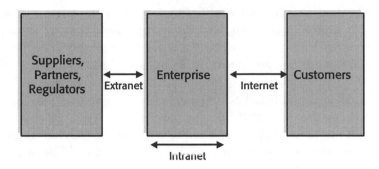

Figure 2.12   The nets of e-commerce.

Within the IT community, most of the e-commerce discussion naturally focuses on the *nets* of e-commerce: the Internet, intranets, and extranets (see Figure 2.12) and the enabling technologies such as HTML, XML, Java, software agents, and TCP-IP. While mastering these technologies is operationally important, it is beneficial to step back from a technology perspective of e-commerce and look at the underlying strategic logic that should guide our daily tactical work. What do we learn about e-commerce when we look at it through a strategy lens?

Advantage and E-Commerce

As illustrated in Figure 2.13, e-commerce is strategically exciting because it is one of those rare entities that transcends all of your choices in building advan-

	Cost	Differentiation	Focus	Execution	Maneuverability
Sustainable Competitive Advantage			E-Commerce		
Temporary Competitive Advantage			E-Commerce		

Figure 2.13   E-commerce enables advantage.

tage. E-commerce is such a rich concept that it can be used to create any of the classes of advantage (cost, focus, execution, differentiation, or maneuverability) in either of the time dimensions (sustainable or temporary). This is a rare occurrence. Most advantage opportunities are self-limiting to a few of the cells in Figure 2.13. The robustness of the impact of e-commerce on a business is such that how you will build advantage with it is constrained only by your imagination. The first way to think about e-commerce strategically is to think of it as a rich and robust platform for the building of a dynamic portfolio of sustainable and temporary advantages. E-commerce should be appreciated as a platform that can mix all the different types of advantage to create limitless attraction to customers and ever-increasing distance from competitors.

Process and E-Commerce

One of the primary ways to build advantage is through execution excellence or process superiority. As shown in Figure 2.14, process embodies the entire product/service customer experience. Some strategists, therefore, argue that the primary focus of strategy should be the nurturing of the business processes that deliver value and satisfaction to customers. The logic of competition should concentrate on how to compete—for example, the continual improvement of process.

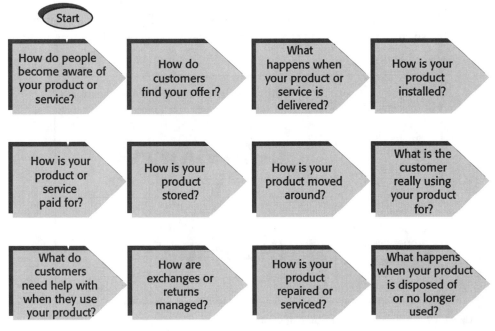

Figure 2.14 Consumption chain.

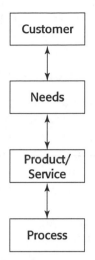

Figure 2.15   Process relationships.

Figure 2.15 illustrates the complicated relationship of process to customers. A customer will have many needs that need to be satisfied and a need may be shared by many customers. A need may be satisfied by multiple products/services, and a product or service may satisfy many needs. Finally, a product or service is delivered through multiple processes, and a process may support multiple products or services. Because of its complexity and importance, process provides a rich opportunity to distinguish oneself with one's customers.

Processes have many important attributes that can be attacked to satisfy customers and distant yourself from competitors. Processes can be judged by the following characteristics:

- speed	- quality	- personalization
- consistency	- learning	- acuity
- exception processing	- costs	- customer satisfaction
- agility	- measurable	- scalability
- innovativeness	- leverage	- frictionless
- accuracy	- productivity	- collaborativenss
- simplicity	- functionality	- starting/ending with customer

What is strategically important about e-commerce is that it can be used to address all these dimensions. In particular, e-commerce is uniquely capable of addressing the attributes of speed, innovativenss, simplicity, lack of friction, productivity, personalization, learning, and collaboration. The second strategic way to look at e-commerce is as a platform for creating attribute-rich processes that interact with customers, interact with business partners, and/or enable internal business activities.

Hyper-Competition and E-Commerce

Hyper-competition means most of all that you must make a war of rapid and disruptive movements replace your traditional strategy of defending your strongholds. There is no safe harbor in retreat. Either you surrender or you become a hyper-competitive predator. Those are your only choices. It is exaggerated, but only slightly so, that maneuverability is the primary type of advantage that a company must have to succeed in a hyper-competitive marketplace.

The problem of hyper-competitive business strategy reduces to being able to continuously turn the "front." Using a military analogy, armies line up against each other across a front (see Figure 2.16). Then, as shown in Figure 2.17, the trick is to turn the front. The obvious reason is to permit your front-line forces to proceed unopposed, but the more compelling reason is that it disrupts the support infrastructure behind the front and displaces all the support systems from their positions. Turning the front ruins the plans of the opponent and causes tremendous friction for the opponent as it tries to reestablish order between the new front and its support infrastructure.

As shown in Figure 2.18, the same logic applies to business strategy. In a hyper-competitive business environment, it is necessary to be able to continually turn the front to create new value propositions for customers or to devalue

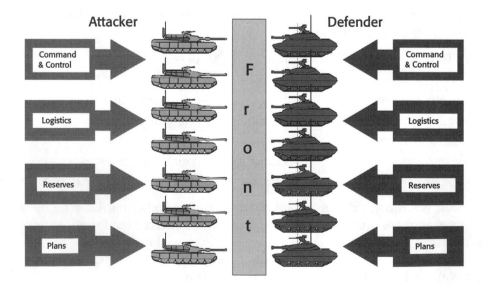

Figure 2.16   The front.

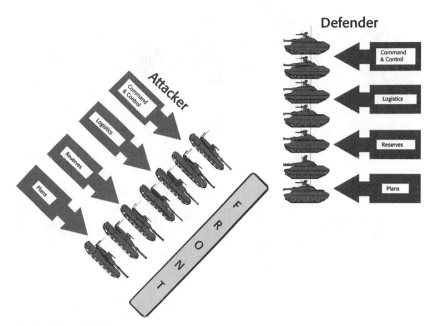

Figure 2.17   Turn the front.

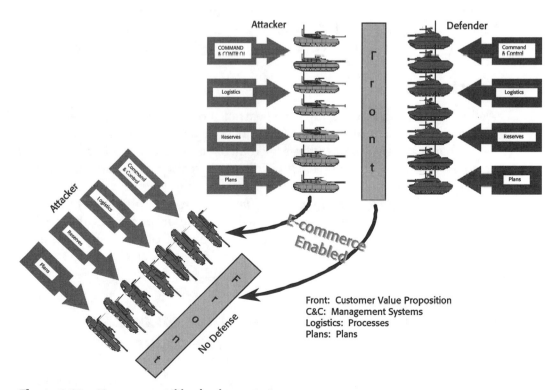

Front: Customer Value Proposition
C&C: Management Systems
Logistics: Processes
Plans: Plans

Figure 2.18   Hyper-competitive business strategy.

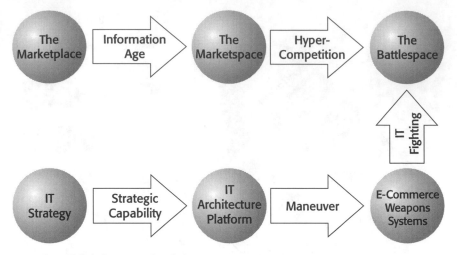

Figure 2.19   IT fighting: A revised view.

the initiatives of your opponents. In the information age, turning the front equates to being able to turn your e-commerce systems. The competitor who has a deeper and more far-reaching strategy for commanding e-commerce will have a definitive advantage in an endless war of turning the fronts. Figure 2.19 shows how Figure 2.5 is revised. IT weapon systems become specific e-commerce weapon systems. E-commerce provides the vehicle to confront the battlespace.

Conclusion

We live in exciting times, and at the heart of those is the rise of the electronic enterprise. An electronic business (e-business) is an enterprise in which all the value chains are electronically intermediated—a business that is built on and operated through e-commerce. How you strategically understand and implement e-commerce will make a dramatic difference to your success. Miyamoto Musashi, in his great strategy classic, *The Five Rings*, wrote, "Essentially the weapon in and of itself is meaningless without the proper applications of its virtues by the warrior." The weapon of e-commerce offers many virtues of advantage. It is your strategic challenge to build e-commerce weapon systems that permit your business to command the battlespace.

Information Technology Substitution and Diffusion: A Primer for the IT Executive

Whether one is doing architecture, data warehousing, or e-commerce, one has to be concerned with what information technologies will be deployed and how to evolve that portfolio of technologies to maximize investment efficiency and effectiveness. The problem of technology management has grown exponentially with the distribution of computing resources. This essay provides a strategy for managing the selection and evolution of the technology portfolio.

As we move into the new millennium, the management of business is becoming increasingly complex and difficult as virulent hyper-competition accelerates. Industry turbulence is being driven by factors such as globalization of competition, slow growth in developed countries, changing customer demographics and value expectations, bypass competition from suppliers, relentless cost pressures, and the advent of new electronic distribution and sales channels. All of these factors are conspiring to expedite the need to reshape and renew all aspects of company value chains. As never before, it is now urgent to concurrently improve the efficiency of all business functions and processes while personalizing service to the customer.

Information technology is critical to addressing these challenges. All typical business functions—such as inventory management, logistics, sales management, store operations, financial management, and human resources management—can be made more efficient and effective by redesigning each function to take full advantage of existing and emerging information technologies. Dramatically improved information movement and management technologies are increasingly the means to achieving improved business ends (customer satisfaction, market share, and revenue growth). Electronic commerce, in particular (as personified by multimedia, the Internet, kiosks, interactive television, and EDI), is becoming the new mandatory information movement and management means of touching, retaining, and selling to extremely fickle customers.

While information technology provides sophisticated tools to overcome the challenges of our times and configure a new, vibrant, and successful organization, it also demands making procurement decisions under escalating uncertainty and risk. There are more information technologies, vendors, and choices than ever before. No sooner is a decision made then a new technology is announced that apparently makes yesterday's champion obsolete. Users and technologists insist that the new challenger must be adopted immediately if the company is to remain competitive. Systems integration becomes a nightmare as the system configurations continue to mutate.

Information technology presents the IT executive with a pressing dilemma. On one hand, it certainly is a significant means to winning the hyper-competitive wars of the new millennium. On the other hand, IT itself is undergoing such rapid change and presents us with such discontinuities that it is increasingly difficult to make selection decisions. What can be done to increase understanding of the evolution of information technologies so that the addition of new technologies and the retirement of dated technologies can be done in an orderly manner? Can we understand the strategic logic of technological change so that the apparent chaos can be mastered and we can make optimum decisions as to what will and will not be in our IT portfolios? Is there a way to know when it is the ideal time to adopt a new technology?

The unanimous answer to these questions is "yes." A discipline of study called *technology substitution and diffusion* provides a theory of how technologies substitute for each other. Embedded in the theory are tools called "S" curves that can be used to assist in making the difficult decisions. Understanding and applying technology substitution and diffusion methods are critical to making the best possible judgments regarding if and when to jump between information technologies.

The remainder of this essay explains technology substitution and diffusion theory. The following subjects are developed:

Technology substitution and diffusion theory. This section explains the logic of the methodology. The primary tool of technology substitution and diffusion theory is called the "S" curve.

An "S" curve analysis. This section analyzes Java, an exciting and emergent technology, in terms of "S" curves.

Course of action. This section provides a suggested prescription for how the IT executive should incorporate "S" curves into his or her decision-making processes.

By prudently applying technology substitution and diffusion theory, IT executives can take command of the technology change conundrum and alleviate the ceaseless procurement turmoil.

Technology Substitution and Diffusion Theory

For decades, researchers have been intrigued about how a new technology replaces an incumbent technology. Is each instance of substitution a unique event, with nothing in common with other substitution instances, or is there a repeatable pattern that can be understood and for which we can plan? Was the process through which steamboats replaced sailboats the same or different from the process through which transistors replaced vacuum tubes? The answer is that the process by which technologies replace each other follows a reasonably predictable sequence of events, and the resulting theory of that research is called "technology substitution and diffusion theory." This theory can explain how, when, and if a new information technology will replace an existing one. It is through this theory that IT executives can take greater command and control of their technology procurement decisions.

Technology substitution is the process by which one technology displaces another technology in performing a function or set of functions for a market. The substitute technology offers the customer an inducement to switch by virtue of an improved value proposition. Diffusion is the process by which a marketplace adopts a substitute technology. Substitution is the process by which one technology challenges and replaces another, and diffusion is the process through which the substitute is accepted or rejected by the marketplace. Substitution and diffusion are the engines and instruments of economic progress. It is through technology substitution and diffusion that new plateaus of wealth creation are obtainable.

Underlying technology substitution is the idea that people have an enduring set of basic needs. The pursuit of substitution is to find ever-better solutions (value propositions) for those relatively fixed needs. There are five basic drivers for new technologies:

Serendipity. An accidental discovery leads to the discovery of a superior technology.

Military research. Military research and development lead to the discovery of a new commercial technology.

Planned obsolescence. Commercial research and development are done to obsolete an existing product in order to renew market sales.

Depletion of resources. The foreseeable depletion of some factor of production leads to research to develop a superior replacement before the resource is depleted.

Competitive pressures. The need to endlessly offer superior value propositions to customers stimulates intense research and development.

The last driver, competitive pressures, impels the subject at hand.

Market diffusion is the dynamics of market acceptance of the substitution of a new product for an existing product. In technology substitution and diffusion jargon, the incumbent product is referred to as the "defender" and the substitute product is referred to as the "attacker." The speed of diffusion is a function of the following:

Value proposition. How far superior is the value proposition of the attacker to the value proposition of the defender?

Infrastructure. How much infrastructure support must be put in place to support the new product?

Learning. What communication channels are used to reach, persuade, and influence the market?

Ease of substitution. How much effort (time, cost, training, etc.) is required to adopt the attacker?

Defense. How does the defender defend itself and, in doing so, alter the comparative value propositions?

Diffusion is usually expressed in terms of market share.

What Is a Product?

A product is understood to be a set of functions built on a technology base that meets some customer need (see Figure 2.20). Therefore, three types of generic technology substitutions may occur:

Function substitution. The attacker displaces the defender in performing some functions but not all. The attacker may also add new functions, as well as replace existing functions. The resulting relationship between the two products becomes complementary.

Product substitution. The functionality of the defender is replaced in its entirety by the attacker. The defender's asset base, however, remains viable.

Asset substitution. Not only does the attacker replace the product, but it is done with a different set of technological assets that obsoletes and destroys the technology competencies and investments of the defender.

Figure 2.21 shows the three points of attack. A substitution attack is not necessarily constant in its target and, depending on situational dynamics, can swing between types.

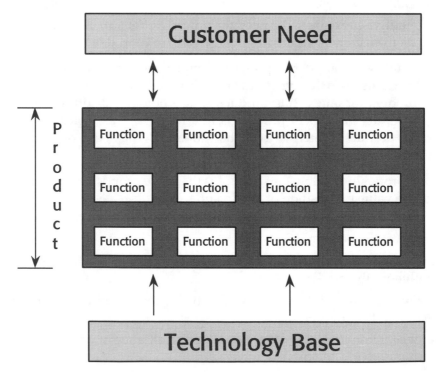

Figure 2.20   A product.

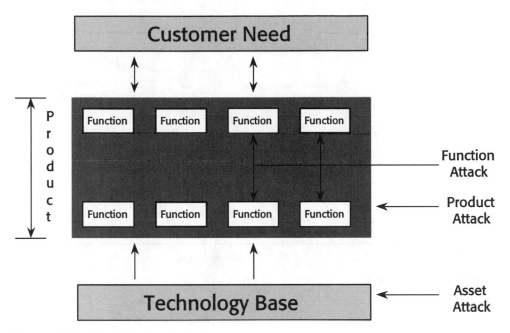

Figure 2.21 A substitute attack.

"S" Curves

The life cycle of a technology is routinely illustrated through the use of "S" curves (see Figure 2.22). The substitution process of two technologies is illustrated using dueling "S" curves (see Figure 2.23). The basic logic of an "S" curve is as follows:

All technologies should/must be understood in terms of performance limits. As investments are made in a technology, that technology's price/performance improvement will follow an "S" curve shape (see Figure 2.22).

At first, in Stage I, the product will be incomplete and expensive and will appeal only to a niche market with very specific objectives for using the product.

In Stages II and III, dramatic improvements are made in the product. For every dollar invested in improving the product, there is a significantly greater return in its value proposition. An intense rush of innovation to improve the product follows.

In Stage IV, the limits of the technology are reached. It is increasingly difficult to squeeze out improvements. For every dollar invested in research and development (R&D), less than a dollar in added value is generated.

Market diffusion also follows an "S" curve pattern, as shown in Figure 2.24. The point at which the diffusion rate is highest is called the point of inflection. At this point, most of the barriers to market acceptance have been overcome,

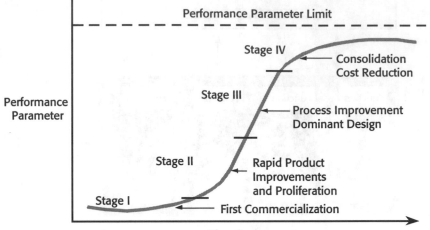
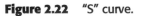

Figure 2.22   "S" curve.

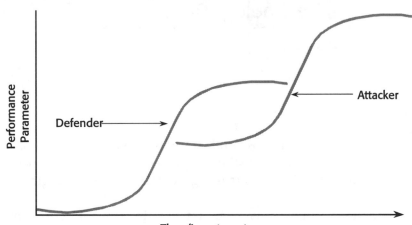

Figure 2.23   Dueling "S" curves.

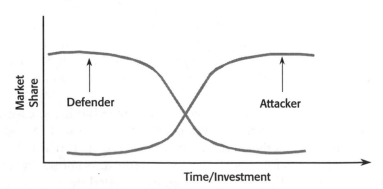

Figure 2.24   Market diffusion.

and a horde of imitators follows the aggressive early pioneers. Customer adoption patterns can be segmented into five types, as follows:

Pioneers. Those customers who have a very specific need for the technology and are willing to cope with its shortcomings to acquire the new features/functionality.

Early adopters. Those customers who wait for some early proof of the concept and then jump at the technology.

The front middle. The average customer who will adopt the technology once it is proven.

The back middle. The same as the front middle, but slower to act because of various constraints on their behavior.

The laggards. Those customers who adopt the technology late, if ever.

What is particularly interesting is that once the diffusion process starts and the product achieves a relatively small percentage of market penetration, the attack process almost inevitably goes to completion (unless the technology is attacked by another attacker and becomes a defender). The reason for this is that if the technology provides clear benefits when it is only at the beginning of its "S" curve, its attraction becomes overwhelming as it dramatically improves while ascending the "S" curve.

The diffusion process often takes decades. For example, consider the diffusion time periods within the United States for the following common technologies:

- Electric lights took approximately 50 years to achieve a 95 percent diffusion level.

- The radio took approximately 35 years to achieve a 95 percent diffusion level.

- The telephone took approximately 80 years to achieve a 90 percent diffusion level.

- Television took approximately 30 years to achieve a 90 percent diffusion level.

By their very nature, information technologies that are capital-, infrastructure-, and skill-intensive require time to diffuse. Diffusion should be measured by steady "S" curve growth in market share, not by market researcher pronouncements that often have no relationship to the governing realities of "S" curve theory.

The Defender and Attacker

It is therefore typical in technology substitution situations for both the attacker and the defender to coexist for a drawn-out time period. The end of the "S" curve for the incumbent is not extinction. The end of the "S" curve for a defeated former colossus is a much harder fate to brave; it is obsolescence.

What must happen if there is to be sustained progress for civilization? At some point on the "S" curve, a new technology must emerge to challenge the existing technology. Fundamental to this replacement technology is that it must have a higher price/performance limit. The attacker, as shown in Figure 2.23, then challenges the defender for the market. One can almost always recognize a strong "S" curve attack by the need of the defender to drastically lower prices. This is exactly what IBM and other mainframe vendors had to do to respond to the open systems client/server attack.

The defender has at least six defenses from which to choose, in any combination and varying depth:

- The defender can search for new and unaffected markets.

- The defender can focus on entrenched customers who will be late, if ever, new product adopters.

- The defender can aggressively improve its product (i.e., improve service, lower pricing, improve warranty).

- The defender can raise fear, uncertainty, and doubt (FUD) to stall the migration.

- The defender can dramatically increase its R&D in an attempt to generally extend its "S" curve or focus the R&D for a "function defense." In a function defense, the defender identifies those function clusters that the attacker will have the most difficulty matching, then enhances them. Thus, the defender attempts to contain and limit the substitution to a function attack. This will result in the two products being complementary, rather than the attacker replacing the defender.

- The defender can accept the inevitable and move to the new "S" curve. This may be done overtly or covertly. When we say covertly, we mean that the product maintains its external name and image but that its internal characteristics are altered to match the attacker's technology. This strategy has certain emotional and psychological advantages with highly committed customers.

The defender generally enjoys the strong advantage of being in harmony with a prevailing "dominant logic." A dominant logic is a widely held set of beliefs and assumptions that guide a community's conceptualization of problems and actions. The correctness of a dominant logic is taken for granted, and actions in conflict with it are held under suspicion. To be successful, the attacker must overcome the prevailing dominant logic that supports the incumbent and must create a superior replacement logic. Consequently, the attacker, to be successful, must offer a clearly superior value proposition. It is not enough for the attacker just to be better; it must offer a premium value over the incumbent.

In practice, defenders often defend quite poorly, and if the attacking technology has a superior "S" curve its victory is preordained. The reasons for a poor defense are as follows:

- Due to sunken costs, the defender is not willing to abandon its investment.

- The existing technology is politically strong. The organization's power system is not even willing to entertain that an attack is occurring, yet alone consider converting.

- The organization's traditions and culture are inwardly focused. It is not conceivable that an alternative solution could exist. This results in a very colored view of the marketplace.

- The organization does not have the will, competencies, or technology assets to change.

- Inertia—the business machine just keeps moving straight ahead, immune to marketplace realities.

In any case, if one studies the history of technology substitutions, one will discover that while it may take considerable time to overcome the barriers and climb the "S" curve, attackers do remarkably well, and defenders routinely fail to adapt and become displaced.

The Paradox of Unit Sales

An interesting and important paradox of technology substitution and diffusion is that the sales of the attacker and the defender can both grow robustly at the same time. The defender often asserts rising sales as proof that a viable attack is not happening. Figure 2.25 shows typical sales curves for dueling "S" curve products. Notice that both products may be growing in unit sales for an extended period. This is quite common in substitution situations and may be due to the following:

- The new functionality of the challenger, with its complementary relationship to the defender, actually stimulates demand for the defender. This attack is a function attack.

- The slower diffusion rate is compared to that of the overall market growth. The rising tide of demand lifts sales for the defender as well as the attacker.

Eventually, however, the attacker continues to grow, and an inevitable decline, not only in market share but also in unit sales, occurs for the defender.

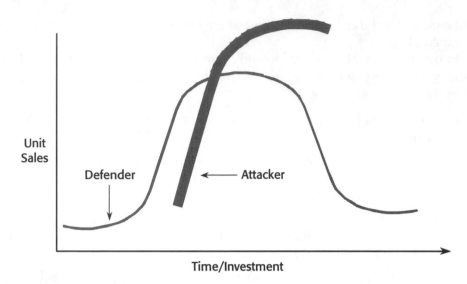

Figure 2.25 Sales curves.

Thus, an interesting paradox exists—a product may be growing in unit sales but concurrently declining in market share. This is exactly what happened to mainframe computers as the network computing revolution accelerated. Obviously, the important element in evaluating the success of an attack is the evolving direction of market share of both the attacker and defender, not their unit sales.

Know-How Curves

Figure 2.26 illustrates that each "S" curve has a corresponding and shadow-like know-how curve that mirrors its life cycle. The know-how curve reflects the accumulated knowledge that has been gathered regarding how to exploit the technology. When one moves between "S" curves rather than jumping curves, one often takes a giant step, where for some period of time one foot is on the new "S" curve but the other foot is on the old know-how curve. It is therefore not surprising that the initial experiences with new technologies almost always prove disappointing; one needs time to develop the missing, but much needed, know-how. Implications for absorbing new technologies are as follows:

- Understand the existence and significance of the shadow know-how curve for each "S" curve.

- Anticipate the paucity of know-how when switching curves, and plan appropriately. One must either plan to throw a test system away (prototyping) or buy assistance from those who already have the know-how.

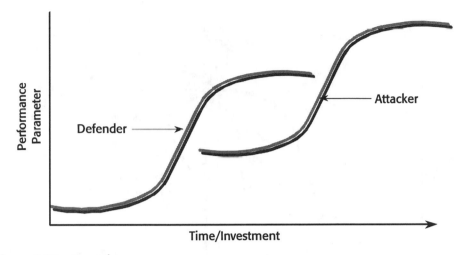

Figure 2.26 Know-how curves.

- Know-how can be a source of competitive advantage. One should carefully consider whether it is truly advisable to share know-how and, by doing so, to enhance the ability of others (including one's competitors) to climb know-how curves quickly, thereby erasing one's hard-won knowledge.

Technologies are available to all. The greatest technological advantage one can possess is often one's knowledge and one's skill in deploying that knowledge.

Thrashing

The reason to jump "S" curves is to achieve new feature/performance benefits within a finite time period. If simultaneous "S" curve attacks occur concurrently (the attacker is being attacked while attacking) and if one jumps curves too often within a finite time period, one may experience the anomaly of "thrashing." Thrashing occurs when, because of too many jumps (even though the potential exists for better price/performance) within one's time window, one is actually worse off than had one not jumped or, at least, not jumped as often.

Figure 2.27 illustrates thrashing. In the example shown, the user would have been best off to make only one jump. By making the second jump, he or she is actually worse off than had he or she stayed with the original technology. Because business success often demands exceptional use of the most advantageous IT, the IT executive must carefully consider the time effect of "S" curve

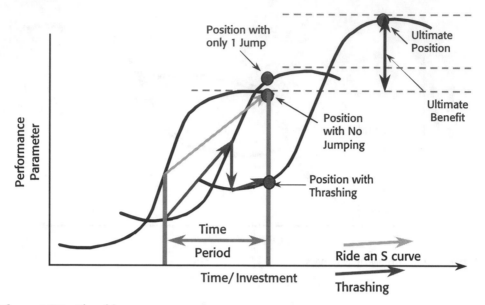

Figure 2.27   Thrashing.

jumps. By jumping too infrequently, one is left in a position of technological inferiority. By jumping too often, one thrashes. Managing IT in an environment of simultaneous "S" curve attacks requires the following:

- A deep understanding of "S" curve theory
- An understanding of business needs to guide one's choice of new technologies
- Seasoned judgment

Thrashing explains why companies that are more conservative in jumping "S" curves are often more successful than the most aggressive companies within a given technological time window.

Paradox

"S" curve analysis explains a number of paradoxes that routinely lead to incorrect analysis of technology change:

- As a product accelerates through the high growth portion of the "S" curve and achieves ever-greater market share, it, paradoxically, also approaches its limits.
- Once a successful "S" curve attack has begun, a defender can be growing in unit sales but, paradoxically, declining in market share. While a defender is growing in units sold, it is dying in market share.

■ The attacker's success, paradoxically, both causes the defender to lower its prices (to the benefit of those who will not convert) and stimulates sales of the defender because of complementary functionality. The laggards, paradoxically, disparage the attacking technology but benefit from it in terms of the improved value propositions it forces from the defender.

Technology substitution and diffusion must often be analyzed in terms of such paradoxes that lead to conclusions that are quite different from those derived from conventional linear thinking.

Summary

Technology substitution and diffusion theory and its chief tool, the "S" curve, provide a rich strategic framework from which to make insightful decisions on whether one should adopt new information technologies. They also explain what is meant when someone asserts that a technology is dead, dying, or a "dinosaur." It means that a successful "S" curve attack is underway and that the fate of the incumbent is foretold. The very act of thinking about technological choices in terms of "S" curves will radically improve one's ability to choose both new technologies in which to invest and when to invest in them.

An "S" Curve Analysis of Java

One of the most exciting and hyped technologies to come along (in an industry that swims in exciting and hyped technologies) is the programming language called Java from Sun Systems. Eric Schmidt, formerly Chief Technology Officer of Sun Systems, said, "Java is bigger than the Internet." A few months later, Steven Ballmer, Executive Vice President of Microsoft, was compelled to say in an interview, "The notion that the PC is dead is the topic of crazy minds." What is going on here?

This is the beginning of an instance of technology substitution and diffusion. Java and a related technology called the WEB or network PC are attacking the defending fat client PC technology based on the products of Microsoft and Intel (often referred to as the WINTEL architecture or fat PC). This attack is of interest to the IT executive because, while the Java/WEB PC environment alleges many advantages over the incumbent, it is in the development stages of its "S" curve. Nevertheless, IT executives are constantly reading about Java and are coming under pressure to introduce it. What is the strategic situation?

We will now perform an "S" curve analysis of Java by referring to the figures just discussed. This will illustrate how "S" curves can be used to structure the technology substitution and diffusion debate within a company and provide needed insights so that optimum (as opposed to emotional) decisions can be made. We will do a tight technology substitution and diffusion analysis of Java by asking a series of "S" curve questions and answering them. Although the related technology of WEB PC is not necessary in order to use Java, we will include it in our analysis. Java alone does not obsolete the fat PC, but Java plus the WEB PC does.

What is Java? (Figure 2.20). Java is an objected-oriented programming language, similar to C++, that was specifically designed for distributed computing environments. It is a product in the sense of Figure 2.20. It is stored on a server computer and is dynamically brought to the requesting client computer at the time of demand. It is compiled into an intermediary state called "byte code" that permits it to be portable across client machines. A virtual Java machine runs on each client computer. It interprets the byte code at the moment of execution.

What is the WEB PC? (Figure 2.20). The WEB PC is an information appliance, a product, designed to work in an Internet environment in which software and content are delivered to the PC at the moment of demand. Unlike conventional PCs (in which all application software is stored on the PC), the WEB PC is basically a dynamic execution environment.

What is the attack? (Figure 2.21). Java alone is a function attack on the WINTEL fat PC architecture. The software at the client site can be dynamically loaded onto the fat PC that can run a virtual Java machine. When you add the WEB PC, the attack becomes an asset attack. It becomes an asset attack because the Java/WEB PC can do everything the fat client can do, plus it offers tremendous improvements in portability, simplicity, and cost of software distribution and administration.

Where are Java and the WEB PC on their "S" curves? What is the new performance limit? (Figure 2.22). Both technologies are in the growth stage. New features that are needed to make Java an operational technology are announced monthly.

The improved performance elements that a Java/WEB PC provides over a fat client Microsoft/Intel environment are the following:

- Simplicity of use
- Dynamic software distribution
- Simplified software administration and customer support and service
- Portability
- Openness
- Less expensive client hardware

How is Java riding the "S" curve? (Figure 2.22). One area in which Java has urgently needed performance improvement has been execution speed.

Since its introduction as a slow, interpretive language, Java's "S" curve execution performance has been improved through source code compilers, "just in" compilers, and byte code compilers. This is an excellent example of how a technology improves as it rides the "S" curve.

What are the diffusion prospects for Java? (Figure 2.24). Java's diffusion will show a gradual *pattern*, per Figure 2.24, for the following reasons:

■ Customers will have to be convinced of its value proposition. In particular, they will be concerned about security, speed of client execution, and ability to interface with legacy technologies.

■ Programmers will have to be taught not only how to program in Java, but how to design Java applications and systems. The latter will prove challenging as delivering software on demand in small applets is quite different from a resident software model.

■ The infrastructure for Java is not yet in place. Virtual Java machines need to be resident on client machines and, equally importantly, high-speed communication is necessary as an infrastructure requirement. The architecture does not work if the client-to-server connection is not broadband.

■ For mobile users, Java may prove not to be a viable alternative in the foreseeable future.

How will the defender defend? (Figure 2.23). WINTEL proponents will vehemently defend their dominant logic. Among other things, they will do the following:

■ Aggressively incorporate Java into their systems to confine the attack to a function attack

■ Raise fear, uncertainty, and doubt (FUD) about the immaturity of Java and the lack of business applications

■ Carry out a function defense by emphasizing the strengths of their platform (i.e., security, performance, and leverage of existing knowledge and technology)

Inevitably, many of the arguments that mainframe proponents made against the PC, WINTEL proponents will now make against the Java/WEB PC. This defense is proving particularly successful against the WEB PC because of the dramatic price reduction of the PC, improvements in software maintainability, and the desire of the user community to maintain and extend their sunken investment in Windows technology.

What about the problem of know-how? (Figure 2.26). This will prove to be a major drag on early progress. Performing client/server functions in a Java/WEB PC architecture will differ from performing those functions in a fat PC environment. Aggressive prototyping and pathfinder projects are called for to gather and then propagate the necessary knowledge.

What about thrashing? (Figure 2.27). Thrashing is not an issue in the foreseeable future. There is no attacker attacking the Java attacker.

Will Java and WEB PC complete a successful attack? I believe that they will and, per Figure 2.24, will gradually displace the fat PC architecture. The advantages offered by the new architecture are sufficient to overcome the dominant logic of the existing one. A good way to test if this is true is to invert the attacker and defender. Per Figure 2.23, pretend that Java and the WEB PC are the defenders against a WINTEL attack. Would that attack be successful? If the Java and WEB PC environment had 14 years of maturity on its side, as does the Microsoft fat client environment, would a fat client PC environment be an attractive alternative to a mature Java/ WEB PC environment?

Other than for people who have slow communications, I think not. I therefore believe, though it will certainly be messy and emotional, that we will witness a normal technology substitution and diffusion event. In the next year or two, we will see experimentation with Java and WEB PCs, and we will see the fat client proponents attempt to position Java as a complementary technology (function attack in Figure 2.21). They will make all of the arguments for the dominant logic technology and will raise a great deal of FUD. Nevertheless, the benefits of portability, cost, simplicity, and administration control far outweigh the early problems. As Java rides its "S" curve, it will win market share, and, not surprisingly, we will see a period of time in which both Java and the incumbent PC technology are both growing.

When should we jump? This is a question of balancing one's business needs against the "S" curve positions of Java and WEB PCs. If one is by nature a conservative user of IT, moving applications to Java now will put one at the front of the curve. Conversely, if one sees opportunities to drastically improve automation or electronic sales through this architecture, one has a business need that motivates one to reconsider one's normal posture. When to jump is an individual business decision that is tempered by an "S" curve understanding of the situation.

Summary

In this section, we have applied "S" curves to analyze Java technology and the associated technology of WEB PCs. What we have seen is that much of the rhetoric about these technologies, as well as about the Microsoft/Intel defending technologies, is fully explainable through an "S" curve analysis. It is our conclusion that Java will prove to be a successful attacker.

Course of Action

Business success will be more and more closely linked with one's selection and deployment of information movement and management technologies. When information technologies were used for just backroom operations, who did it better did not make the difference. As information technologies are used increasingly to touch and influence the customer, technology choice can make a strategic difference.

My recommendation is simple and straightforward. Technology selection and adoption are too important to be left to the emotional preferences of the staff and the competing screams of the vendors. An anchor of reason is necessary. Technology substitution and diffusion theory provides such an anchor.

I strongly recommend that IT executives take the following actions:

- Train staff in "S" curves.

- Insist that new technology proposals include an "S" curve analysis. Have the staff perform the "S" curve analysis across time (i.e., the situation today, six months from now, and a year from now).

- Insist that suppliers present information in terms of "S" curves. Ask them what they are attacking, what kind of attack it is, and how gathering the know-how can be accelerated. In addition, how will they overcome the dominant logic?

- Have some team members take the role of the defenders. Let them explain how they will defend against the attack. Why will the attack fail?

- Reverse the roles of the attacker and the defender. Could the defender as the attacker win? Could the attacker as defender uphold its dominant logic?

- Keep the debate on adopting new technologies centered on "S" curves. This will eliminate the emotionalism that is common in technology substitution situations.

All of this is remarkably simple to do and will radically improve a group's ability to make insightful decisions about new technologies.

Conclusion

In the coming years, the rush of new technologies offering promise to businesses will accelerate. While the risks and rewards associated with technology decisions both increase, time windows for making these decisions will shorten. People will want to know now. They will want to know why what is being done is being done. Whether one chooses to implement the new technology or defer, some interest group will want a cogent explanation.

In the chaos of business in the new millennium, "S" curves can provide an anchor for a fast and substantive analysis of emerging technologies. They supplement existing methods and provide a strategic perspective that many popular approaches do not consider. The efficacy of the technology selection process will be dramatically improved with the incorporation of "S" curve analysis.

Commitment in Information Technology Strategy

Most information technology analysis understandably focuses on technologies. Experience has shown that, more often than not, success is more tightly linked to the commitment of the implementation teams to their technology efforts. The human part of the information technology equation usually makes the difference. This essay focuses on the people aspects of information technology evolution.

The debate over whether information technology (IT) is strategic has come to an abrupt end. As the information age accelerates and new value creation dramatically shifts to those who can, with superiority, move and manage bits as opposed to move and manage atoms, information technology strategy has taken on a new urgency to the business. As shown in Figure 2.5, most businesses are discovering that information technology and its fuel, software, are the new source of sustainable and temporary competitive advantage. It is increasingly through information technology that consumer attraction and loyalty are accomplished while competitor initiatives are muted. It is therefore not surprising that business strategy is more and more influenced by, enabled by, and dependent on information technology strategy.

As would naturally be expected, much of the focus of information technology strategy has been on *technology*. As a consequence of this, IT strategy often focuses almost exclusively on the *nonhuman*; for example, IT strategists exhaustively debate operating systems, databases, the Web, object technologies, Java, wireless communications, and convergence. What they do not debate, but is often the deciding variable in strategy success, is the human element of IT strategy, and, in particular, the issue of building and sustaining organizational commitment to the selected technology strategy. Though exaggerated, but only slightly so, we would assert that IT strategy may need to focus on technology, the nonhuman, but its ultimate execution success is more tightly dependent on its ability to manage the human issues of organizational and individual commitment. A mediocre technology strategy, implemented with a deep and far-reaching organizational resolve, will be a brilliant success while an exceptional technology strategy, implemented with apathy, will be a failure. The strategic performance of the IT assets will be greater if IT strategy shifts from an unqualified absorption with the nonhuman to an appreciation of the human.

Commitment has become so fundamental to IT strategy because the hyper-competitive nature of the information age has converted strategy into a war of movement. Regardless of the portfolio of advantage that you will create through IT, it will constantly need to be refreshed. The absence of commitment creates *friction* to agility and maneuverability, and it retards speed. Friction is the onerous counter-force that pushes back on effort. It saps the strength from initiatives. IT strategy as commitment means that one understands that IT strategy must be concerned with the nonhuman, but for the nonhuman to succeed, the human issues of building and sustaining commitment must be addressed to minimize friction.

Commitment Planning

A commitment plan is a specific set of actions taken to establish and sustain credibility. It is a set of actions taken to alter beliefs and redirect the actions of others in support of your technology strategy. It demonstrates the commitment of the leadership team to the strategy and, by doing so, influences and shapes the commitment levels of the staff to the strategy. A commitment plan complements the technology plan.

Commitment is willingness by individuals and organizational entities to execute high levels of effort and sacrifice over an extended period of time to overcome obstacles and challenges on behalf of a shared agenda. The strategic logic of commitment is that commitment yields trust, trust yields belief, and belief yields effort—effort that proceeds without the depleting effects of organizational friction. It is by approaching friction-free effort that strategic performance is accelerated through commitment planning.

It certainly would be best of all if no commitment planning were necessary. If it can be anticipated that the organization will enthusiastically and automatically embrace your technology initiatives, you have a highly unusual and favorable situation. Unfortunately, this is often not the case. As a result of previous half-hearted efforts, constant shifting of priorities, and a collapse of trust due to downsizing and other anti-people efforts, many IT managers find themselves with a staff with the following friction-packed attitudes:

- They are jaded, skeptical, and cynical; they regard each new initiative and strategy as the "Strategic Program du Jour." The staff maxim is "Don't bother, this too shall pass."

- Based on a rich history, they believe "Management believes deeply in little and is committed to less." Management appears to suffer from attention deficit disorder.

- Based on previous experiences where they devoted themselves only to have their efforts canceled and discarded, their feelings about management are that "It is not that they do not have the strength of their convictions, it is that they don't have any convictions to have strength about."

In essence, the staff has become adept in a friction-full game of pretend in which you pretend to believe in your strategy and they pretend to execute it. Commitment planning is necessary to move from pretense to effort and from muddling mediocre performance to exceptional strategic performance.

Types of Commitment

Though typically presented and discussed as a nondecomposable idea, commitment can be partitioned into the three subclassifications of intellectual commitment, emotional commitment, and political commitment. Intellectual commitment is the rational understanding of an effort. It appeals to logic and reason and is normally the easiest to obtain. A person who is intellectually committed is a person who understands the flow of thinking and evidence that supports the initiative and is satisfied with that chain of thought. Due to the technical and precise nature of their work, members of an information technology community pride themselves on their reasoning abilities and will not support initiatives unless they have seen, critiqued, and come to satisfactory terms with the evidence.

Emotional commitment represents how an individual feels about an initiative. An initiative may present opportunity, but it may equally invoke fear. People ask themselves the emotionally loaded commitment question, "What does this mean to me?" If this strategy is followed, they speculate "What will it mean to my job status, my mobility, my skills and competencies, my relationships, my personal ambition?" Emotional commitment is a very personal type of commitment, and the same set of actions will conjure up as many responses as people being affected.

People who are emotionally uncomfortable with a strategy will often engage in desperate logic. Desperate logic is the attempt to find any and all possible refutations and lump them together as a rebuttal. Though normally presented in a more hidden manner, an overt example of desperate logic would be as follows:

Person A loans person B her car. When B returns it, person A tells her that it has a new dent to which person B replies "The car had the dent when I borrowed it, and I did not return the car with a dent, and, in any case, I did not borrow your car."

A person who engages in desperate logic is very uncomfortable with a situation and will grope for any reasons to reduce his or her emotional discomfort and will certainly not commit.

Political commitment is the willingness of individuals to use their organizational power to make something happen. Organizations divide, as do all social institutions, into political interest groups based on factors such as division of work, resource allocations, shared mental models, training and skills, shared experiences, career aspirations, and job levels. Strategic change will, by definition, alter status, power, resource allocations, and importance of job positions in the organization. As a consequence, some political groups will perceive the strategy as a threat, some will prefer the status quo, and even those who would win by successful implementation will often be cautious due to the risks associated with obtaining a new political order. By their nature, political groups focus on the continued well-being of their group. The group interest supersedes organizational interest, and the groups are not interested in change, regardless of merit, which has a negative impact on their group's standing. As a consequence, political groups will try to control what will be debated, the legitimacy of the proposed strategy, and the degree of commitment. Political commitment is, consequentially, the hardest to achieve.

In summary, we suggest that commitment sits on a continuum with two extremes. At one end are the fully committed who understand the strategy; they like it and are willing to use their power to make it happen. At the other end are the noncommitted. They think it is nonsense, they believe that it is no good for them, and they will use their political power to stop it. For your information technology strategy to succeed, you must achieve a favorable position along the continuum that mobilizes enough commitment. By enough commitment, I mean enough sustainable effort to overcome all the external obstacles and challenges to achieving the strategy plus remaining internal organizational friction to your efforts.

Commitment Design

Commitment is too important to be assumed, left to chance, or be the product of wishful thinking. You must explicitly design a commitment strategy as part of your overall technology strategy. The objective of a commitment strategy is to build, sustain, and compound organizational and individual commitment to your technology strategy by overcoming overt and benign intellectual, emotional, and political opposition. You engage a commitment strategy to reduce friction to your efforts.

Figure 2.28 exhibits an eight-step process that can be used to design commitment into your efforts in an anticipatory manner, as opposed to reacting to friction in a frenzied and ill-prepared manner when it inevitably occurs. The methodology strings together a set of strategy frameworks that help you think about the problem. As is the case with all strategy frameworks, the success achieved from utilizing it depends on your sensitivity, understanding, and imagination in applying it as opposed to mechanically filling in the blanks.

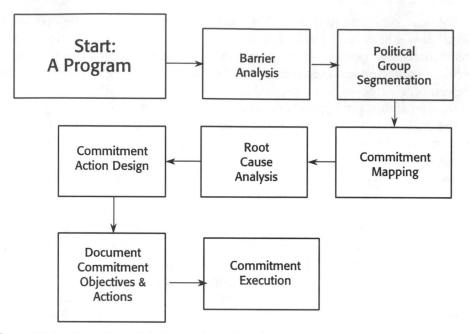

Figure 2.28   Commitment design methodology.

Step 1: A Technology Plan

An IT strategy will require a commitment strategy if its realization will mate-rially alter the status quo. As illustrated in Figure 2.29, such a strategy will fall within people's "zone of critical evaluation." People will not commit to actions

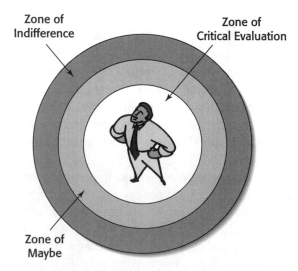

Figure 2.29   Zone of critical evaluation.

	Barrier 1	Barrier 2	Barrier 3	No Commitment	Barrier N
Objective 1					
Objective 2					
Objective N					

Intersection?
Need commitment strategy

Figure 2.30   Barrier Analysis Table.

that fall within their zone of critical evaluation unless a satisfactory level of intellectual, emotional, and political commitment is achieved.

Step 2: Barrier Analysis

A Barrier Analysis Table (see Figure 2.30) should be developed, creating a matrix of strategy objectives against anticipated barriers to success. The intersection of objectives with the "commitment" barrier confirms that lack of commitment will be an obstacle that needs to be addressed in an anticipatory manner.

Step 3: Political Groups Segmentation

As shown in Figure 2.31, each political group should be segmented and analyzed as to its potential commitment to the IT strategy. Emotional or intellectual commitment levels could also segment groups, but political is the preferred grouping. The questions of interest are the following:

- What defines the group? What are the attributes that create this grouping of people? What is their agenda?

- What is their interest? What public and private agendas are they trying to achieve?

Objectives	What defines the group?	What is their agenda?	Intellectual Commitment L M H	Emotional Commitment L M H	Political Commitment L M H	Summary: Committed? Y N
Objective 1						
Objective 2	N/A	N/A				
Objective N	N/A	N/A				

Figure 2.31   Political group segmentation.

- What are the group commitment levels? Where do they stand on each type of commitment as well as their overall commitment reaction to the strategy?

All groups that are material to your success should be segmented and analyzed.

Step 4: Commitment Map

As shown in Figure 2.32, each political group should be placed on the commitment map. This visualizes the current commitment levels that are confronting you—H (high) or L (low). For groups in supportive positions, you may wish to devise commitment actions to sustain their commitment. For groups in adverse positions, you will need to develop commitment actions to move them to more favorable positions. While a position of (H, H, H) would be best for all groups, the pragmatic objective is to reduce resistance (friction) to a manageable amount as opposed to completely eliminating it. If your IT strategy is taking deep and far-reaching actions, it will disenfranchise some. The problem is not to achieve an unachievable state of 100 percent commitment but enough commitment to succeed.

Step 5: Root Cause Analysis

In order to move nonsupportive groups to more favorable commitment positions, it is necessary to understand why they oppose the strategy. As shown in Figure 2.33, the technique of root cause analysis can be used to perform this analysis. Root cause analysis is built on the medical model of illness diagnosis. What presents and is most visibly discernible are the signs and symptoms. These represent the external manifestations of the problem. Treatments at this

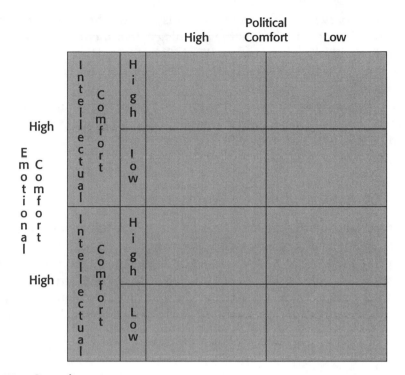

Figure 2.32   Commitment map.

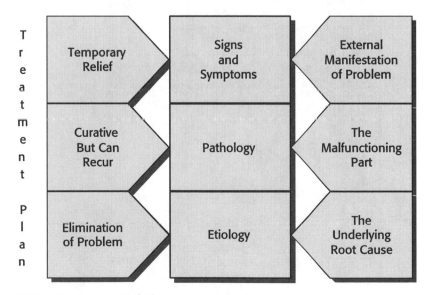

Figure 2.33   Root cause analysis.

level provide only temporary relief. What is causing the signs and symptoms is a malfunctioning part. This is the pathology. Treatment at this level is curative, but the pathology can reoccur. Underlying the pathology is the etiology or root cause of the problem. Treatment at this level permanently eliminates the problem.

Root cause analysis should be done for both supportive and adverse political groups. For supportive groups, one should analyze the root cause of their support so that it can be sustained. For noncommitted groups, all three layers of analysis should be done.

Step 6: Commitment Action Design

Commitment action design is the heart of the commitment design process and the most creative activity. The first action is to draw a Before and After Commitment Map (Figure 2.34) that visualizes the commitment repositioning that you wish to achieve (i.e., the desired future state of commitment). Strategy is often conceptualized as movement between positions. In Figure 2.34, we show the commitment positions we covet for each political group. Notice that on the arrows, which illustrate the repositioning, it is good practice to itemize either

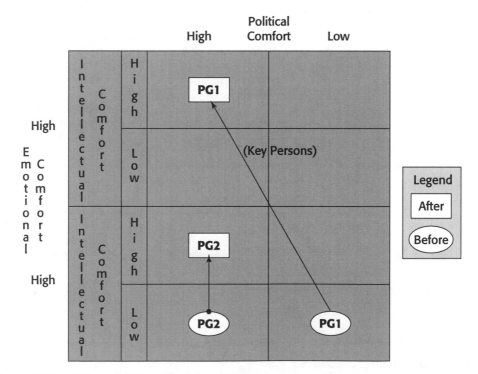

Figure 2.34   Before and After Commitment Map.

the influential roles and/or people that need to be persuaded to make the repositioning occur.

Having set the repositioning objectives on the Before and After Commitment Map (see Figure 2.34), it is now necessary to itemize the specific actions that you will take to make the change commitment positions occur. This can be documented on a Root Cause Action Map (see Figure 2.35). As shown in Figure 2.35, for each political group, you can itemize the previously completed root cause analysis (see Figure 2.33) and document the treatment plan (actions) that you will take by root cause level.

The actions you take are a function of your sensitivity and intimate understanding of your company, culture, and the specific situation. Typical commitment actions may include education, expert testimony, changes in the internal rewards and recognition systems, changes in the way the internal economy works, building of alliances, opening opportunities for participation, and using carrot approaches as well as bully pulpits.

Of particular importance is the development of a set of executive commitment actions that send a strong and unambiguous signal to the community of the senior management's commitment to the plan. Infrequent verbal promises made by fickle executives do not equate to skin in the game. If executive commitment begins and ends with just the nodding of their heads, the organizational proletariat will question the staying power of their management. Substantive commitment actions are required by senior management to change a skeptical staff's expectation of management's sincerity about the strategy. The organization must come to believe that management will execute the strategy

	Political Group 1		Political Group 2		Political Group N	
	Analysis	Treatment	Analysis	Treatment	Analysis	Treatment
Signs and Symptoms						
Pathology						
Etiology						

Figure 2.35   Root cause action map.

with extended and genuine effort before they will commit and extend their effort. To establish such credibility, management must have historically established a reputation that has earned them commitment respect (in such a case, establishing commitment is relatively easy), or they must establish such respect by taking actions that make it hard for them to reverse themselves.

Step 7: Document Commitment Objectives and Actions

The net results of the previous six steps can be succinctly documented using the Objective and Action forms shown in Figure 2.36. There should be an objective for each political group and at least one action to achieve it. As is expected in documenting objectives and actions, both require a target date and method of measurement, to verify that it has occurred. The meaning of each data item in Figure 2.36 will be explained in Chapter 4, "Strategy."

Step 8: Commitment Execution

As shown in Figure 2.37, the commitment actions are converted into implementation programs and associated projects. Periodic monitoring that includes

```
Commitment Objective:


Description


Measure:                        Date:
```

```
Move:

Description

Owner:       Champion      Priority:     Measure      Date:
```

Figure 2.36 Commitment objectives and actions.

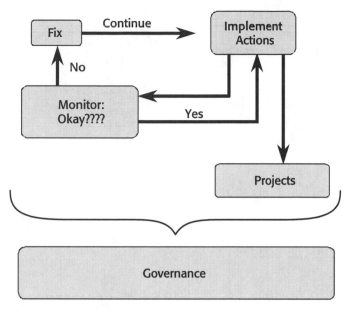

Figure 2.37 Commitment execution.

updated commitment maps must be done to adapt the commitment plan to the constantly evolving times and circumstances.

Summary

This section has presented an eight-step process that can be followed to develop a commitment plan to enable your IT strategy. While the process has been presented in the context of supporting an IT strategy to reduce friction, it can support any strategic effort where lack of commitment is an anticipated obstacle. Though the process has been illustrated as a linear process, it is, in practice, highly iterative.

As shown in Figure 2.38, what you are trying to do is change the payoff matrix of each political group. Before execution of your commitment plan, the minimax (minimum maximum lost) of their payoff matrix tells them that they have the least to lose potentially by not committing. The number in each cell is the payoff for each group by executing that cell. What your commitment plan does is change the minimax payoff so that they have the least to lose by committing. In essence, a commitment plan works by changing the reward/loss structure for each political group so that it minimizes its maximum potential lost though commitment, effort, and collaboration rather than indifference, resistance, and friction. In this way, strategic performance is enabled.

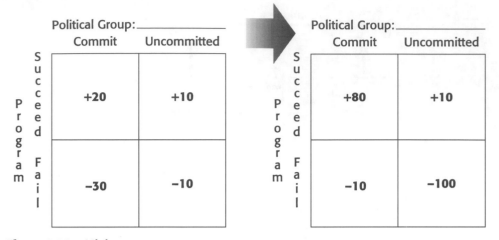

Figure 2.38 Minimax.

Conclusion

The strategy for any company that must cope with turbulence boiling over to the point of chaos is a strategy of agility, surprise, dislocation, and exploitation. It a strategy of swift movement with opportunistic zigs and zags. For an IT strategy to be beneficial in the new millennium, it will be a strategy that enables the business to continually reconfigure its IT assets in order to repeatedly enrich the value proposition for the customer. IT assets will have to become like water, a shape shifter, able to constantly morph into different shapes as and when necessitated in response to a fluid marketplace. In such an environment it will not be enough for IT to enable the business to be fast; it must enable the business to be quick.

If IT is to be the weaponry of choice that permits the business limitless adaptive maneuverability, your IT strategy cannot be restrained by self-caused friction. Friction will wear away and deplete both your energy and your will. To minimize friction, IT strategy must embrace, as an equal concern, the human as well as the nonhuman. Those who will go forth where they do not expect it and attack where they are unprepared will do so by complementing their visionary information technology plans with equally insightful commitment plans. This is the path to exceptional strategic performance.

There are many things that you can buy. You can buy technology, you can buy advice, you can buy assets, and you can even buy time. What you cannot buy is commitment. You cannot pay anyone enough that they will be willing to die for you. Commitment is given by each as he or she emotionally, intellectually, and politically embraces the strategy. Commitment is something that is earned and must be won. It is something that must be planned for and managed. The absence of commitment, not the poor selection of technology, is often the primary cause of IT strategy failure.

Breeder Strategy

It is common to talk about information technology strategy, but often neglected is the question of how we develop good IT strategists. Strategy is only as good as the team of technologists who envision it. This essay addresses the challenge of developing a team of highly capable IT strategists.

Executives in all industries are being bombarded with change. Customer demographics are changing, consumer expectations of products and services are changing, supplier relationships are changing, and the tools and technologies used to touch and service markets are changing. With so much accelerating change, coupled with the associated risk and confusion, it is not surprising that a growing and prosperous advice industry has been born.

Many, in jest, have referred to our times as the advice age. There is so much uncertainty and chaos that decision makers aggressively seek wisdom from advice givers. Nowhere are there more gurus, pundits, oracles, seers, market researchers, academics, consultants, prophets, diviners, and soothsayers prepared to offer sagacious advice than in the area of strategy. The advice, however, can often be as confusing as the problems. Among a seemingly endless list, the decision maker is advised to implement teams, implement total quality management, reengineer his or her processes, implement an enterprise IT architecture, recentralize, decentralize, outsource, focus on customer satisfaction, or focus on alignment; the key is cost, the key is focus, or the key is customization. The list is not only infinite, but often contradictory. Who should the decision maker listen to and what should the decision maker do?

It is my response that the first action that must be taken to respond to the ongoing turbulence of our times, the hyper-competitive information age, is to become strategically competent. The information age will be characterized by continuing upheaval; it is doubtful that things will ever settle down again. All businesses will have to cope with turbulence as business as normal. The nature of an interactive multimedia society lends itself to change, speed, nimbleness, and entrepreneurship. A set of actions conceived at a moment of time, however wise, will not be sufficient. What is first and foremost required is the ability to assess, develop, and implement strategy in a manner consistent with ever-changing times and circumstances. The first response, and the response from which all other responses germinate, is to develop strategic acumen.

The Problem and Opportunity

Where does strategy come from? Strategy is the harvest of strategic thinking. If we repeat this question recursively in an attempt to discover the first mover, we now ask, where does strategic thinking come from? The answer is that people accomplish strategic thinking. It is the creative output of individuals, who through a natural gift of intuition or training, mentoring, study, and experience, have mastered the art.

Prior to the information age, strategic thinking and strategy formulation were formally limited to the top of the corporate hierarchy. Senior management developed, managed, and communicated strategy. The rest of the organization was responsible for the tactical details of implementation. There is a great deal of controversy over the wisdom of this strategy model, but, for better or worse, it is an accurate portrayal of what was done in practice.

Many changes have occurred that challenge the continued wisdom of this approach. The following interlocking events have raised the question of whether it is now prudent to deconcentrate strategy and disperse strategic thinking and strategy formulation throughout the entire organization and, especially, to those units that face the customer.

> **Hierarchy failure.** Strategic planning, under the command-and-control structure, has not worked nearly as well as hoped for or needed. One just needs to chart the changing fortunes of once great companies to see the paucity of strategic acumen. As the issues in the strategy mix have grown (globalization, technological discontinuities, consumerism, hyper-competition, mergers, acquisitions, spin-offs, and accelerated cycle times), it has become more evident that a few remote executives do not have all the answers and, in many cases, are too far removed from the mayhem of the marketplace to truly hear and understand the voice of the customer.
>
> **Democratic organizations.** In response to competition, the need for speed and agility, the recognition that the hierarchy does not have all the answers, the rise of process management as the preferred organizing structure, social/cultural demands by employees for more say, and information-age technologies that facilitate collaboration and promote the knowledge organization, many organizations are moving to more democratic structures. Though they go by many different names such as participation management, teams, self-managing work groups, and empowerment, they all share the same fundamental idea that decision making should be pushed down, placed closer to the customer, and put in the hands of those who know and do the work.
>
> **The information age.** Strategic thinking and strategy are a response to conflict. Without conflict, business reduces to a problem of efficient administration. Strategy and strategic thinking become of interest when, and only

when, competition arises. If you have a monopoly, your strategy is maintaining the monopoly. The nature of the information age creates an incredibly contentious environment. As the tempo of the game quickens, speed and flexibility of response, not hierarchical position, become crucial. As Sun Tzu said:

As a rule, you need to change tactics a hundred times. To talk about government orders is like going to announce to your superiors that you want to put out a fire. By the time you get back with an order, there is nothing left but ashes.

The competitive nature of the information age propels strategic decision making to the point of action. It propels it to those who intimately know what's happening.

The resulting notion that emerges from these three concurrent events is that strategy and strategic thinking should be dispersed and executed throughout the organization. By dismantling the command and control of the hierarchy, those closest to the customer and the situation will be empowered to strategize and act. As one proponent of dispersing strategy formulations states:

Strategic management is a task for the whole organization all the time, not the province of specialist or a once yearly undertaking.

What they believe is that the aggregate decisions of many associates, exercising individual judgment, even if frequently mistaken, is likely to do less harm than the detached decisions of a hierarchical management and, in any case, through proximity of seeing the results and hustle, will be corrected briskly. To put it in the fighting words of the times, *everyone and anyone is to be a strategist.*

While this is all very liberating and promoted with enthusiasm by the advice community, it does raise three serious questions to the attentive observer:

Synthesis. The heart of strategic thinking is not decomposition; it is synthesis. The dispersal of strategy responsibility raises question about how holistic thinking and action will be accomplished. Who will see and synthesize the whole picture and speak and think for the whole?

Quality of strategy. If the few in the hierarchy couldn't do it well, why should we expect that the masses would? If strategy and strategic thinking become everyone's responsibility, how does it happen that everyone is an able strategist? Popularization of anything normally results in the creation of a large group of average people. When a large group of people do anything, the result is a huge cluster at the center of a bell curve. We want strategic excellence. Rather than improving the situation, the great transfer of strategy to the organizational rank and file could just as well result in mass strategic mediocrity.

Suitability. Everyone will not necessarily make a very good strategist. The following is a list of qualities one would normally associate with a capable strategist:

- Holistic thinker: The individual views problems from multiple perspectives and integrates those perspectives.

- Abstract thinker: The individual is comfortable dealing with conceptual ideas.

- Acceptance of ambiguity: The individual can tolerate that he or she will always have to analyze, synthesize, and make decisions based on inadequate and incomplete information.

- Working with models: The individual is comfortable analyzing the real world through abstract models of it.

- Interpret metaphors: The individual is able to translate metaphors and aphorisms into practical meanings.

- Open-minded: The individual can cast aside his or her views and consider new and contradictory positions without prejudice or bias.

- Humble: The individual feels the responsibility and burden of the consequences of his or her duties and is humbled by them.

- Research-oriented: The individual is interested in continual learning and improving his or her strategic acumen.

- Curious: The individual's favorite words are why and how.

- Multi-axial thinking: The individual can think in multiple dimensions at a time.

- Paradoxical thinking: The individual can cope with the discomfort of paradox.

Are these the characteristics of your average employee?

Although there is much to be optimistic about in the dispersal of strategy and strategic thinking, there is also reason for caution and concern.

Breeding Strategy

My response to this issue is what I call a *breeder strategy*—a bold action to distribute strategic thinking capabilities across the enterprise. If we are going to dispose of the command-and-control model, we must not replace it with a substitute form of mediocrity, but with a superior capability. The superior capability is an organization with dispersed strategy responsibilities that has created excellence in breeding strategy. By a breeder strategy, I mean a deep and far-reaching competence in strategic thinking, strategy formulation, strategy execution, and the ability to continually procreate new strategies in harmony with changing times and circumstances.

Sun Tzu set the objectives for a breeder strategy:

Victory over the multitudes is unknowable by the multitudes. Everyone knows the forms by which I am victorious, but no one knows the form by which I ensure victory. They know the traces of attainment of victory, but do not know the abstract form that makes for victory. Victory is apparent to all, but the science of ensuring victory is a mysterious secret, generally unknown.

It is the objective of a breeder strategy that as many people in your organization as possible master *the abstract forms and mysterious secrets that make for victory.*

The idea is to create an army of awesome strategic thinkers. A cadre of imaginative thinkers who are not constrained by what has been or what is. Competitive superiority is not about winning today's contests; it is about prepositioning to win tomorrow's contests, contests that are most often not simple linear extrapolations of the present. Accounting logic will provide you with a score card, but it is strategic thinking that will tell you the opportunistic paths to follow. How much more sweeping are the possibilities when we increase the community of people who can fruitfully engage in the *mysterious secret.*

The dispersal of strategy responsibility, without a plan on how you are going to educate and elevate the acumen of the new strategists, is magical thinking. Magical thinking occurs when you think something and your belief is what makes it happen. Declaring everyone a strategist is exciting for the moment, but unless one takes pains to train and mentor the newly sprung army of junior Sun Tzus, the results will be next year's strategic planning problem. You will create a muddle larger than the one that you had hoped to escape.

A breeder strategy, on the other hand, has the raw potential to make strategy a strategic configuration of power. If you have dispersed strategic excellence and if numerous individuals and teams throughout your business can engage in creative strategic thinking and action on a daily basis, you will have created a powerful organization. Sun Tzu described strategists as follows:

They do not wander when they move. They act in accord with events. Their actions and inactions are matters of strategy . . . A leader of deep wisdom and ability lays deep plans for what others do not think about.

An entire organization of people who do not wander, who act in accord with events, and whose every action spurs strategy is an organization that has turned strategy into a strategic configuration of power.

A breeder strategy is a long-term infrastructure strategy to raise the tide of strategic perfection throughout the organization. It consists of four complementary actions:

Education. Most of your staff probably has little or no formal education in strategy. It will be necessary to provide formal foundation education with ongoing special-topic seminars as the students achieve advanced readiness. Strategic thinking is a difficult subject. If you are not willing to train your people, do not expect the dispersal of strategy responsibility to accomplish anything other than dispersing mediocrity.

Basic strategy education can be accomplished in a one-week course. Subjects covered would include strategic thinking, strategic frameworks, strategic planning methodology, schools of strategic thought, classics of strategy, and case studies. More advanced courses would focus on special subjects such as positioning, change management, alignment, or use of sophisticated frameworks. Special seminars would consist of group discussion of the classics of strategy such as *The Art of War* by Sun Tzu and *The Five Rings* by Miyamoto Musashi and relating the studied sections to current business problems.

Study. A strategist becomes a student of strategy. The reward and recognition system must encourage continual learning and further mastery of the art. Employees must be encouraged to join professional associations, attend strategy conferences, read strategy books and journals, and participate in industry consortia concerned with strategy issues. You must study because study increases your receptivity to learning and understanding the deeper teachings of the great masters. As Musashi said:

> *Remember that what I say and how you perceive what I say can be completely different depending upon your* awareness *of yourself and the level of skill that you have attained. The need for constant study and thought is essential for understanding the way of the warrior.*

Study helps create *aware* individuals. Aware individuals see what others do not see, know what others do not know, and perceive the formless. This is the optimum return for your breeder strategy investment.

When I conduct strategy workshops with clients, I sometimes ask them to do the "I wish" exercise. When your team engages in "I wish," you make a list of the five key things you would most wish for your business. People wish for all sorts of things. Most often, they wish for the gifts of collaboration, leadership, speed, and alignment. If I were ever on an "I wish" team, my wish would be different. I would wish for awareness.

Mentoring. Strategic thinking is very hard. Having a mentor makes the seemingly impossible possible. Promising strategists should be culled out and assigned to your best strategist for tutoring and development. When you start a breeder strategy, you will not know who will excel. As time progresses, who is thriving and who is dog paddling will become evident. You must reinforce success. Through mentoring, you can accelerate the mastery of your junior people.

Practice. Reading and talking about strategy can get you only so far. As is true with mastering any other discipline, it is necessary to be a practitioner. Your aspiring strategists need to be given assignments appropriate to their development to stretch and grow their skills. Briefings, presentations, and analysis should all provide opportunities to exhibit their growing strategic acumen.

One of the most noticeable things about organizations that have trained their people in strategy is how the daily debates change. All work takes on a strategy flavor. The language, the frameworks, and the way of thinking permeate the organization and change their approach from whatever was being done to a strategic approach.

I never cease to be amazed at how money is spent on things of much less enduring value while a breeder strategy is deemed controversial. How better can you spend your money than by raising the tide of strategic excellence of your business? Many organizations averaged two weeks of training per employee on total quality management and other passing strategic fads. What they got for their money was people trained in one, and only one, specific strategic action—a strategic action being coexecuted by all their competitors that at best would yield competitive parity. Having spent all that money and time, all that happened was that the bar got raised for all and all were prepared to reach the new height. If you spent two weeks training all your employees on strategy, as you did for quality, you would have a group of people who on a daily basis would begin breeding a strategy distinct to your business. Is that not a far more superior result?

All your employees will not achieve the same level of excellence. As is true with everything else, there is a distribution of achievement based on many factors. Some will do better and lead, and the rest will do better than they did before. The bell curve will still be a bell curve, but it will have shifted dramatically to the right. You should anticipate that your staff's skills will distribute across the following four levels of attainment:

Indifference level. These staff members are disinterested to the point of overt negative reactions. They prefer to deal with pressing substantive problems of the immediately-in-your-face variety. While there will be little practical gain from their education, they nevertheless will absorb some of the education and, in spite of their negativism, will understand your future strategic actions better than before.

Cognitive level. These employees will understand and be interested in the material but will have practical problems in applying what they have learned. Their appreciation of strategy will drastically reduce friction as they will comprehend the intents of your future strategic initiatives.

Execution level. These employees will both understand what they have learned and be able to apply it. They will provide the greatest part of the rising tide as they will internalize what they have learned and apply it to all their endeavors.

Gifted level. These employees, few and far between, will be exceptional strategists. They will reach a level of intuitive strategic grace where they will sense the subtlest linkages of the cause-and-effect web of relationships. Having employees who can function at this level of excellence is a prize that should be closely guarded.

Competitors will not like to compete against a business that is executing a breeder strategy. They will not relish competing against such a company because who wants, on a daily basis, to compete against team after team of people who think in terms of friction, speed, disruption, paradox, concentration, surprise, maneuver, commitment, and alignment in everything that they do. As your dispersed strategic excellence grows in force, the strategic distance between you and your competitors expands, and their ability to maintain your tempo of action will decay. They will be subjected to an ever-intensifying, deteriorating situation that will place constantly increasing stress on all their planning and delivery systems. At best, they will come to realize that they are confronting a formidable opponent, lose heart, and turn their market attentions elsewhere.

The struggle of business is the struggle for advantage. The objective is to find a way, short of brute force, to accomplish your aims. A breeder strategy is a way to create advantage, not as an episodic event, but as the daily routine. It is a deep and far-reaching response to the challenges of the information age. Imagine an entire organization where *every action and inaction are matters of strategy*. Such an organization would be truly awesome—an organization that can cope with the unknowable as well as the knowable.

Before concluding, we can also investigate the logic of a breeder strategy from a very simple and pragmatic perspective. Let's assume that the information age blooms more or less as hyped. Perhaps time will show that rather than being over-hyped, the impact of information convergence has been under-hyped. In the forthcoming years, all information, regardless of form, is online and readily accessible by point and click from robust desktop browsers. Global networked interactive multimedia has become a reality. Your employees have instant access to anything and everything they need. The digitized multimedia databases of the world are at the mercy of their high-performance search engines that can search not only on word strings, but on sounds, partial images, and video clips. Information is available to anyone, anywhere, and in any form.

The problem is, of course, that the exact same information (less your secured corporate digital libraries) is also available to your competitors. The hierarchy of interest to you is data, information, knowledge, and wisdom. Each begets the next. The raw availability of more information does not necessarily increase the ability to create knowledge or wisdom. It may, in practice, have the reverse effect as the average employee is overwhelmed by the seemingly unlimited hypermedia from which to choose. Rather than being able to create new knowledge, the average employee becomes lost in a rat's maze of information as he or she is unable to cull out the subtle and buried webs of advantage.

The availability of mass information to all has the natural effect of creating a higher but still level playing field. To acquire advantage, it is necessary to take actions that elevate and distinguish your employees' abilities to interpret the information in a superior manner. The creation of new knowledge and wisdom requires insightful analysis and synthesis of the information. This is where strategic thinking is invaluable. Strategic thinking can provide a powerful zoom lens through which your employees synthesize the newly available information in ways more creative than your competitors'. Access to more information alone is of limited value; you must raise the tide of everyone's competence in strategic interpretation. You can accomplish this pragmatically through a breeder strategy.

Conclusion

In the Star Trek progeny that have followed the original series, there is a computer simulation playhouse called the holodeck. The holodeck can simulate, in complete detail, any fantasy that you wish. It simulates your story with all the accompanying props, dialogue, and actions in perfect life-like response to your actions.

The holodeck is the ultimate retail entertainment product because, unlike in real life, your holodeck life-like actions have no real-life consequences. When the simulation period is over, regardless of what you did or didn't do, nothing really happened. It was all wonderful make-believe. So the holodeck creates a fantasy world where actions have no consequences. You can do it over and over again, without any harm to anyone or any negative repercussions, until you get the exact outcome you seek.

We, unfortunately, do not live in an Eden-like holodeck world. In real life, actions and inactions do have real consequences. As we all know, all too well, it really does matter what we do or don't do. If we could live in a holodeck world, strategy would be superfluous. Therefore, we are suggesting that because we must conduct ourselves in a real world where real actions result in real consequences, a breeder strategy is an artful action. It is an artful action because the consequence of a breeder strategy is that the strategic utility of the staff's actions improves dramatically with a corresponding increase in the utility of the consequences of their actions.

A breeder strategy satisfies the imposing standard that strategy must be deep and far-reaching. It is a deep and far-reaching strategy because it results in procreating an entire community of people who can create deep and far-reaching strategies. What could possibly be a deeper and more far-reaching action than an action that multiplies deep and far-reaching actions?

I believe that companies ultimately will have but two choices. You can continue to execute mass-market strategic advice, or you can breed your own advice. In the former case, you do what everybody else does and engage in a game of who can do the same thing a little bit better. In the latter case, you do a customized set of actions that are designed and executed by you for only you. It may not work, but it certainly is well worth the try. Companies have poured millions into ideas that had much less potential of a comparable payoff.

It is my contention that in our turbulent times the first knowledge is strategic thinking. It is the business knowledge that enriches all other business knowledge. Advantage is integrated at the heart of every decision. Strategic thinking provides the missing nexus between all improved means and improved ends (market share, revenue, and customer satisfaction).

In the play *Amadeus*, Salieri, Mozart's antagonist, is revered by the classical music audiences of Vienna, and Mozart is shunned. Mozart's music is chastised for having *too many notes*. Salieri, however, knows the stark truth that Mozart is the vastly superior composer. Toward the end of the play, Salieri, paradoxically, rejects his own fame, criticizes the uneducated rejection of Mozart by the public, and bemoans the mediocre taste of the music-going public when he laments:

> *What does it mean or matter to be viewed as distinguished or undistinguished by those who, in all truth, are hopelessly unable to distinguish?*

Salieri, cursed with musical knowledge, understood the vast difference between what an audience of average musical acumen would applaud and what a knowledgeable audience would applaud. Had Vienna audiences been students of music rather than simple consumers of music, they would have been able to distinguish the genius of Mozart from the mediocrity of Salieri.

In the information age, our employees have to be able to distinguish. The problem will not be the availability of information; the challenge will be the compiling of the relevant slivers, fragments, and shreds that create knowledge and wisdom. They cannot be just simple consumers of information; they need to be students of strategy who can see in the information what others do not see. They need to see in the information what has not yet taken shape or form. They need to sense with strategic insight what is invisible to the less prepared. They need to be aware individuals. You need a breeder strategy to attain this.

You need a breeder strategy to win the business wars of the future. You need a breeder strategy so that in a commodity world, you can stand out.

IT Strategy as Structure

One of the most visible parts of IT strategy is organizational structure. People work as individuals, in groups, and in teams within the context of an organizational structure. Organizational structure is one of the fundamental thrusts of any IT strategy. This essay addresses the fundamental strategy question of how does one decide how to organize.

For most employees, strategy is equal to organizational structure, or more precisely, the changing of organizational structure. While they are most often not privy to the grand strategy of the business or are presented with only isolated and disjointed pieces of it, they personally observe and feel the impact of reorganizations. For most people, the announcement of another reorganization is the start flag signaling that business strategy is going into motion. Organizing and reorganizing to align and realign is the most common and visible sign of strategy to the organizational rank and file.

Sun Tzu said:

> *Structure follows strategy. Forces are to be structured strategically based on what is advantageous.*

Sun Tzu recognized then, as astute strategists do today, that organizational structure is critical to facilitating strategy. The organizational design defines the structural distribution of resources that will be mobilized to execute your strategy. How will you be able to execute if your organization's structure stands in direct opposition to your efforts?

Information-age IT organizational design has the following pressing objectives:

Heightened collaboration. The design should promote the various organizational units to work harmoniously together toward the shared competitive aims.

Speed in everything. The design should enable the business to execute all actions with swiftness.

Responsiveness. The design should permit the business to promptly react to changing times and circumstances.

Flexibility. The design should permit the organization to be adaptive.

Innovation. The design should leave room for people to be innovative in solving customer problems.

Permeability. The design should enable new ideas to enter and disperse throughout the organization. It should enable the business to learn.

Leverage. The design should permit the business to achieve economies of scale and reuse where appropriate.

Execution. The design should facilitate doing. It should lubricate action and eliminate the exhausting resistance of friction.

Spontaneity. The design should permit the organization to dynamically evolve to stay in harmony with the changing environment. This is called spontaneous self-reorganization.

Accountability. The design should make it clear who is responsible for what.

Authority. The design should make it clear who has the authority to make decisions and allocate resources.

Control. The design should balance spontaneity with the need for control.

The turbulence that accompanies the information age makes achieving these design points particularly important. An IT organization that cannot act means that you have a business that cannot compete.

Strategy is, to a large degree, not a problem of managing a large group but a problem of orchestrating advantageous coordination across groups. It is not surprising therefore that everyone includes organizational design as a required strategic configuration of power. It is mandatory that the organization be designed with speed, flexibility, and the alleviation of friction so that the business can maneuver to engage in IT fighting.

Organizational design remains an art. It is usually necessary to select a strategic dimension that is most relevant to the current times and circumstances (geography, function, process, market, etc.) as dictated by your strategy. The selected dimension is set as the anchor of the design and remaining design choices are made by revolving them about this primary factor.

Of particular concern in designing organizational structures is the elimination of friction. In most organizations today, if nothing was done but eliminating the massive organizational drag on action, most organizations would experience tremendous increases in productivity. The retarding resistance of organizational friction slows any and all actions, yet alone the execution of bold actions, actions of indirection, or surprise maneuvers. What must often be overcome in redesigning IT organizations to permit graceful maneuverability is the ingrown structures that promote friction.

The history of IT organizational design is the history of a structure in place: The whistle blows, a game of musical chairs ensues, a new structure is created, and the game continues until the next whistle. As organizations strive to balance stability and productivity against flexibility and innovation, they periodically restructure en masse to respond to the environmental stimuli. We suggest that an IT organization structure that mixes the ideas of mini-businesses and the internal marketplace can provide a dynamic balance, replace episodic restructuring with continuous restructuring, and position the IT organization in a state of heightened capability.

Last, we would like to reemphasize that structure follows strategy and is not strategy, but the facilitation of strategy. In general, organizational restructuring is the last issue to be addressed when developing a strategic plan. One first focuses on what is to be achieved and the required actions to accomplish your ends, and then, and only then, does one address how to organize to facilitate those ends. Setting an organizational structure in place before you have completed your strategic thinking unnecessarily constrains your freedom. Organizational design is the first result of strategy, not the aim of it. It is common among the organizational multitudes to believe that the reorganization that they are going through for the nth time is literally the business strategy. If they are right, you are probably in a great deal of trouble.

Basic and Alternative Organizational Designs

The challenge of designing an information-age organizational structure for the IT organization exists at two levels. These levels may be referred to as the macro and micro design problems. The macro problem addressees the number of IT organizations, their roles and responsibilities, their placement relative to the business units they serve, and their governance relationship with other IT entities within the business. The micro problem addresses the question of how a specific IT organization should internally organize within itself to efficiently and effectively deliver its products and services to its customers.

The Macro Problem of IT Organizational Structure

Figure 2.39 illustrates the macro problem of IT organizational design. The basic organizing unit of the modern enterprise is the strategic business unit (SBU). A strategic business unit is the foundation building block of a global enterprise structure and has the following characteristics:

- It is a collection of related businesses.
- It has a distinct mission.
- It serves well-defined markets.
- It has a distinct set of competitors.
- It has the resources and opportunity to deliver value to its market.
- It has a distinct management team.
- It has profit and loss responsibility.

IT Macro Structure

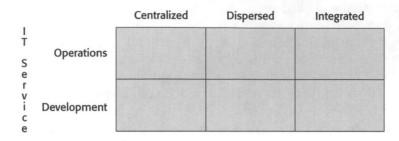

Figure 2.39   Macro organizational design.

The distinct business units may cooperate extensively with each other or be quite independent in their actions. We refer to the degree of collaboration as a strategic position along a continuum between a pure union or a pure multistate strategy. In a union strategy, the business units collaborate extensively in terms of sharing and leveraging processes, competencies, product development, and marketing initiatives. In a multistate strategy, each business addresses its marketplace unilaterally. The design point for the union/multistate decision will be strongly influenced by the following factors:

Market position. To what extent do market segments across SBUs and product lines overlap? To what extent will the business share brand names, advertising, customer image, and other marketing elements across products/markets?

Product/service position. To what extent is their synergy between SBU product lines?

Competitive moves. To what extent is advantage accrued by linking competitive moves across SBUs?

Cost position. To what extent does cross-SBU collaboration lead to cost advantage (i.e., reuse, leverage, economies of scale)?

After analysis, a business takes a considered position somewhere along the continuum between the extremes of a pure multistate or a pure union.

Against the background of this macro organizational structure of the business, a macro IT organizational structure must be designed. An IT organization provides two broad sets of products and services to its customers—life cycle application development and support services and production operations. For each of these, there are three basic structures (with endless mutations) from which to choose:

Centralized. A single and centralized IT organization provides these services to the SBUs.

Dispersed. Independent IT organizations provide these services to designated SBUs.

Integrated. Independent but coordinated IT organizations provides these services to designated SBUs.

For each considered alternative macro design—centralized, dispersed, integrated, or mutation mixture—it is necessary to consider the following four basic questions to arrive at an optimum design:

- How many IT organizations will the corporation have? Will each SBU have its own, or will they share IT service providers?

- What will be the roles and responsibilities of each IT organization? Table 2.5 shows a simple taxonomy of information systems. Which cells are each IT entity responsible for, and are they responsible for development and/or operations? A similar mapping must be done in terms of allocation of databases.

- Will the IT entities be separate entities apart from the SBUs they serve, or will they be entities within the business units? If they are apart, what will be the economic rules for exchanging goods and services?

- How will multiple IT entities be governed? For issues of common concern such as architecture, corporate communications networks, and human resource policies, what governance mechanisms will be deployed to maintain synergy?

In this way, you design a macro IT organizational structure of a centralized, dispersed, integrated, or mutated structure for both development and operations that aligns itself with the macro SBU structure and union/multistate strategy of the business.

Table 2.5   Roles and Responsibilities

	TYPE OF SYSTEM				
Domain of System	**Transaction on Processing**	**Data Warehousing**	**Information Sharing**	**Workgroup Productivity**	**Individual Productivity**
Corporate					
Shared SBU					
SBU					
Divisional					
Department					
Personal					

The Micro Problem of IT Organizational Design

The micro problem of IT organizational design starts where the macro problem ends. For each IT entity that will exist, it is necessary to design an internal structure that will deliver operations and/or development in a fast, flexible, and friction-free manner. If the internal structure does not become a strategic configuration of power, then all efforts to make IT maneuverable will fail because it will not be possible to mobilize the IT resources in an effective and efficient manner.

Although there are endless mutations and variations, there are six basic micro design structures to choose from, as follows:

Functional structure (Figure 2.40). Employees are grouped strictly vertically based on functional skills and expertise.

Matrix structure (Figure 2.41). Employees are grouped in a grid-like structure with multiple chains of authority.

Product structure (Figure 2.42). Employees are grouped into self-contained, product-driven structures that are responsible end to end for a given family of products.

Geographic structure (Figure 2.43). Employees are grouped into self-contained structures that deliver all products and services to a geographical region.

Front-end/Back-end structure (Figure 2.44). Employees are grouped into customer-facing functions that serve customers and use products and services developed and supported by back-end functions.

Process structure (Figure 2.45). Employees are grouped into horizontal teams that deliver products and services by process.

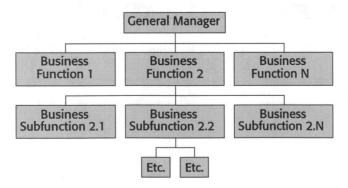

Figure 2.40   Functional Structure.

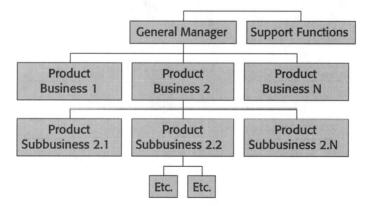

General Manager		Functional Structure			
		F1	F2	F3	Fn
Project/Product Structure	P1				
	P2				
	P3				
	Pn				

Figure 2.41   Matrix Structure.

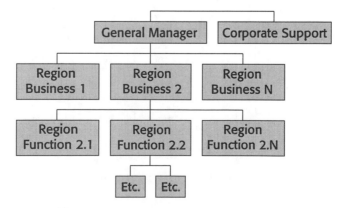

Figure 2.42   Product Structure.

Figure 2.43   Geographic Structure.

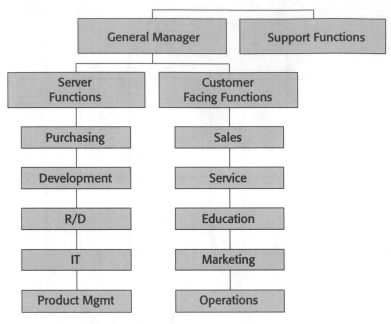

Figure 2.44 Front-end/Back-end Structure.

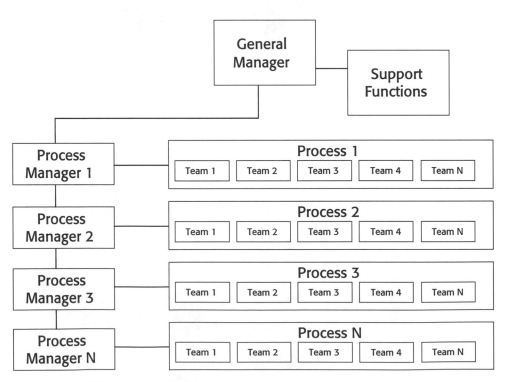

Figure 2.45 Process Structure.

Table 2.6 summarizes the generic advantages and challenges of each structure.

The problem for the information-age IT organization is to define a structure that balances conflicting needs. While we need stability and formality for short-term efficiencies, we need flexibility and spontaneity to cope with the turbulence about us. We need to be organic rather than bureaucratic.

Table 2.6 Advantages and Challenges

ORGANIZATIONAL STRUCTURE	ADVANTAGES	CHALLENGES
Functional	1. Efficiency 2. Centers of excellence 3. Focus 4. Ease of management	1. Efficient decision making 2. End-to-end accountability 3. Functional loyalty 4. Lack of flexibility
Matrix	1. Provides attention to multiple dimensions of organization design 2. Coordination 3. Considered allocation of resources 4. Horizontal communications	1. Difficult to implement and manage 2. Power battles 3. Delineation of authority 4. Costs of communication
Product	1. Product/customer focused 2. Accountability 3. High product-level coordination 4. Decision making at product level	1. Cost inefficiencies 2. Horizontal product coordination. 3. Responsiveness to local needs
Geographic	1. Market sensitivity 2. Decision making and authority at market level	1. Cost inefficiencies 2. Cross geographic coordination 3. Local loyalties
Front End/Back End	1. Single customer interface 2. Customer responsive 3. Promotes many-to-many relationships	1. Linking front ends to back ends efficiently and effectively 2. Cost allocations 3. Decision making
Process	1. Efficiency 2. Customer focus 3. Productivity	1. Process leadership 2. Cross-process coordination 3. Functional expertise 4. Process fiefdoms

The Problems with Traditional IT Organizational Designs

Most traditional IT organizations are a structural combination of functional and product design structures. MVS people supported the mainframe environment while UNIX people supported the UNIX environment and PC people supported the PC/LAN environment. Operations people supported specific technological smokestacks. Developers were organized by product teams to serve specific customers. Figure 2.46 illustrates this structure.

This made reasonably good sense during the industrial age of IT. Because the IT technology platforms were vertically segregated, functional centers of excellence to achieve stability and efficiency were a good choice. Each functional unit could strive to optimize its individual environment for the welfare of the customer and the corporation. There was little need for cross-environment collaboration, coordination, and information flow.

Two things have gone wrong with this model. First, the technology that we wish to deploy—that is, interactive multimedia across distributed and heterogeneous computing environments—is horizontal in nature. To make it work requires extensive horizontal collaboration and coordination across functional specialties. The traditional IT hierarchical smokestack structure not only is inappropriate for this, it actively works against it as employees are loyal to their specific vertical technological environment rather than cross-environment needs.

Second, the traditional smokestack IT organization was designed for stability and predictability. Its structure was designed to preserve rather than change. During the industrial age, change was very slow and predictable. The smokestack structure took on a mechanistic and bureaucratic flavor as it pon-

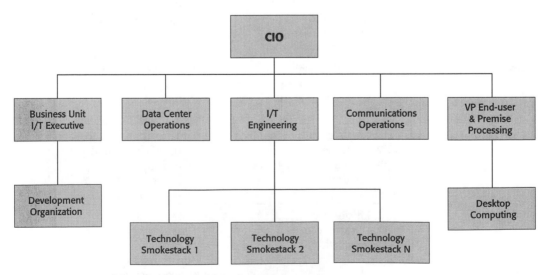

Figure 2.46   Traditional IT organization design.

derously would introduce or experiment with new technologies. Change was formally viewed as a threat rather than an opportunity.

The problems with the traditional IT structure do not therefore require elaborate or extensive debate. Its shortcomings are dual:

- It was designed to optimize, through economies of scale, the delivery of vertical IT products and services.
- It was designed not to change but to preserve.

The result of this is obvious to everyone in our field. IT organizations are viewed as slow, inflexible, and a business obstacle to be overcome. They are not viewed favorably because their inherent micro organizational structure is misaligned with the horizontal technological needs of the information age. They are misaligned because they create tremendous friction to change for the business. They cannot cope with continual change and the rapid horizontal introduction and utilization of gregarious information technologies.

Proposed Solution

The proposed solution to this problem is to design a new micro IT organizational structure built on three interrelated ideas:

Centers of competency (COC). Employees are grouped into logically related sets of skills.

Process. All work gets done through processes.

Internal marketplace. An internal marketplace is established in which centers of competency buy and sell products and services to each other.

We will develop the proposed micro organizational design structure by building on these ideas as follows:

Centers of competency (COC). A center of competency is a logical group of employees with a related set of skills. It is often also refered to as a center of excellence or a knowledge center. The center of competency provides an administrative home for employees, provides a place to learn skills and receive specialty mentoring, and a facility to investigate and develop best practices.

A center of competency is a mini-business, a boutique service provider. As shown in Figure 2.47, it provides a group of services to other IT centers of competency. Its manager or coach is the business manager, who is responsible for developing the center of competency so that its employees can find work. The coach/manager, like any other businessperson, owns capabilities and must find utilization opportunities for them. A center of competency is therefore a mini-business. It is not unlike an SBU. It has products to sell, a

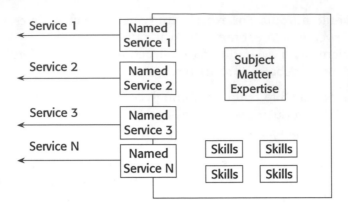

Figure 2.47   Center of competency.

marketplace, the need to earn revenue, and the need to continually upgrade its products and services to maintain its customer base.

Process. All work is the result of executing processes. Process owners hire individuals from centers of competency and form teams to develop processes. Product managers, marketing/sales managers, and senior management hire members of the centers of competency to execute processes. Figure 2.48 shows how a team is formed. The buyer hires individuals with the necessary skills from each center of competency.

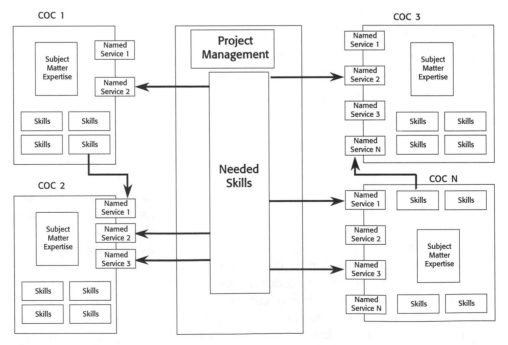

Figure 2.48   A team.

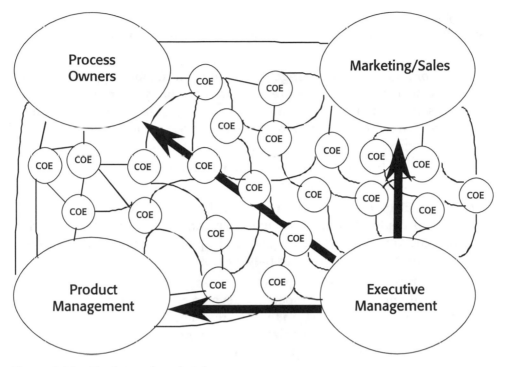

Figure 2.49 The internal marketplace.

Internal marketplace. As shown in Figure 2.49, the IT organization runs on the model of an internal marketplace. The marketplace works as follows:

- Senior management negotiates budgets with product managers, marketing/sales, and process owners.

- Centers of competency are mini-businesses that need to earn revenue. They do not receive a budget. They have a cost and earning projection.

- The economy runs by the four centers with budgeted money (i.e., product managers, marketing/sales, process owners, and senior management), buying products and services from the centers of competency. This would generally involve the hiring of a project manager who would, in turn, shop for desired services in the internal marketplace. Centers of competency, in turn, also buy products and services from other centers of competency.

What we have now done is turn the traditional hierarchical, mechanistic, and bureaucratic IT organization into a vibrant and dynamic economic entity where there are buyers, sellers, and a sustainable, strong motivation to cooperate and continually improve products and services.

Why is creating an internal marketplace built on boutique centers of competency a desirable structure for the information-age IT organization? I would suggest the following reasons:

The IT organization is no longer shielded from the marketplace realities. It also feels the day-to-day pressures to continually upgrade its products and services. If a center of competency wants to stay in business, it must continually improve the products and services it sells to other centers of competency.

The core structure for execution is a horizontal team. This team is formed using marketplace mechanisms.

The normal marketplace mechanism of how you spend your money is used to foster alignment. As management, product managers, marketing/sales, and process owners shift their spending patterns, the centers of competency must respond, or they will lose revenue.

The structure lends itself to spontaneous reorganization. As spending patterns shift or centers of competency develop new products or services, the structure naturally adjusts to the new realities. You do not blow a whistle and say reorganize. Reorganization in the internal marketplace is occurring dynamically as some products and services win and others lose.

The structure is very scalable. Successful centers of competency can be grown, shrunk, or replicated as needed.

There is a marketplace. Centers of competency will thrive only if they can find buyers for their services. Product managers and marketing will thrive only if they employ processes to deliver products and services that SBU customers want. Everyone has a customer.

Customers can evaluate, measure, and negotiate terms and conditions of purchase. Suppliers need to continually refine their offerings to maintain satisfied customers. Members of a center of competency work for their customers, not their vertical boss.

The structure lends itself to virtual structures or, if desired, outsourcing. In both cases, one would decide which service offerings are better performed by noninternal providers, but those services must be designed into the overall internal economy.

Centers of competency have extreme motivation to cooperate with each other. Only through horizontal collaboration on a customer-focused team are they able to accrue revenue.

Centers of competency improve value for buyers by integrating products and services across centers. Buyers can buy basic products and services or more finished goods.

The traditional IT organizational structure suffers from a gross inconsistency. The external customer-facing business units have to cope with the battlespace everyday. They have to be adaptive and fast. The mechanism that causes concern for speed, flexibility, service, value, and quality is the marketplace mechanism of choice and selection. Traditional IT organization units have functioned bureaucratically in the comfort of entitlement. They delivered products and services but did not have to win the business. The boutique structure of centers of competency, integrated with the notion of an internal marketplace, addresses this shortcoming.

Conclusion

The problem of designing an information-age organizational structure for the IT organization is a problem of coordination. How do you design the micro IT organization so that horizontal products and services can be delivered rapidly, flexibly, and without friction? I propose that the best mechanism to do that is an internal marketplace based on center of competency boutiques that are subject to normal marketplace mechanisms. If you want speed and agility, you must submit the IT organization to marketplace pressures.

Specifically, the proposed design addresses the pressing design issues as follows:

Heightened collaboration. The unit of delivered work is the team. Centers of competency remain viable only if they can work together on successful teams.

Speed in everything. The internal marketplace rewards efficiency and speed. Centers of competency are motivated to continually improve their offerings, with speed being a prime buying factor for purchasers.

Responsiveness. Centers of competency earn their living. As with any supplier in a marketplace, urgency in meeting customer needs is critical.

Flexibility. Centers of competency are adaptive to meet the current needs and emerging needs for which buyers will pay. The problem for the center of competency is not what do I want to provide but what will a customer pay for.

Innovation. Centers of competency are rewarded for constantly upgrading and innovating by the growth of their center.

Permeability. There is little advantage to maintain the status quo. Centers of competency search for new ideas and ways to remain prosperous.

Leverage. Centers of competency mentor and teach their preferred skills to others. Processes are reused and tuned to promote efficiency in execution.

Execution. Execution is accomplished through the unit of the team. Noncooperation is rewarded by replacement.

Spontaneity. The design lends itself to spontaneous self-reorganization. As money and opportunities are made available, entrepreneurial centers of competency hustle to the new opportunity.

Accountability. Buyers are accountable for what they buy.

Authority. Buyers make informed purchase decisions.

Control. Management can expand, contract, or reposition the internal economy at will, based on how it changes its spending patterns.

I submit that the internal marketplace structure is superior to the other six structures that we have discussed in this essay. It is superior because it is fast and flexible and because it removes friction. It is superior because it repositions the IT organizational structure so that the business can continually change and adapt to the battlespace.

Strategic Implications

There are many implications from these essays. They certainly argue for the importance of IT architecture, the necessity of implementing a robust e-commerce environment, or the importance of commitment to realizing your aims. There is, however, one dominant implication that transcends all of the essays; that implication is the priority of achieving a state of strategic alignment between IT and the business.

The digital enterprise of the 21st century is an enterprise that is built on its IT capabilities. Few business strategies can be successfully executed without the superior use of the information technology resources. IT must be in alignment with the business because more and more, IT is the mechanism through which the business expresses itself.

What does it mean for IT to be aligned with the business? IT is in alignment with the business when it becomes a weapon system that enables the business to fight a hyper-competitive information-age war of movement. IT is no longer viewed as an expense to be frugally applied merely to automate business processes; it is used as the fuel of advantage both to create and exploit opportunities in the battlespace. IT is aligned with the business when the business can use IT to create, disrupt, and exploit markets through IT fighting.

As illustrated in Figure 2.50 (left side), in military strategy there are four fundamental strategic options:

- You can fight a persistent war of combat against an opponent's army.
- You can fight a persistent war on the logistics infrastructure of your opponent.

- You can fight a raiding war against your opponent's army.

- You can fight a raiding war against the logistics infrastructure of your opponent.

Businesses also have four fundamental strategic options, as illustrated in Figure 2.50 (right side):

- They can fight a war of attrition using sustainable competitive advantages.

- They can fight a war of maneuver using sustainable competitive advantages.

- They can fight a war of attrition using temporary competitive advantages.

- They can fight a war of maneuver using temporary competitive advantages.

As shown in Figure 2.50, the contest is moving from the marketplace (a war of attrition fueled by sustainable competitive advantages) to the battlespace (a war of maneuver fueled by an endless stream of overlapping temporary advantages). The digital enterprise engages the battlespace through IT fighting and must be in a state of perfect alignment with the business if the business is to prevail over its competitors.

This state of alignment does not appear out of thin air. It requires strategy to create and position the IT resources so that they become a business weapon. Strategy precedes alignment, and that is what the rest of this book is about. It is about teaching the methods of strategy and strategic thinking so that you can build an IT organization that is in a state of superior alignment with the business. The business must be able to move with speed, alacrity, and the absence of friction. This is the path to managing IT for competitive advantage.

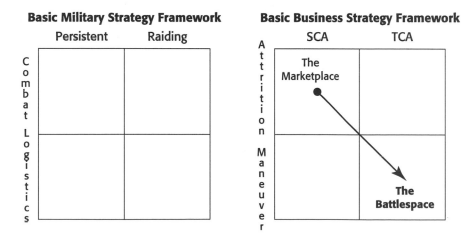

Figure 2.50 Basic military and business strategy frameworks.

The strategic intent of IT strategy is to enable the business to win in the battlespace every day with every customer and with every transaction. By careful positioning of the IT resources, you will empower your employees so that they can routinely delight and excite your customers. Through unique appreciation of the value of the IT assets, you will elevate your IT capabilities to the point where they become a compelling and durable contributor to the competitive advantage of the business.

To be successful, any competitive business must address four fundamental drivers:

- There must exist a market for your product/service and that market must exhibit one or more compelling needs.

- You must have a portfolio of competitive advantages that satisfy the compelling needs.

- You must have a way to exploit/leverage your competitive advantages.

- You must have a way to control costs.

IT has become strategic because IT can now address these issues. These essays provided insight into how to accomplish that goal.

CHAPTER 3

Assessment

The purpose of this chapter is to explain the assessment step of the strategic planning process. *Assessment* is the thorough analysis of the business environment to decide what to focus on. There are an endless amount of detail and numerous petitioners competing for management attention. Assessment filters the candidates to a preferred set that demands strategic attention and response. In executing this step, as is true for all the strategic planning steps, we view the IT organization as a "business." Figure 3.1 is an enlargement of the assessment step. We explain this step in the following manner:

Business scope and alignment. This section defines the notion of a business scope. A *business scope* defines the key describers of the IT business. A corollary concept to a business scope is alignment. *Alignment* is the process of ensuring that all business functions operate in harmony with each other to support the business scope.

Directives and assumptions. This section explains how the IT function aligns itself with the greater business through the notion of directives and assumptions. The strategic planning for the IT organization takes place within the context of an overall business that the IT function must support. The business strategic planning function provides directives and assumptions that bound (guide) the IT effort.

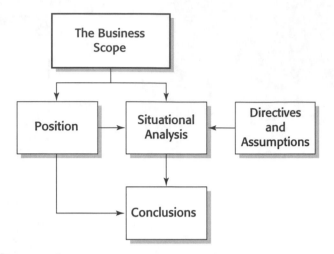

Figure 3.1 Assessment.

Position. This section explains the concept and development of positioning the IT business. *Positioning* illustrates the state of one or more business areas. Position answers the question "Where are we?"

Situational analysis. This section explains how to perform a situational analysis. *Situational analysis* is the collection and analysis of information about the business for developing conclusions about the state of the business. Situational analysis is performed by using various analytical methodologies.

Conclusions. This section explains the notion of conclusions, which are the culmination of the assessment step. *Conclusions* are explicit statements describing the overall situation of the business. They represent a set of imperatives requiring remedial or exploitative strategic action.

If you know others and know yourself, you will not be imperiled in a hundred battles; if you do not know others but know yourself, you will win one and lose one; if you do not know others and do not know yourself, you will be imperiled in every single battle.

—*Sun Tzu*, The Art of War

Sun Tzu teaches that assessment is the necessary preamble to a winning strategy:

The one with many strategic factors in his favor wins, the one with few strategic factors in his favor loses. . . . Observing the matter in this way, I can foresee who will win and who will lose.

Table 3.1   Sun's Tzu's Seven Strategic Factors

SUN TZU'S STRATEGIC FACTOR	DEFINITION	MODERN DAY EQUIVALENT
1. The Way	Inducing the people to share the same aims as the leadership through justice and benevolence	Culture, ethos, ethics
2. The Leadership	Intelligence, sternness, trustworthiness, humanity, and courage	Same
3. The Weather	The seasons	Industry dynamics
4. The Terrain	The lay of the land	Competition
5. Discipline	Organization, chain of command, and logistics	Management systems, capabilities, and processes
6. Troop Strength and Training	Number and competence of troops	Same
7. Reward and Punishment System	Procedures for rewarding valor and punishing disobedience	Human resource architecture

Sun Tzu's seven strategic factors, in order of importance, and their modern equivalents are listed in Table 3.1.

Adaptation to events takes place within the context of the assessment of these factors. It is remarkable that these strategic factors remain as relevant today as they were 2500 years ago. It is these factors that must be assessed.

The first step of strategic planning, therefore, is assessment, the act of knowing oneself and all other aspects of the business environment. Without assessment, we would proceed without forethought—a sure formula for failure.

Business Scope and Alignment

We understand the IT business as consisting of a business scope and a set of organizational units to realize that business scope. The business organizes into units to accomplish the business scope. Relative to each other and the business scope, functional units may be in a state of alignment or misalignment. Figure 3.2 illustrates these ideas.

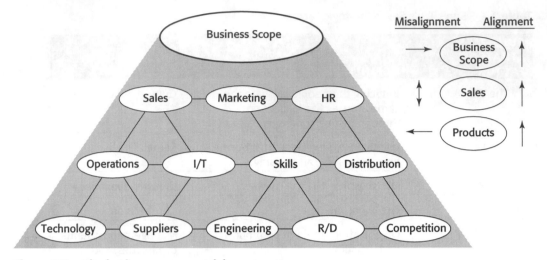

Figure 3.2   The business scope model.

Business Scope

Table 3.2 itemizes the attributes of a business scope. After reviewing a business scope, one should clearly understand the nature of a business. Each attribute of a business scope is now explained:

Vision. Provides a guiding theme that articulates the nature of the business and its intent for the future. A vision should be informative, shared, competitive, empowering, and worthy of an extended personal commitment.

Mission. Clearly defines the purpose of the business. It should remove any doubt as to what intents are to be accomplished.

Values. Describe what the business believes in. Values are important for success from at least two perspectives:

- Values are the root system for staff behavior. Management cannot expect winning behaviors to develop throughout the organization without building a foundation of values, which stimulate and support desirable behaviors.

- Values provide the basis for autonomous action by empowered employees. Executive management cannot be everywhere all the time, making every decision. If teams are to make rapid decisions without endless top management review, they require a framework of values to guide their decision making.

Customers/markets. Defines the recipients of products and services.

Products/services. Defines the IT products and services that are delivered to the business.

Geography. Defines the "space" of the battlespace. As companies compete globally, space takes on increased strategic significance because financial systems, standards, products, human resource practices, and capabilities all have to adapt to the new geography of the battlespace.

Strategic intent.[1] Describes the long-term ambition of our efforts. It may be viewed a grand selfish vision. A strategic intent has the following attributes:

- It is the long-term stable ambition of a winner. It defines winning and is worthy of an extended corporate attention plan.

- It represents ambition out of all proportion to the resources and capabilities of the organization. It promotes leveraging the resources of the organization to reach the intent rather than settling for limited objectives.

- It provides a compelling target for organizational commitment and effort.

- It provides a future to fold back against. One must constantly ask, "What must I do now to get closer to my strategic intent?"

Strategic planning cycles, therefore, are not disconnected. Each planning cycle should be understood as a stepping stone to the strategic intent. Challenges and hurdles are addressed in each planning cycle to move us closer to the stable long-term intent. As illustrated in Figure 3.3, the business does not wander from planning cycle to planning cycle but moves forward toward a defined end—the end of a winner.

Given that the purpose of IT is competitiveness, the strategic intent of an IT organization must include the realization of a reach/range/maneuverability architecture. By moving ever closer to a reach, range, and maneuverability architecture, an infrastructure is put in place that permits rapid IT system development, deployment, and evolution.

An ancillary concept to strategic intent is that of "market leader." One may assert that there are three types of companies:

- Those that ask customers what they want and are perpetual followers

- Those that temporarily succeed in leading customers in directions they don't need to go

- Those that lead customers where they need to go—market leaders

A strategic intent-driven company is always the latter type of company; it anticipates what customers will need rather than selling customers what they wanted/needed six months or a year ago.

Table 3.2   Business Scope Definition

BUSINESS ATTRIBUTE	DEFINITION
Vision	Business guiding theme
Mission	Purpose of the business
Values	Distinguishing beliefs—ethos
Customer/markets	To whom we sell
Products/services	What we sell
Geography	Where we sell
Strategic intent	Long-term ambition of our efforts
Driving force	Primary determiner of products/services and markets
Sustainable competitive advantage	Asset, capability, process, etc., which attracts us to our customers and deters our competitors

Market leaders are often vision-driven.

What everyone knows is what has already happened. What everyone knows is not called wisdom. What the aware individual knows is what has not yet taken shape; what has not yet occurred. If you see the subtle and notice the hidden so as to seize victory when there is no form, this is really good.

Sun Tzu, The Art of War

Visionaries provide insights that allow for discontinuous improvements in the strategic situation of a business. Much can be gained if you can take action while to most "there is no form."

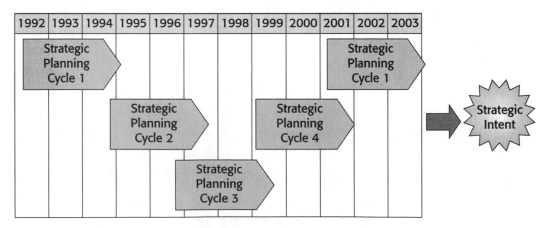

Figure 3.3   Strategic intent.

Table 3.3   Driving Forces

DRIVING FORCE	DEFINITION	EXAMPLE
Products offered	Continue to produce and deliver products similar to those it has	Automobile manufacturer
Market needs	Provide a range of products to meet current and emerging needs in the markets it serves	Hospital supply
Technology	Offers only products derived from its technological capability	Pharmaceutical
Production capability	Offers only products driven by its production know-how/capability	Lodging
Method of sale	Selects products and serves markets based on its primary method of sale	TV home shopping
Method of distribution	Selects products and markets based on its distribution channels	Catalog house
Natural resources	Offers products and services based on its natural resource asset	Oil company
Size/growth	Provide a range of products to meet size/growth objectives	Mergers and acquisitions
Return/profit	Provide a range of products to meet return/profit objectives	Conglomerate

Driving force.[2] Is an explicit statement of what will be the primary determiner of the scope of future markets and products. Table 3.3 illustrates a variety of driving forces from which a firm may choose. The selection of a driving force is a pivotal decision because it will have a great influence on day-to-day decision making throughout the organization.

Sustainable competitive advantage (SCA). This includes the resources, capabilities, assets, and processes that provide the enterprise with a distinct attraction to its customers and unique advantage over its competitors. Table 3.4 lists the seven attributes that describe an SCA. An SCA may result in an advantage in cost/productivity, value-added/differentiation, or customer focus. The assessment, development, nurturing, and compounding of SCA is a major thrust of strategy development. SCA defines how the business will win. Table 3.5 may be used to analyze existing and candidate SCAs for potency.

Complementing sustainable competitive advantages are temporary competitive advantages (TCA). TCAs have the same attributes, but they lack durability.

Table 3.4   Sustainable Competitive Advantages

ATTRIBUTE	DEFINITION
Customer perception	The customer perceives a consistent difference in one or more critical buying factors.
SCA linkage	The difference in customer perception is directly attributable to the SCA.
Durability	Both the customer's perception and the SCA linkage are durable over an extended time period.
Transparency	The mechanics/details of the SCA are difficult to understand by competitors.
Accessibility	The competitor has unequal access to the required resources to mimic the SCA.
Replication	The competitor would have extreme difficulty reproducing the SCA.
Coordination	The SCA requires difficult and subtle coordination of multiple resources.

TCAs require continual refreshment. With the advent of hyper-competition, for the typical IT organization, the portfolio of SCAs is dwindling and being replaced by short-term TCAs.

A business scope defines the essential characteristics of a business. It encapsulates the idea, concept, and formula of the business.

Alignment

A business accomplishes its objectives by mobilizing all the units toward realizing its business scope. To be successful, a business must realize a tri-state of alignment:

Table 3.5   SCA Evaluation Matrix

SCA	CUSTOMER PERCEPTION	SCA LINKAGE	DURA-BILITY	TRANS-PARENCY	ACCESSI-BILITY	REPLI-CATION	COORDIN-ATION
SCA 1							
SCA 2							
SCA 3							
SCA 4							
SCA 5							
SCA N							

- The business scope is internally aligned between its elements.
- All internal business units are aligned with each other.
- The aligned internal business functions, as a whole through the aligned business scope, are aligned with the needs of the external battlespace.

The essence of alignment is coordination, perseverance, and concentration of effort toward a shared set of objectives. A business that is aligned is said to be in a state of "strategic fit."

Strategic fit or alignment should be understood as a continuum of states, which include the following key data points in increasing achievement of alignment:

Entropy (chaos). Gross misalignment. Collaboration within and between functions, processes, and the external battlespace is a rare accident.

Misfit. Collaboration between functions and processes is minimal.

Mixed. There exists a mixture of alignment and misalignment. A reasonable number of functions and processes are "kind of" going in the same direction.

Threshold (minimal). A minimal level of alignment exists so that products and services can move through the value chain and to the customer. Businesses at less than a threshold level will eventually implode if the state is not improved.

Harmony. General and continuing collaboration.

Perfect alignment. Not only does a state of harmony exist, but the state has been achieved in a manner that provides sustainable competitive advantage to the firm.

As will be presented in the next section, achieving a level of strategic fit at and preferably superior to threshold is a foundation requirement of strategy.

Alignment does not mean automatons marching mindlessly in straight lines. Alignment is a wide highway, not a thin line. Alignment includes skunk works and "crazy money," and it encourages creative independence. Alignment may include parallel projects as well as contradictory projects. The issue is that it is purposeful from the perspective of the whole rather than the individual optimizations of individual parts at the expense of the whole.

As shown in Figure 3.4, strategy crosses all functional areas. It is therefore not possible to develop or execute strategy without an objective of forcing a strategic fit. Without alignment, a business proceeds in a state of chaos with each unit optimizing its own provincial view of the world at the expense of the whole business (see Figure 3.5).

Those whose upper and lower ranks have the same desire are victorious. . . . Those skilled in strategy achieve cooperation in a group so that directing the group is like directing a single individual with no other choice.... Employ the entire force like employing a single individual.

Sun Tzu, The Art of War

Alignment is best conceptualized as the civilizing (throttling) of intra-organizational conflict to a point where a shared agenda and common purpose can be established. Alignment beyond that point is probably detrimental. Just as external competition provides the overall impetus to improve products and services, healthy and spirited debate during both the assessment and strategy steps leads to maximizing creative and innovative responses. This is the consequence of the clash of competing ideas. When fortune inevitably changes, new necessities will demand fresh responses. The novelty of these responses springs from the breadth of organizational diversity rather than from the depths of uniformity. For the execution step to succeed, however, a state of civilized alignment must be obtained, or we will expend and exhaust our energies battling each other rather than our competitors. Alignment must therefore

Figure 3.4 Strategy is comprehensive.

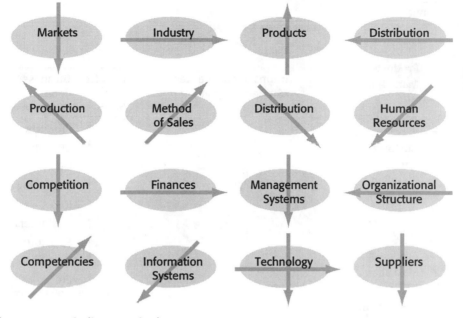

Figure 3.5 Misalignment is chaos.

walk a delicate balance, maximizing current uniformity while not squashing the diversity required to seed tomorrow's adaptability.

As shown in Figure 3.6, a fundamental activity of strategic planning is moving the organization from its current state of alignment, whether it be a state of harmony, entropy, or mixed, into a strategic fit state with the new business scope. A continual effort to reach alignment is imperative. While immediate business needs and opportunities will often cause misalignments as functions and processes move forward on varied schedules, if an effort is not maintained to reassert alignment then the seeds of future strategic problems will be sown. It is hard enough for the business to react to external change beyond its control without having to take strategic actions to rectify problems created by its own negligence to maintain synergy. The nature of alignment is best understood as an endless race to achieve, rather than an effort to maintain. Alignment is a continual journey, not a one-time event.

It should be obvious from this discussion of business scope and alignment that a potentially traumatic event for any organization is a change, however small, in any element of the business scope. If any business scope element is redefined, all the functional units have to realign themselves. It would then logically follow that the worst thing that could happen to an organization is concurrent and major shifts in all (or almost all) of the business scope elements. Massive business scope redefinition would cause a transition state of chaos as the business functions struggle to achieve a new state of alignment.

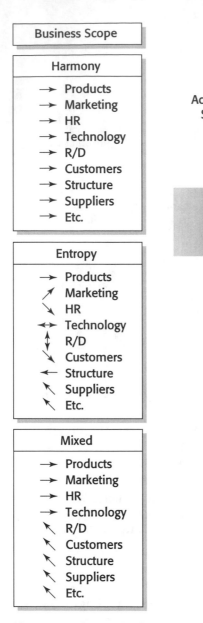
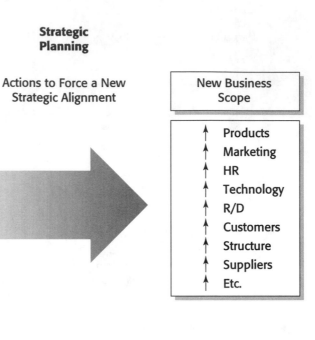

Figure 3.6   Strategic alignment.

This is exactly what is happening to many IT organizations today. As illustrated in Table 3.6, many of the business scope elements are being redefined in response to the IT pincer we discussed in Chapter 1, "Strategic Planning for Information Technology." It is therefore not surprising that IT organizations find defining an identity for the new millennium difficult when they are in a state of such mass transition.

Table 3.6 Changed IT Business Scope

BUSINESS SCOPE ELEMENT/ BUSINESS ATTRIBUTE	OLD IT BUSINESS SCOPE	NEW IT BUSINESS SCOPE
Vision	Cost efficiency	Advantage efficency
Mission	Build functional organizational systems	Build enterprise systems
Values	Optimize IT	Serve the business
Customers/markets	Data center user	Workgroup, departmental, and corporate user
Products/services	One size fits all	Cut-and-paste network computing
Geography	Domestic	Global
Strategic intent	IT as basis for advantage for IT	IT as basis for competitive advantage for the business
Driving force	Production capability/ products	Market needs
Sustainable competitive advantage	Internal monopoly	World-class efficiency and effectiveness of the IT resource

Summary

Strategy is a problem of coordination, not of masses.

Sun Tzu, The Art of War

The basis of success is not the quantity of resources employed but the manner of employment. The business scope provides an unambiguous shared agenda for the organization. Alignment provides the vehicle to bring all functions into accord with the shared agenda. The objectives of the business as a whole are primary; the agenda of each unit is secondary. All strategic actions take place in the context of optimizing the business as a whole. Strategies of the individual units have purpose only toward that end.

Directives and Assumptions

The IT organization exists to provide competitiveness to the rest of the business. Its direction, as a whole, needs to be in alignment with the needs and requirements of the greater business. All strategic thinking and actions take place in the overriding context of meeting the information movement and

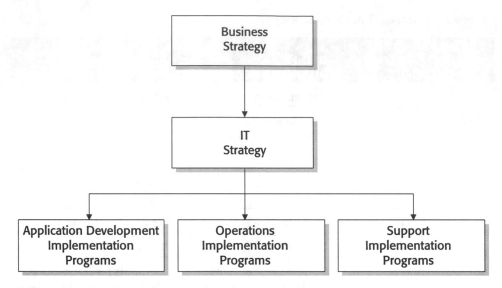

Figure 3.7 Direction and assumption planning chain.

management needs of the customers. Though not constantly restated, whether one is doing business scope development, positioning, objective definitions, or commitment plan, all of strategic planning is done in constant (even when silent) reference to serving customers' needs.

It should therefore be anticipated that the strategic planning effort of the business, as a whole, will provide directives and assumptions to guide, prioritize, lead, and shape the IT strategic planning effort, which will initiate various implementation programs (see Figure 3.7). These directives and assumptions bind the strategies that are permissible for the IT organization to undertake and, in so doing, help ensure a strategic fit between the business and the IT function (see Figure 3.8). The more valued a business partner the IT organization is viewed by the functional business units, the greater participation and influence the IT organization will have in shaping overall business strategy and in bounding IT directives and assumptions.

The optimum strategic planning situation would therefore have a high degree of concurrency and interlock between the business strategic planning activities and those of the IT organization. In this situation, the IT planning would occur slightly staggered but in parallel to the business planning, with the chief IT strategist (the CIO) actively participating in the business planning. In this and only this situation is the degree of collaboration, coordination, communication, and alignment maximized.

Unfortunately, there is often an absence of a formal strategy statement by the business to provide the needed directives and assumptions. This short-

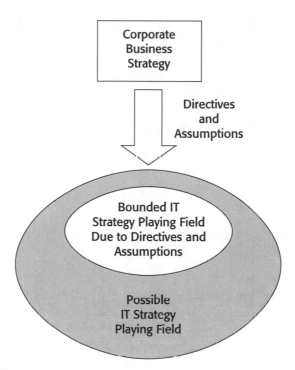

Figure 3.8 Binding strategy.

coming can be addressed by performing an alignment analysis. To do an alignment analysis, we need to understand four definitions:

Business drivers. External forces to the business of such importance that the business must respond creatively and aggressively to them. Sample business drivers would be regulation, globalization, or the advent of new distribution channels (electronic storefronts on the WWW).

Technology drivers. IT industry forces of such importance that the IT organizations must respond creatively and aggressively to them. Sample technology drivers would be the Internet, selective outsourcing, or technology standards.

Major business initiatives. Classes of responses to the business drivers. Sample business initiatives would be to provide premier customer care, simplify business processes, or serve a global customer.

IT requirements. Impact of business initiatives or technology drivers on the IT organization. Sample IT requirements would be to provide a single view of the customer, re-skill the workforce, or balance build versus buy for new software systems.

The logic of alignment is therefore as follows: Because of the business drivers, it will be necessary for the business to undertake major business initiatives. To execute the business initiatives, certain IT requirements must be met. IT requirements must also be met to react creatively to technology drivers that create new technology opportunities for the organization and/or obsolete existing technology investments.

This analysis can be aided by using three matrices as follows:

- Step 1: Matrix business drivers to business initiatives, as illustrated in Table 3.7

- Step 2: Matrix business initiatives to IT requirements, as illustrated in Table 3.8

- Step 3: Matrix technology drivers to IT requirements, as illustrated in Table 3.9

These completed matrices will provide you with a clear understanding of how the business and technology will drive your strategic decision making. In performing this alignment analysis, what one will surely find is that the business initiatives will center on becoming more "innovative." Continual innovation is a primary requirement for coping with hyper-competition. Innovation is the ability to convert novel ideas into revenue and profits by developing new products, processes, and/or business models. Innovative businesses promote creativity, are resourceful and inquisitive, and look for relationships across previously unrelated objects. Because most innovations will require the use of IT to express themselves, a key challenge for IT strategy is positioning IT resources so that innovation can be quickly converted into operational systems.

Table 3.7   Business Drivers to Business Initiative Matrix

	BUSINESS INITIATIVES				
Business Drivers	Initiative 1	Initiative 2	Initiative 3	Initiative 4	Initiative "n"
Business driver 1					
Business driver 2					
Business driver 3					
Business driver 4					
Business Driver N					

Table 3.8   Business Initiative to IT Requirements Matrix

	IT REQUIREMENTS				
Business Initiatives	IT Require-ment 1	IT Require-ment 2	IT Require-ment 3	IT Require-ment 4	IT Require-ment "n"
Business initiative 1					
Business initiative 2					
Business initiative 3					
Business initiative 4					
Business Initiative N					

Position

A *position* is an illustration of the state of a strategic area along one or more strategic dimensions. Position is best expressed graphically, quantitatively, and qualitatively. A *strategic dimension* is a variable that is critical to business success. Positions are descriptive of the state of the business, and their correctness should not be argumentative. Position analysis yields a series of position

Table 3.9   Technology Drivers to IT Requirements Matrix

	IT REQUIREMENTS				
Technology Drivers	IT Require-ment 1	IT Require-ment 2	IT Require-ment 3	IT Require-ment 4	IT Require-ment "n"
Technology driver 1					
Technology driver 2					
Technology driver 3					
Technology driver 4					
Technology Driver N					

charts that cross all strategically important business areas and collectively answer the question "Where are we?"

The underlying notion of this technique is that the strategic position (Position) of a business, $P_{BUSINESS}$, can be expressed as a set of positions:

$$P_{BUSINESS} = (P_{MARKET}, P_{FINANCIAL}, P_{TECHNOLOGY}, P_{SALES}, P_{OPERATIONS}, P_{DISTRIBUTION}, P_{ENGINEERING}, etc.).$$

A position may also reflect the state of a resource such as a competency or process capability. Positioning is a recursive concept, and any position, P_{XYZ}, may itself be expressed as a set of positions. This point will be fully demonstrated later in this section when we discuss positioning of a product.

Any business area can be positioned. The strategic planning team has the responsibility to do the following:

- Define which areas are to be included in the analysis and require positioning
- Define what are the strategic dimensions that illustrate the status of the area
- Collect the required data to do the positioning
- Define the presentation format, preferably graphically, of the position

Positioning, like situational analysis, needs to be done in multiple dimensions:

Current (period ending) position. What is the collective strategic position of the business as of the ending of the current period?

Strategic intent position. What would be the position of the business if the strategic intent was reached?

Competitor position. What is the present situation and what is projected to be the position of the collective competition?

Desired future-state position. What positions does the business wish to attain by the end of this planning cycle?

The resulting gaps between the current position and the other positions are used to develop conclusions, objectives, and strategic moves.

Positioning forces "fantasy convergence." The graphical format of a position and the explicit statement of the position force clarity and eliminate confusion. A shared agenda cannot be developed if agreement isn't reached on the present state of the organization or if there is gross misunderstanding among those who are trying to reach agreement. Positioning addresses this problem and forces resolution of the differences we possess on the state of the business.

A business area must be positioned in a manner that provides understanding and insight into its strategic dimensions. The remainder of this section demonstrates the positioning of multiple business areas or resources of particular importance to the IT function. These are common but exemplary positionings. Each positioning is developed using the following structure:

- *Definition* of the business area or resource being positioned
- *Description* of the business area or resource being positioned
- *IT strategic planning impact* analysis of the implications of the positioning to the IT strategic planning activity

A strategic area, which is selected and positioned, is said to be under "position management."

Financial Position

Definition: Financial position is used to display the financial state of the business. It is the most common and readily understood type of positioning.

Description: There are numerous ways to illustrate financial position—balance sheet, revenue and expense, forecasts and history, per unit revenue and expense, and net margin as well as multiple financial ratios. These include such ratios as the following:

- Liquidity ratios measure the firm's ability to meet short-term financial obligations.
- Profitability ratios measure performance.
- Leverage ratios measure the extent of debt and equity funding.
- Activity ratios measure resource utilization.

All these candidate financial measures may be point-of-time- and time-line-oriented.

IT strategic planning impact: The critical issue is to define and reach consensus on which are to be the measures of performance for the IT function. Is the IT organization to be measured on return on investment (ROI), cash flow, expense/employee, IT as a percent of revenue, cost savings, or some other measure? Financial performance has been and remains the measure of success (or failure). Financial positioning therefore demands the explicit definition of which measures are the ones against which IT success is to be judged. The most traditional measure is the unit cost of product or service.

Market Position

Definition: Market position defines the market segmentation and associated position for each IT product and service.

Description: For each IT product and service, a market position defines the following:

- The size of the market
- The market compound annual growth rate (CAGR)
- The market share
- Market shares of major competitors' products

This information is often illustrated in the form of a pie chart, as shown in Figure 3.9. Market segmentation is important because it clearly identifies the following:

- What we are selling
- To whom we are selling
- What need(s) we are attempting to meet

Market segmentation is also important because many of the positioning techniques and situational analysis techniques are best executed at the market segment level.

With the emergence of reach/range/maneuverability architectures, market segments are fragmenting. *Segmentation* presents the idea of a group of users with the same need. *Fragmentation* represents the idea of users with very distinct needs. Because Internet computing permits "cut-and-paste" solutions, users will start demanding information appliances and technologies that specifically optimize their business practices. There will be a shift from the question of what technologies to offer that make it easiest for the IT organization to the question of what technologies to offer that maximize the end users'

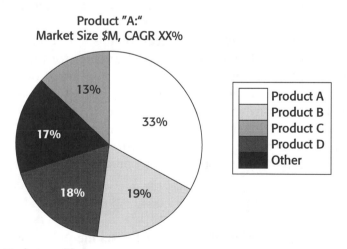

Figure 3.9   Market position.

competitive advantage. This has a number of important implications for IT providers:

- Systems integration skills grow in importance.

- Architecture will be critical to define the "bonding" mechanisms among the specialized solutions.

- The number and types of IT technologies that will have to be supported will proliferate.

- A versatile staff will be more valuable than a specialized staff.

- The services provided will be more valuable to the customer, lack the traditional economies of scale, and thus be premium priced.

- Fragmentation is both an advantage and a disadvantage from the perspective of competition. Competitors will lose economy-of-scale advantages and expertise in competing for the in-house account, but conversely, smaller, boutique vendors will become rivals.

Fragmentation represents a major paradigm shift to the IT organization that historically operated on "one size processing fits all," and it will require a number of organizational realignments to deal with the change from one big user segment to multiple user fragments.

IT strategic planning impact: A market perspective creates a proper customer/supplier relationship between the IT organization and the users. The internal IT user community is now viewed as a battlespace with needs that the IT organization has to meet through competitive products and services.

Market research is critical to successful market positioning.

What enables an intelligent leader to overcome others and achieve extraordinary accomplishments is foreknowledge. All matters require foreknowledge.

Sun Tzu, The Art of War

The better one understands customer needs, the better one can position one's products and services to satisfy them.

The ideal way of understanding one's customers is to understand them strategically. Recursively, do a strategic analysis of each customer. What are that customer's critical success factors? What are the cost drivers in the value chains? What are the threats and opportunities? What is the basis of sustainable competitive advantage? If you understand your customer strategically, then you can begin to design IT solutions and introduce emerging technologies that directly contribute to building the customer's sustainable competitive advantage. You will then be regarded as a cherished partner rather than an expense.

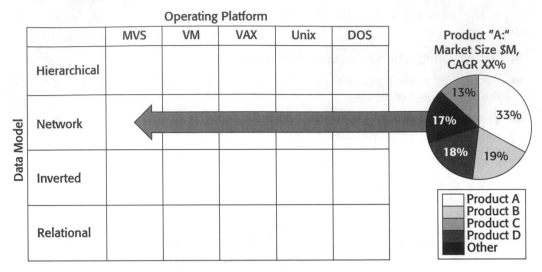

Figure 3.10   Traditional DBMS market segmentation.

Course of action: Market segmentation is done in the following manner:

1. Identify key variables that segment the market (i.e., product feature, buyer type, cost, geography, distribution channel, etc.)
2. Assign discrete values for each segmentation variable
3. Construct a segmentation table ($\frac{2}{3}$ dimensions)
4. Test the segmentation table for validity by positioning the industry competitors in the table

Figure 3.10 illustrates how database management system (DBMS) products have traditionally been segmented by the key variables of operating platform and the data model supported.

Core Competency

Definition: Core competency represents the collective learning of the organization, especially hard-to-coordinate diverse skills, which integrate multiple streams of technologies.[3]

Description: Core competencies provide "roots" for competitive advantage because they can be leveraged to support multiple products and services in multiple market segments. A core competency has four primary attributes:

- It provides access to a wide variety of markets.
- It makes a significant contribution to the customer's perceived benefits of the product.

- It is difficult to imitate.
- It is often the complex coordination of multiple technologies and applied skills.

Figure 3.11 illustrates the power of the core competency concept. The foundation competencies are leveraged into multiple core products, which in turn are multiplied into numerous end products, which are then sent out into the market. Core products are highly reusable building blocks. End products are families of differentiated products (premium, customized, enhanced, cost-reduced, basic) to meet diverse customer needs (see Figure 3.12). An end product consists of three layers:

- The core layer satisfies the overt user need.
- The tangible layer includes attributes of the product such as functionally, quality, price/performance, branding, and size.
- The augmented layer includes attributes of distinction such as reputation, warranty, service, and investment protection.

By designing success around competencies, a company uses skill investment as opposed to capital investment as the basis of advantage. A company can therefore position itself so that a portfolio of competencies supports a portfolio of products for a portfolio of markets (customers).

IT strategic planning impact: The pressing question is what is the set of core competencies that the IT organization requires to be successful in the new millenium, given the challenges we outlined in Chapter 2, "Managing IT for

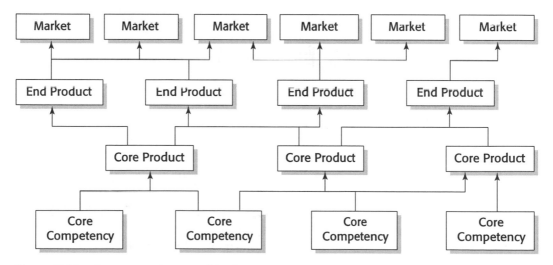

Figure 3.11   Core competency architecture.

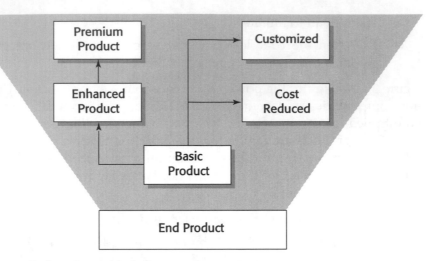

Figure 3.12 End product exploded.

Competitive Advantage." Figure 3.13 illustrates a candidate core competency architecture. Core competency and capabilities (which follow) are two major frameworks from which an organization can be managed and positioned strategically.

Course of action: Existing and candidate core competencies can be evaluated using Table 3.10. Care must be taken to prevent core competencies from becoming dated core rigidities, which prevent adaptation to changing customer needs.

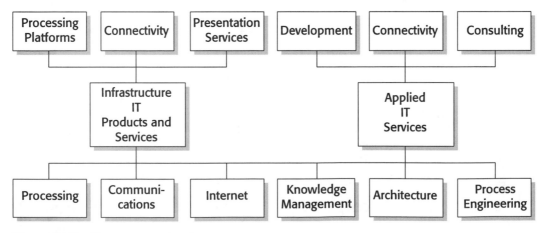

Figure 3.13 IT core competencies.

Table 3.10   Core Competency Evaluation Matrix

CORE COMPE- TENCY (CC)	MARKET ACCESS	DIRECT RELATIONSHIP TO CUSTOMER'S PERCEIVED VALUE	DIFFICULT TO IMITATE	COMPLEX COORDINATION OF SKILLS/ TECHNOLOGIES
CC 1				
CC 2				
CC 3				
CC 4				
CC N				

Capabilities

Definition: Capabilities is a strategic framework that asserts that the focus of strategy is the nurturing of the primary business processes and practices that deliver value and satisfaction to the customer. Strategic positioning should concentrate on enabling the infrastructure to support robust capabilities and selecting the capabilities on which to compete.[4]

Description: A capabilities perspective asserts that the logic of competition is not *with whom* to compete nor *with what* to compete nor *for whom* to compete but is *how* to compete. Success therefore depends on transforming key processes into strategic capabilities that consistently provide superior value to the customer. A capability has six attributes:

Speed. The process can quickly respond to customer demands and the incorporation of a stream of new ideas and technologies (the capability must be maneuverable).

Process consistency. The process can unfailingly produce a product, which meets or exceeds customer expectations.

Agility. The process is highly malleable to accommodate unique customer requirements. (The capability must deal with market fragmentation.)

Cross-functional. The process crosses multiple business areas in its execution.

Begins and ends with the customer. The process is a closed loop starting with acquisition of a customer need and ending with satisfying that need.

Complements core competencies. The process puts core competencies into motion and in doing so translates the competency into value for the customer.

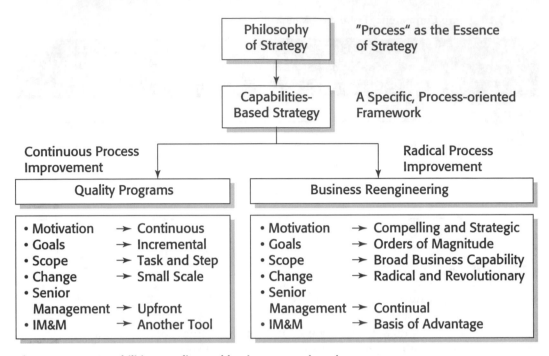

Figure 3.14   Capabilities, quality, and business reengineering.

Capabilities put two other contemporary business practices into a broader perspective. As illustrated in Figure 3.14, capabilities link quality initiatives and business reengineering to strategy. Capabilities provide a specific strategic framework that emphasizes process as the winning strategic dimension. Quality programs provide a tactic to continuously improve capabilities while business reengineering provides an approach to overhaul processes radically.

THE MAJOR FRAMEWORKS

Capabilities, along with core competencies, strategic alignment, and sustainable competitive advantage, represent the major contemporary paradigms of what should sit at the foundation of strategy. Table 3.11 itemizes the primary attributes of each competing perspective. Frameworks complement each other; as shown in Figure 3.15, strategic alignment provides a necessary foundation layer for success while core competencies and capabilities are often the basis of sustainable competitive advantage.

Figure 3.15   Integrating frameworks.

IT strategic planning impact: What are the critical capabilities for the IT organization for the new millennium? The following starter list is suggested:

Systems integration. The ability to build complex operational systems through the integration of heterogeneous technologies.

Project management. The ability to manage large and complex projects.

Network computing operations management (the Internet). The ability to operate complex network computing systems in an effective and efficient manner.

Configuration management. The ability to manage the bill-of-material of complex network computing architectures composed of components from a heterogeneous set of vendors.

Infrastructure development. The ability to rapidly amend and append the IT infrastructure with ever-changing opportunistic technologies.

Supplier management. The ability to work closely with selected suppliers to create a high-performance IT environments.

Course of action. Use Table 3.12 as an aid to evaluate existing and candidate capabilities. Refer to the **Description** section for definitions of the table column heading attributes.

Table 3.11   Major Frameworks Compared

CORE COMPETENCIES	CAPABILITIES	STRATEGIC ALIGNMENT	SUSTAINABLE COMPETITIVE ADVANTAGE
Market access	Process speed	Coordination	Customer perception
Customer perception	Process consistency	Perseverance	Linkage
Difficult to imitate	Agility	Concentration	Durability
Coordination	Cross-functional	of effort	Accessibility
	Begins and ends	Commitment	Transparency
	with customer		Replication
	Relationship to		Coordination
	core competency		

Table 3.12 Capabilities Evaluation Matrix

| CAPABILITY | PROCESS SPEED | PROCESS CONSIS- TENCY | AGILITY | CROSS-FUNCTIONAL | |
				BEGIN AND END WITH CUSTOMER	RELATED TO CORE COMPETENCY
Capability 1					
Capability 2					
Capability 3					
Capability 4					
Capability N					

Human Resource Position

Definition: Human resource (HR) position defines the alignment of human resource systems and practices with the strategic direction of the business.

Description: Values define what a company believes in. Behaviors are the daily way that employees individually and collectively express the values and operationilize them. Human resource systems provide the linkage between the two. As shown in Figure 3.16, the human resource systems serve a dual purpose, which are:

- The traditional tactical mission of administering a functional responsibility
- The strategic mission of motivating and stimulating desired behaviors in the populace

As shown in Figure 3.17, each HR system should be positioned so that the following occur:

- Its tactical and functional purpose is clearly understood.
- The inclusion of behavior incentives to stimulate desired behaviors is present.

As a consequence of the preceding, a high-powered HR environment is created where each desired behavior is stimulated through multiple HR systems, and each HR system supports the development of multiple desired behaviors.

IT strategic planning impact: IT strategic planning in conjunction with the HR organization needs to do the following:

- Identify the value set
- Develop and reach consensus on the desired behaviors set

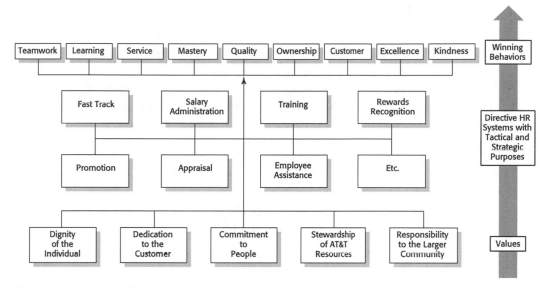

Figure 3.16   HR architecture.

Source: "Implementing Client/Server Computing: A Strategic Perspective," Bernard H. Boar (McGraw-Hill, 1993). Reprinted with the permission of the publisher.

- Take inventory of human resource systems
- Identify the current tactical purpose of each HR system
- Design into the HR systems incentives to stimulate winning behaviors

The HR architecture provides the strategy team with "knobs" to turn to influence staff behaviors. This becomes extremely important as part of the change management plan to encourage cooperation during the execution step of the strategy process.

HR System Name	
Tactical and Functional Purpose	
← Strategic Incentives →	
Behaviors	Incorporated Incentives
Behavior 1	
Behavior 2	
Behavior 3	
Behavior 4	

Reinforcement Practices for Desired Behaviors

Figure 3.17   HR System exploded.

IT Position

Definition: IT position defines the state of the IT resource. This state is presented in the context of an encompassing IT architecture.

Description: IT is often a resource in a state of chaos. Table 3.13 provides a framework to position the "greater" IT resource. Along the strategic dimensions of infrastructure, information, applications, and organization, it is important to understand the following states:

Inventory. What exists?

Principles. What are the established high-level rules that guide decision making?

Models. What are the structural models (data models, organization structures, business models, etc.) that illustrate the IT assets?

Standards. What are the agreed-to products, methods, vendors, and interfaces that bond our IT environment together?

The "infrastructure" row in Table 3.13 is commonly referred to as the IT technology architecture, and it is this architecture that we suggest is best realized by extending the reach of IT, the range of data that is accessible, and the maneuverability of the IT components. It is obvious that the matrix serves only as a conceptual placeholder and that positioning an IT architecture requires exploding each cell in a manner consistent with the contents of that cell.

IT strategic planning impact: The positioning of IT is of vital importance to IT strategic planning. For IT to achieve its strategic objective of competitiveness, it is necessary for IT management to have control and knowledge of what they are managing. The IT architecture provides the required framework. Changes in IT equate to reconfiguring the architecture. IT management can therefore understand the before and after pictures of proposed changes.

The information contained in Table 3.13 has been what most IT organizations have historically equated to IT strategy. While it is obviously important,

Table 3.13   IT Architecture

STRATEGIC DIMENSION	INVENTORY	PRINCIPLES	MODELS	STANDARDS
Infrastructure				
Information				
Applications				
Organization				

Source: CSC/Index.

alone it is insufficient. It is part, but only part, of the overall strategic thinking and plan required. It is inadequate to manage the business strategically.

Strategic Progress

Definition: Strategic progress is a point-of time-report of the status of existing strategy implementation programs from previous strategic planning cycles.

Description: Strategy implementation programs are often multiyear projects. The state of existing projects is of prime importance from four perspectives:

- Are present strategy implementation programs working?
- Do programs in progress or programs in the planning stage need to be modified?
- What has been learned from these experiences?
- Does current data collection indicate that the present portfolio of actions is still a preferred set of actions?

For each outstanding project, it is important to know its due date, current implementation status, planned implementation status, and lessons learned.

Although we are very interested in current status, we are not bounded by it. Each planning period should be "zero based." Just like the budgeting method of zero-based budgeting in which all financial expenditures must be cyclically reevaluated and compete for new funding and resources, the same is true for strategy. What is in progress has no halo effect; all problems start with equal rights to our attention and resources.

IT strategic planning impact: As discussed in Chapter 5, "Execution," strategic moves are implemented through projects. The selected project management system must meet the standard requirement of status reporting.

Five Force Model

Definition: The Five Force model is an analytical method used to determine the state of competition at an industry or business level.[5]

Description: The Five Force model asserts that competition in an industry is a function of the dynamic interplay of five forces, and they are as follows:

Supplier power. The power of industry suppliers to control prices, quality, and the overall conditions of purchase.

Buyer power. The power of the customers of an industry to exploit their position to influence pricing, quality, and the overall conditions of purchase.

Threat of entry. The ease of entry of new competitors.

Substitute products. The availability and attractiveness of substitute products.

Rivalry of existing competitors. The intensity of competition among the incumbent players.

Figure 3.18 illustrates the Five Force model. When "the industry" is in the center, the Five Force model analyzes the overall competitive situation of the industry. When "your business" is put in the center, it can be used to understand the competitive situation of your business alone, relative to its external environment. The business is in a constant battle to improve or at least maintain its overall competitive position. To do this, it must undertake initiatives to improve its position relative to some Five Force. Likewise, it must be on vigilance to react to the initiatives of others who are trying to reposition themselves at the enterprise's expense. Tables 3.14 through 3.18 summarize the factors that compose each Five Force. Figure 3.19 graphically depicts a Five Force model and its associated factors.

At any given time, the Five Forces may be affecting the business in any of the following ways:

No impact. A Five Force factor is dormant.

An act by another. A supplier, customer, or rival takes an action to improve its position at your expense.

An act by you. You initiate an action to improve a Five Force position.

An external act. An event outside the immediate Five Force domain (war, economic swing, etc.) occurs that can alter the balance of the Five Forces.

The Five Force model points out the competitive primacy of being able to maneuver, adapt, and change.

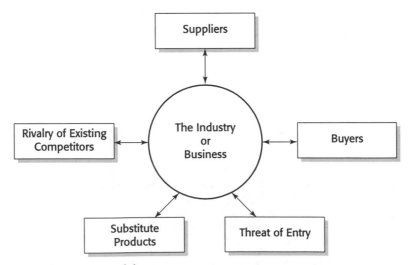

Figure 3.18   Five Force model.

Supplier force is the degree to which a supplier can determine the conditions of purchase including price, feature/functionality, service, and quality.

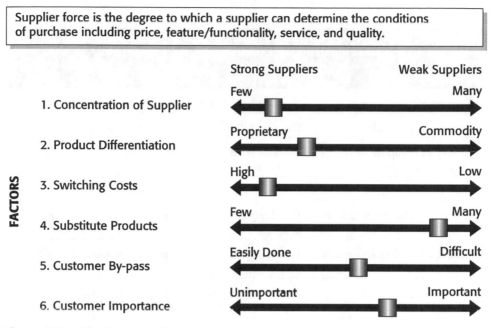

Figure 3.19 Five Force positioning example.

Table 3.14 Supplier Power

SUPPLIER POWER IS THE DEGREE TO WHICH SUPPLIERS CAN DETERMINE THE CONDITIONS OF PURCHASE	
FACTOR	**DEFINITION**
Concentration of suppliers	The number and equality of suppliers
Product differentiation	The degree of commodity or proprietariness of the product
Switching costs	The total costs incurred by the buyer to switch to a different product
Substitute products	The existence of alternative products providing equal or better feature/functionality at equal or better price/performance
Customer by-pass	The degree to which the supplier can by-pass the customer and sell directly to the customer's customer
Customer importance	The importance of the customer to the supplier

Table 3.15 Buyer Power

BUYER POWER IS THE DEGREE TO WHICH THE BUYER'S BARGAINING POSITION CAN DETERMINE THE CONDITIONS OF PURCHASE	
FACTOR	DEFINITION
Concentration of buyers	The number of buyers and size of purchase
Product is commodity	The degree of commodity of the product
Product as component of buyer's cost structure	The influence of the product on the cost structure of the customer's product
Buyer's profitability	The current financial performance of the buyer
Product's importance to buyer	The degree to which the product is important in adding-value
Product viewed as an expense	The degree to which the product is viewed as a cost and only a cost
Supplier by-pass	The degree to which the buyer can buy from the supplier's supplier or do it themselves

Table 3.16 Threat of Entry

THREAT OF ENTRY IS THE DEGREE TO WHICH THERE IS A VIABLE PROBABILITY THAT NEW ENTRANTS WILL JOIN THE BATTLESPACE	
FACTOR	DEFINITION
Economies of scale	The costs associated with achieving the necessary economies of scale to achieve competitive pricing
Product differentiation	The differentiation of incumbent products and their associated customer loyalty
Switching costs	The total costs of switching products
Capital requirements	The amount of up-front investment required to enter the battlespace
Distribution channel access	The openness the distribution channels to a new player
Government policy	The degree to which government policy and laws control market entry
Retaliation of incumbents	The degree to which incumbents have demonstrated a willingness to protect their markets

Table 3.17 Substitute Products

SUBSTITUTE PRODUCTS CONSTRAIN THE ABILITY OF AN ENTERPRISE TO CONTROL THE TERMS OF PURCHASE BECAUSE AT SOME POINT THE CUSTOMER MAY SWITCH	
FACTOR	**DEFINITION**
Strong substitute	The degree of equal or better feature/functionality
Price/performance	The degree to which the substitute offers equal or better price/performance
Profitability of substitute industry	The degree to which the industry of the substitute product is profitable
Competitive rivalry of substitute industry	The degree to which the level of competition in the substitute industry encourages migration to new markets

Table 3.18 Rivalry of Existing Competitors

RIVALRY IS THE DEGREE TO WHICH EXISTING COMBATANTS "BATTLE" FOR MARKET SHARE	
FACTOR	**DEFINITION**
Number and equality of competitors	The number of competitors and their equality
Market growth	The market growth or decline
Product differentiation	The degree to which competitor products can substitute for each other
Switching costs	The total expense a customer incurs in switching competitors
Fixed costs	The degree of fixed costs and/or perishability of the product
Unit of capacity increment	The amount of additional product produced per investment in unit capacity increase
Exit barriers	The degree to which all competitors play by established rules.
Diversity of corporate personalities	The degree to which all competitors play by established rules

IT strategic planning impact: The key impact of the Five Force model on IT strategic planning is that by using it for each market segment competed in, the user can do the following:

- Understand which competitive factors determine competitive balance. These are the drivers of competition.

- Develop the actions needed to achieve a more favorable position.

- Develop blocking actions to prevent Five Force antagonists from achieving more favorable positions at their expense.

Supplier Position

Definition: Supplier position is used to illustrate the strategic status of the suppliers to the IT organization.

Description: The management of the relationship with suppliers is increasingly important as the IT organization moves toward Internet/network computing. The internal IT organization will increasingly operate as a systems integrator; consequently, the depth of the vendor relationship will have a profound effect on the IT organization's ability to offer end-to-end network computing solutions.

The status of existing and candidate strategic suppliers can be identified by the following factors:

Common objectives. The supplier and the IT organizations share specific measurable and dated objectives.

Common actions. The supplier and the IT organization engage in shared and coordinated actions to achieve the common objectives. Examples of this might include electronic commerce (EDI, e-mail, video conferencing, database access), on-site inventory, exclusive distribution rights, cooperative multivendor support teams, dedicated support teams, guaranteed service levels, early access to new technology, best-price agreements, and interfirm employee rotation.

Shared commitment. The supplier and the IT organization management engage in visible and substantive programs to demonstrate mutual commitment to the partnership.

Critical component. The product provided by the supplier is a critical factor in the final product created by the IT organization in the eyes of the user.

Value chain improvement. The supplier and IT organization value chains are interlocked to provide continuous improvement in productivity and value-added.

Preferred status. The supplier has a publicly avowed and demonstrated preferred status.

The essence of a preferred supplier is the overlapping of strategy to help each accrue superior future strategic positions. A strategic supplier is thus best understood from the dimensions of trust, durability of relationship, information sharing, and common governance.

IT strategic planning impact: The crucial issue in selecting strategic suppliers is that they provide "critical components." In the new millennium, the strategic suppliers will be those who provide the building blocks of successful systems integration: DBMS, distributed transaction monitors, advanced user interfaces, middleware (bonding software), and e-commerce technologies.

Internal Business/IT Economy

Definition: The business/IT economy is the explicit design of the intrabusiness processes for the production and exchange of IT services.

Description: An economic system includes the processes used for the production and exchange of goods and services. Any economic system must address three fundamental problems:

- What will be produced? How much and when?

- How will it be produced? Who will provide the products using what resources and technologies?

- For whom will the products be produced? Who will receive the products and in what proportion?

At one extreme, some societies solve these problems by command-and-control central planning economies where the government takes all decision-making responsibility on itself. At the other extreme, *laissez-faire* market economies work through a system of prices, markets, profit and loss, and incentives.

A business, as a self-contained economic entity, has to define an economic system to govern intrabusiness production and exchange of services between organizational entities just as a society does. Historically, large host-centered computing shops leaned toward a monopolistic command system. The IT organization was granted by the government (the executive business decision makers) monopolistic market power to determine what technologies would be used, when they would be used, the price of the services, and who would receive the services (usually done through a priority-setting council). As explained in Chapter 1, "Strategic Planning for Information Technology," competitive pressures have caused many businesses to reevaluate their internal IT economy and begin to move it toward the free-market model.

While some explain this movement as the evolution of the IT function from a cost center to a profit center, it is better stated as the movement from a monopolist to a competitor. It is better stated this way because what is really wanted is not so much that the IT organization make profits, but that the IT organization's behaviors reflect those of serving the customer. This is characteristic of a free-market system and is markedly different from the insular behavior that is characteristic of an internal monopoly.

An appreciation of the current design of the internal IT economy and probable change is extremely important to the IT organization because the economic model used to govern intrabusiness IT services has massive realignment implications on competition, budgeting and chargeback, organization design, staff behaviors, and more. The pivotal economic design points are as follows:

Allocation system. How is market demand governed? Does a central planning council decide what will be maintained and developed, or do user organizations, individually and in consortiums, dictate their wishes by control of their own IT dollars?

Market system. Are the user organizations free to choose any supplier, or must they use the internal IT organization? Is the internal IT organization free to choose *not* to supply desired services? Is the IT organization free to sell its services to external customers? To what degree is the choice of technologies that may be used regulated?

Resource (budgeting) system. Do the user organizations have control over their own IT budget, or does a central planning board allocate IT expense as overhead (a corporate tax)? Does IT get its own budget, or does it receive revenue from its products and services (chargeback) from which it funds itself? Is the IT organization free to grow and contract based on demand for its services, or is the IT budget used as a way to throttle IT expenses?

Supplier system. How does the IT organization interact with its customers? Is it a sole supplier that is an order taker, or does it operate using the market processes of a competitive business (i.e., sales organization, distribution channels, contracts, etc)?

The answers to these questions represent the intrabusiness/IT economy position.

IT strategic planning impact: The impact of the redesign of the intra-business IT economy is as follows:

- The full intensity and pressure of competition as the catalyst for entreprenuership, innovation, and productivity are being applied to the IT organization.

- It is being applied by the redesign of the internal economy from a command model to a market-system model.

- The importance and impact of this change cannot be overstated. All strategic business areas must be reevaluated to deal with a free-market economy.

- Understanding, influencing, and anticipating movements of the economy is a new major point of strategic focus for the IT strategist.

Two arguments that immediately arise in reaction to a free IT economy are how will IT infrastructure investments be funded and how will cross-functional systems be orchestrated. There are three answers to the first question. Infrastructure may be funded by the following:

- Including in chargeback rates a sufficient margin to fund infrastructure investment

- Making a case to the corporate governing body for a corporate-level IT investment

- Making a case to the corporate governing body for a loan

Cross-functional systems are developed by a creation of consortia. Customers with common objectives form a consortium to fund a shared system. If consortiums can't be formed, then there is no customer for the cross-functional system.

While endless arguments can be made for why the IT organization should maintain its historical economy privileges (some cynics would say self-serving arguments), it is best to mourn their passage quickly and get on with adapting to the new economic order.

The compelling need for competitiveness has led the business decision makers to decide the following:

- Each individual business unit knows best what will meet its needs and maximize its satisfaction.

- The aggregate of these individual satisfactions will provide the maximum IT benefit for the enterprise.

- The free-market system provides the best mechanism to make needs known and satisfied.

IT sovereignty has been passed to the user organizations.

Product/Service Position

Definition: A product/service position is a series of interlocking matrices and graphs that collectively illustrate the position of a product or service. Product/service positioning is an example of the recursive attribute of positioning whereby:

$P_{Business} = (P_{Market}, P_{Competency}, P_{Human Resources}, P_{Strategy Progress}, P_{Products/Services}, P_{Others})$, but

$P_{Products/Services} = ($ a set of 13 interlocking graphs and matrices$)$.

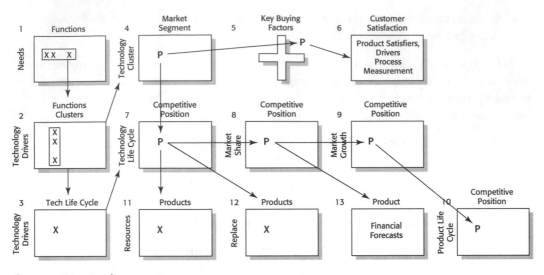

Figure 3.20 Product map.

Description: While strategy strives to satisfy the customer, the locus of strategy is the product. Meeting customer needs, incorporating new and advantageous technologies, battling competition, attacking markets, capturing revenue, and planning new products all revolve around "the product." Figure 3.20 provides a relationship map for the 13 graphs and matrices. As a collective position, the product map begins with the customer need(s) being satisfied and progresses to competitive, technological, financial, resource, and customer satisfaction views of the product. Each element of the product map is individually explained in the following sections. Each section has a matrix purpose, an accompanying figure, which is explained, and a map trace of where the matrix is relative to other matrices.

Need/Function

Purpose: This matrix, number 1 in Figure 3.20, illustrates customer needs as a set of functions required to meet each need. A set of functions, which satisfies a need, is called a *function cluster* (matrix 2). Documenting customer needs in this manner separates transient products and technologies from the functional requirements that have permanence. Products and enabling technologies have to be continually evolved to better meet the needs of the function clusters.

Figure 3.21 cell content: An "x" in a cell indicates that the function is required to meet the selected need.

Functionality

	Function 1	Function 2	Function 3	Function 4	Function 5	Function N
Need 1	X		X			X
Need 2		X	X		X	
Need 3	X	X				
Need N		X	X	X		

Function Clusters

Figure 3.21   Customer need/function matrix.

Function/Technology

Purpose: This matrix, number 2 in Figure 3.20, illustrates the current set of technologies that is being used to satisfy a function cluster. A function cluster is satisfied through a set of driving technologies. Driving technologies are the primary technologies that deliver the required function. The set of technologies that delivers the requirements for a function cluster is call a *technology cluster*. The IT organization must continually upgrade and evolve its driving technologies so that it maintains a rich portfolio of technologies from which to build technology clusters to better satisfy functional needs. This is why all IT technologies are inevitably tactical; they are destined to be replaced as soon as a superior substitute is available.

Figure 3.22 cell content: An "x" in a cell indicates that the technology is required to meet the function cluster requirements.

Map trace of Figure 3.20: A customer need (matrix 1) is documented through a function cluster (matrix 2), which is satisfied through a technology cluster (matrix 4).

Function Clusters

	Cluster 1	Cluster 2	Cluster 3	Cluster 4	Cluster 5	Cluster N
Tech. 1	X	X			X	
Tech. 2		X	X	X		
Tech. 3	X	X	X			X
Tech. N					X	X

A Technology Cluster

Figure 3.22   Function cluster/driving technology matrix.

Technology/Technology Life Cycle

Purpose: This matrix, number 3 in Figure 3.20, assesses the technology life cycle position of each driving technology and the collective life cycle position of each technology cluster. All of the driving technologies are plotted against the technology life cycle. From this one can get a picture of the evolutionary state of each of the key technologies. For each technology cluster (from matrix 2, discussed in the previous section), a technology life cycle position should be assigned as the composite life cycle position of each technology cluster. A common rule is to assign the technology life cycle position of the dominant technology in fulfilling the function cluster requirements.

Table 3.19 cell content: An "x" in a cell identifies the life cycle position of the selected technology.

Product Position

Purpose: This matrix, number 4 in Figure 3.20, positions a product as the intersection of a market segment and a technology cluster. We interpret this matrix as meaning that a given product is targeted to a given market segment and is composed of a given technology cluster.

Table 3.20 cell content: The cell contents should be a product or service.

Map trace of Figure 3.20: A given product, P, is targeted for a market segment (matrix 4). The product is composed of a technology cluster, which satisfies the needs defined by a function cluster (matrix 2), which documents a customer need (matrix 1).

Table 3.19 Driving Technology/Technology Life Cycle Matrix

TECHNOLOGY DRIVERS	TECHNOLOGY LIFE CYCLE STAGE					
	Embryonic	Development	State of the Art	State of the Market	Mature	Decline
Technology 1						
Technology 2						
Technology 3						
Technology 4						
Technology 5						
Technology N						

Table 3.20   Product Position Matrix

TECH-NOLOGY CLUSTERS	MARKET SEGMENTS					
	Segment 1	**Segment 2**	**Segment 3**	**Segment 4**	**Segment 5**	**Segment N**
Technology cluster 1						
Technology cluster 2						
Technology cluster 3						
Technology cluster 4						
Technology cluster 5						
Technology cluster N						

Key Buying Factors

Purpose: This graph, number 5 in Figure 3.20, illustrates the positioning of a product against key purchase decision parameters. A product is designed to satisfy certain key buying factors. As many key buying factor charts are developed as required to illustrate how the product was designed along each key purchase decision-making dimension.

Figure 3.23 graph content: A product, P, is positioned along the service factor axis, which is measured from high (H) to low (L), and the price factor axis,

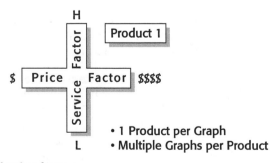

Figure 3.23   Key buying factors.

which is measured from inexpensive ($) to expensive ($$$$), to illustrate the positioning.

Customer Satisfaction

Purpose: This entry, number 6 in Figure 3.20, illustrates the level of customer satisfaction with a product. Customer satisfaction is measured through a Customer Satisfaction Measurement System (CSMS), as illustrated in Figure 3.24. The CSMS defines a product-specific set of measurements as follows:

1. The major customer satisfiers for a product are identified (i.e., quality, value, service, etc.).

2. For each of the satisfiers, a set of satisfier drivers are identified (i.e., for value it would be cost). Both item 1 and 2 are done from a customer view of the product.

3. The internal value chain processes (capabilities) that support the product are identified.

4. Measurements are identified by value chain process and correlated to a satisfier driver (i.e., by improving this measurement, we can positively influence the driver and thereby improve customer satisfaction). Items 3 and 4 are done from an internal perspective.

The net result of this approach is the installment of a measurement system that directly correlates internal system measurements to customer satisfaction.

The structure of the customer satisfaction entry in the product map would look as follows:

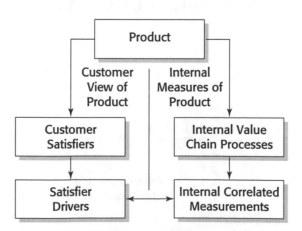

Figure 3.24 Customer Satisfaction Measurement System (CSMS).

I. Customer Satisfier 1	II. Customer Satisfier 2	N. Customer Satisfier N
A. Satisfier Driver 1	A. Satisfier Driver 1	A. Satisfier Driver 1
a. Internal Value Chain Process 1	a. Internal Value Chain Process 1	a. Internal Value Chain Process 1
1. Measurement 1	1. Measurement 1	1. Measurement 1
2. Measurement 2	2. Measurement 2	2. Measurement 2
N. Measurement .n	N. Measurement .n	N. Measurement .n
b. Internal Value Chain Process 2	b. Internal Value Chain Process 2	b. Internal Value Chain Process 2
1. Measurement 1	1. Measurement 1	1. Measurement 1
2. Measurement 2	2. Measurement 2	2. Measurement 2
N. Measurement N	N. Measurement N	N. Measurement N
n. Internal Value Chain Process n	n. Internal Value Chain Process n	n. Internal Value Chain Process n
1. Measurement 1	1. Measurement 1	1. Measurement 1
2. Measurement 2	2. Measurement 2	2. Measurement 2
N. Measurement N	N. Measurement N	N. Measurement N
B. Satisfier Driver 2	B. Satisfier Driver 2	B. Satisfier Driver 2
a. Internal Value	a. Internal Value	a. Internal Value

An example of a customer satisfaction entry for production operations would be as follows:

- Customer Satisfier is determined by product quality.
- Satisfier Driver is determined by product availability.
- Value Chain Process is determined by production operations.
- Measurement 1 is the mean time between failures.
- Measurement 2 is the mean time to repair.
- Measurement 3 is 95 percent response in less than two seconds.

A product must be measured periodically to measure the change in customer satisfaction over time and the changes in internally correlated measurements. An important strategic implication of the CSMS is that process improvement should be justified based on how the investment will improve the correlated measures, not just the traditional cost and benefit analysis. Customer satisfaction is of primary importance and must be included in all product maps.

Technology Life Cycle/Competitive Position

Purpose: This matrix, number 7 in Figure 3.20, illustrates the relationship of the competitive position of a product with the collective technology life cycle position of the product's technology cluster.

Table 3.21 Technology Life Cycle/Competitive Position Matrix

COMPETITIVE DRIVERS	TECHNOLOGY LIFE CYCLE STAGE					
	Embryonic	Development	State of the Art	State of the Market	Mature	Decline
Strong						
Medium						
Weak						

Table 3.21 cell content: Each product, P, is positioned in the cell that reflects the intersection of the collective technology life cycle position of the product (from matrix 3 already discussed) and its competitive position.

Competitive Position/Market Share

Purpose: This matrix, number 8 in Figure 3.20, illustrates the relationship of the competitive position of a product with the market-share position of a product and its competitors.

Table 3.22 cell content: The product and all its major competitors are placed in the appropriate cell of the matrix.

Competitive Position/Market Growth

Purpose: This matrix, number 9 in Figure 3.20, illustrates the relationship of the competitive position of a product with the market growth for the targeted market segment.

Table 3.23 cell content: Products are placed in the appropriate cell of the matrix.

Table 3.22 Competitive Position/Market Share Matrix

	COMPETITIVE POSITION		
MARKET SHARE	STRONG	MEDIUM	WEAK
High			
Medium			
Low			

Table 3.23   Competitive Position/Market Growth Matrix

MARKET GROWTH	COMPETITIVE POSITION		
	STRONG	**MEDIUM**	**WEAK**
High			
Medium			
Low			

Competitive Position/Product Life Cycle

Purpose: This matrix, number 10 in Figure 3.20, illustrates the relationship of the competitive position of a product with the life cycle position of the product.

Table 3.24 cell content: Products are placed in the appropriate cell of the matrix.

Map trace of Figure 3.20: This matrix, together with the prior three matrices, provides a comprehensive competition view of the product.

Product/Resource

Purpose: This matrix, number 11 in Figure 3.20, illustrates which capabilities and core competencies support the product.

Table 3.25 cell content: An "x" in a cell indicates that the selected core competency or capability supports the corresponding product.

Product Replacement

Purpose: This matrix, number 3 in Figure 3.20, identifies which products are in development to replace the current product set.

Table 3.24   Competitive Position/Product Life Cycle Position Matrix

COMPETITIVE POSITION	PRODUCT LIFE CYCLE STAGE			
	INTRODUCTION	**GROWTH**	**MATURE**	**DECLINE**
Strong				
Medium				
Weak				

Table 3.25 Product/Resource Matrix

CAPABILITIES & CORE COMPETENCIES	PRODUCT 1	PRODUCT 2	PRODUCT 3	PRODUCT N
Capability 1				
Capability 2				
Capability 3				
Core Competency 1				
Core Competency 2				
Core Competency N				

Table 3.26 cell content: An "x" in a cell indicates that the selected current product will be replaced by the indicated future product.

Product Financial History and Forecast

Purpose: This graph, number 13 in Figure 3.20, illustrates the historical and projected financial results for the product. (See Figure 3.25.)

IT strategic planning impact: These 13 matrices and graphs provide a comprehensive picture of the current state of a product. Starting from any perspective of interest, the analyst can move through the product map to understand the overall state or position of the product. The strategy team is responsible for designing a product map appropriate to their situation. All the graphs and matrices illustrated here need not be included, and others may be added (critical success factors, cost structure, method of sales and distribution, benchmark results, sustainable competitive advantage, and supplier relationships). Using this map, one can address the crucial question: Are my products meeting my customers' needs?

As an aside, product maps provide an excellent tool for developing a meaningful picture of core competencies. Core competencies is one of the emerging

Table 3.26 Product Replacement Matrix

FUTURE PRODUCT	PRODUCT 1	PRODUCT 2	PRODUCT 3	PRODUCT N
Future Product 1				
Future Product 2				
Future Product 3				
Future Product N				

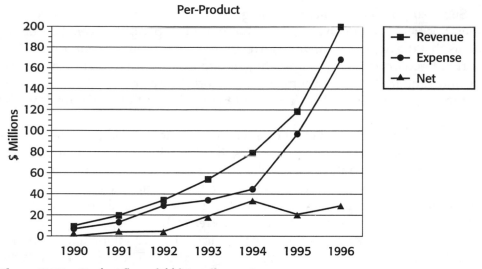

Figure 3.25   Product financial history/forecast.

leading strategic paradigms, but there is little guidance in developing the model. A product map-based approach would be as follows:

1. Develop product maps for all the products.

2. Work the core competency model backward from the product maps by identifying the following:

   - Your markets
   - Your end products
   - The core products that enable those end products
   - The competencies that enable the core products

3. Repeat step 2 as many times as necessary and synthesize the result.

This technique replaces struggling with core competencies, which is usually unfamiliar to the assigned team with products that are usually much more familiar and intuitive. If one performs this activity with the current product maps and the future product maps, the required evolution of core competencies for the organization can be ascertained.

Summary

In ancient times, those known as good warriors prevailed when it was easy to prevail. Their victories are not flukes. Their victories are not flukes because they position themselves where they will surely win, prevailing over those who have already lost.

Sun Tzu, The Art of War

Sun Tzu goes on to state that the greatest warriors are unknown because they positioned themselves with such daunting superiority over their opponents that the opposition always surrendered or retreated without battle. They surrendered or retreated because they recognized the gross inferiority of their position and that victory in combat was forlorn. The acme of skill, therefore, is not to engage in combat but "it is best to win without fighting"(Sun Tzu, *The Art of War*).

The most appropriate metaphor to express this intent and purpose of positioning is chess. Among grandmasters, the loser is seldom defeated by an explicit checkmate; rather, he or she resigns. Though checkmate may take many more moves to occur and its inevitability is not clear to most game observers, the resigning player foresees that his or her board position is hopeless and, unless the opponent makes a gross error, defeat is the only end.

What has occurred is that the victor has achieved a fundamentally superior board position along a winning strategic dimension. Through control of the center of the board, control of key rows or diagonals, or piece advantage, the victor achieves a winning position, which precedes the anticlimactic winning of the game. The opponent, recognizing the inevitability of defeat by virtue of an inferior position, resigns, and the actual act of checkmate is not required.

This is the exact notion and understanding of strategic business positioning that is sought. The objective is to position strategic business areas along their strategic dimensions in such a formidable way that the battlespace battle becomes anticlimactic. By focusing and concentrating on those strategic areas, those that decide victory, "You will surely prevail over those who have already lost." Repetitive success is not the consequence of wishful thinking, good luck, magic, prayer, or chance. It is the consequence of creating and nurturing winning positions.

Those who embrace positioning as the path to success have more in common with the political strategist than the military strategist. The military strategist believes that the objective of war is to eliminate the opponent's military capability to resist. The political strategist views the purpose of war to be the creation of a better and more enduring peace; a political strategist takes "the long view." Similarly, a mundane business view of strategy would suggest that the purpose of strategy is to improve margins, rectify weakness, parry threats, and so on. A positioning strategist would view the purpose of strategy to be creation of an enduring set of business positions that will sustain business success over an extended period.

Situational Analysis

Situational analysis is the collection and analysis of information about the business, from both an internal and external perspective, for the purpose of developing conclusions about the state of the business. It is performed by applying a robust set of analytical methods, which aid in structuring the process of insight and discovery. Situational analysis is both a data-intensive and a process-intensive activity.

This section explains 11 analytical methods. These are not the only methods available, but they do represent a popular and strong sampling. As was the case with positioning, we analyze the IT business in the dimensions of current situation, competitive situation, and future situations.

Strength/Weakness/Opportunity/ Threat Analysis

Purpose: Strength/Weakness/Opportunity/Threat (SWOT) analysis is the analysis of the state of the business from the dimensions of the following:

Strength. A collective organizational competency, asset, or capability, for which the organization has achieved a high level of proficiency.

Weakness. A collective organizational competence, asset, or capability that is competitively inferior and consequently provides a vulnerability for competitors to exploit.

Opportunity. A trend or event that could lead to a positive change in position if addressed by a strategic response.

Threat. A trend or event that could lead to a negative change in position if not addressed by a strategic response.

The considerations of the intelligent always include both harm and benefit. As they consider benefit, their work can expand; as they consider harm, their troubles can be resolved.

Sun Tzu, The Art of War

Table 3.27 SWOT Analysis

INFOR- MATION	IMPLICA- TIONS	STRENGTHS	WEAK- NESSES	OPPOR- TUNITIES	THREATS

Description: The approach to performing SWOT analysis is illustrated in Table 3.27. The process is as follows:

1. Information is collected about a business area or resource.

2. Implications are developed that interpret what the information means.

3. The implications are summarized as a strength, weakness, opportunity, or threat.

The results of multiple individual SWOT analyses are summarized in a SWOT table that provides a composite picture (see Table 3.28).

IT strategic planning impact: SWOT analysis findings provide the basis for conclusions; one should leverage strengths, eliminate weakness, exploit opportunities, and deflect threats.

Critical Success Factors

Purpose: Critical Success Factors (CSF) identify specific competencies, capabilities, and processes that an organization must do well to be successful. CSFs often focus on customer requirements and competition.

Description: Development of CSFs is similar to SWOT analysis (see Table 3.29). Information is collected about a subject area. This information is analyzed to extract key implications. The implications are then summarized as CSFs.

Table 3.30 illustrates a typical set of CSFs for a DBMS vendor from the dimensions of customer satisfaction and competition. Not surprisingly, what satisfies your customers and blocks your competitors often overlaps, and one could argue over the placement of any one factor. What is important is not

Table 3.28   SWOT Table

STRENGTHS	WEAKNESSES
1.	1.
2.	2.
3.	3.
4.	4.
OPPORTUNITIES	THREATS
1.	1.
2.	2.
3.	3.
4.	4.

Table 3.29   Critical Success Factors

INFORMATION	IMPLICATIONS	CRITICAL SUCCESS FACTORS

where the factor is placed, but that actions are taken to ensure that all CSFs are met.

It should be noted that CSFs do not equate to SCA. CSFs identify what must be done well. SCA identifies what you have decided to focus on to provide distinct advantage. Although they are certainly related, they do not equate.

IT strategic planning impact: CSFs can be viewed as encapsulating the "ante" for competing. If you satisfy your customers and block your competitors, you certainly are well on the road to sustained success.

Root Cause Analysis

Purpose: Root cause analysis is a methodology used to uncover the underlying etiology of a problem.

Description: Figure 3.26 illustrates this analytical method. The process proceeds as follows:

1. Signs and symptoms. The complaints of interviewed people are viewed as symptoms or signs of a problem. They describe the most external

Table 3.30   CSF Example

CRITICAL SUCCESS FACTORS	
COMPETITION	**CUSTOMER REQUIREMENTS**
1. Price/performance	1. Developer productivity
2. Name recognition	2. Developer flexibility
3. Support	3. Portability
4. Training	4. Scalability
5. Distribution channels	5. Standards adherence
6. Feature/functionality	6. Vendor viability
7. Market presence	7. Architecture robustness

Temporary Relief	Signs and Symptoms	External Manifestation of Problem
Curative but Can Recur	Operational Problems	Malfunctioning Part
Elimination of Problem	Root Cause	The Underlying Etiology

Figure 3.26 Root cause analysis.

manifestation of a problem but do not necessarily indicate or externalize the underlying cause.

2. Operational problem. Analysis of the symptoms and signs leads to the identification of the "operational problem," that is, the malfunctioning object.

3. Root cause. Further analysis is then undertaken to identify the "root cause" of the malfunction.

This type of analysis is important because the enduring effect of the strategic actions undertaken have very different efficacy depending on where in the root cause chain they are targeted. Actions, which address signs and symptoms, offer only temporary relief. Actions, which target the operation problem, are curative of this instance of the problem, but it can reoccur. Actions, which address the root cause, correct the problem systemically and prevent reoccurrence.

IT strategic planning impact: Actions should be carefully designed to attack problems at the root cause level. Attacking problems at the other two levels provides temporary satisfaction but does not contribute to developing sustainable advantage for the organization.

Matrix Analysis

Purpose: Matrix analysis is a generic analytical method whereby one attempts to develop insight and understanding by analyzing the intersection (relationship) of two strategic business areas or between a strategic business area and its attributes.

Description: Matrix analysis is used to better comprehend relationships. Use Table 3.31 to clarify which core competencies (a major strategic positioning framework) are put in motion by which capabilities (another major strategic positioning framework). Table 3.32 illustrates how matrix analysis could be used to assist in understanding the state of organizational alignment, which was previously discussed. Populate the cells that are not in alignment with a

Table 3.31   Core Competency versus Capability Matrix

	CAPABILITY 1	CAPABILITY 2	CAPABILITY 3	CAPABILITY N
Core Competency 1				
Core Competency 2				
Core Competency 3				
Core Competency n				

statement of why they *are not* in alignment (the root cause) and what possible actions could be taken to move toward alignment. Note in Table 3.32 that business areas are aligned both with each other and with the business scope.

This example raises the general problem of analytical depth of decomposition. In this example, the analysis is done at the macro organizational entity level. It is perhaps the case that better insight would be developed by doing the analysis at subunit levels. The general rule is to do the analysis at the highest possible level without sacrificing understanding. Experience, judgment, and operational problems in doing the analysis all contribute to help identifying when a further decomposition may be advantageous.

IT strategic planning impact: Matrix analysis is simple but powerful. Both the absence of intersections and the existence of intersections provide opportunities for insight.

Table 3.32   Alignment Analysis

	BUSINESS SCOPE	HR	TECHNOLOGY	MARKETING	SALES	ENGINEERING	OTHER
HR		Not applicable					
Technology			Not applicable				
Marketing				Not applicable			
Sales					Not applicable		
Engineering						Not applicable	
Other							Not applicable

Technology Forecasting

Purpose: Technology forecasting is the construction of models of possible futures with associated insights into those futures.

Description: A quality forecast contains the following:

- A statement of the forecast
- The rationale of the forecast
- Dates, values, and probabilities of occurrence
- Opportunities and threats presented by the forecast
- Impact of the forecast on strategic positions

Forecasting has earned a generally negative reputation. It is often characterized as error prone, not more than a guess, and it suffers from historically poor track records and a mindless "law of upward motion." The etiology of this infamous reputation is as follows:

- Forecasters often become more concerned with the elegance of the mathematical models they are creating than the subject of the forecast.
- Forecasters become seduced by a technology high. Their enthusiasm for new technology overshadows the use of common sense and business sense in making realistic forecasts.
- Due to the preceding points, forecasters ignore the basics of market success:
  - What is the customer need being meet?
  - What is the cost/benefit of the technology?
  - How will the established technologies defend themselves?
  - Is the value-added of the new technology worth the additional cost?
  - Is the need being addressed enduring or a fad?
  - What are the switching costs to adapt the new technology?
- Forecasters talk too much to each other, creating and reinforcing a "heads in the clouds" club.
- Being optimistic to a fault, forecasters ignore the practical issues of product commercialization, product diffusion, and creation of supporting and enabling infrastructures.

While all of these caveats are of concern, it is impossible to develop strategy in a dynamic area such as IT and ignore the future. A prudent approach to utilizing forecasts would be as follows:

- Be primarily concerned with the direction, degree of magnitude, and probability of occurrence of the forecast. Do not be concerned with the precision of the dates and values.

- Look for interforecast synergy, and determine if independent forecasts confirm each other.
- Test the forecasts against the market basics itemized previously.

Forewarned, but not dissuaded, we now review four representative methods of forecasting: the multivariate analysis methods, the "S" curve technology models, the Delphi technique, and creating scenarios.

Multivariate Analysis Methods

This refers to a set of mathematical methods where one or several variables are functions of some other known variables. Because we know the mathematical relationship, the values of the unknown variables can be computed. Typical multivariate forecasting methods include conjoint analysis, discriminant analysis, automatic interaction detection, canonical analysis, and simple relationship trending.

"S" Curve Technology Models

Pragmatic experience has indicated that technologies frequently follow "S" curve life cycles. For a given performance parameter, a technology evolves through predictable steps of initial commercialization, proliferation, standardization of design, and consolidation, as shown in Figure 3.27. The trick with "S" curve forecasting is to jump to a replacement technology with a better performing "S" curve at the right point. Figure 3.28 illustrates the application of "S" curves to human interface and DBMS technology. Multiple "S" curves may be summarized in a technology life cycle chart, as shown in the bottom of Figure 3.28. "S" curve modeling is a powerful approach to understanding the evolution of technologies and their replacements. In building "S" curves, exact values are not critical. The technique is of particular value as a way to illustrate for a large community the technology shifts that are occurring.

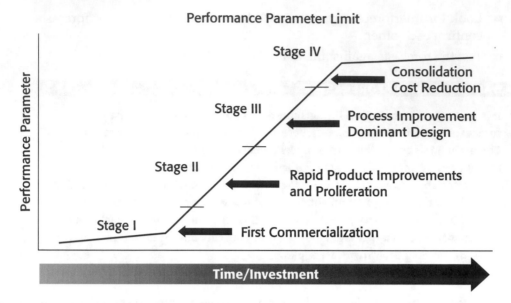

Figure 3.27   "S" Curve technology model.

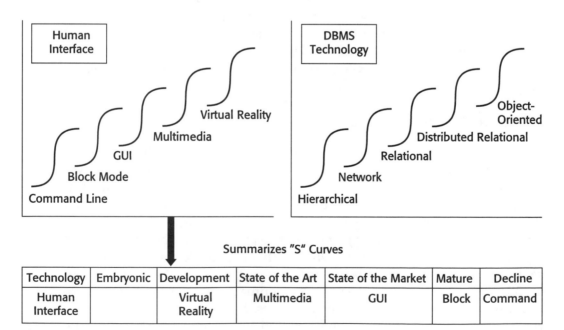

Figure 3.28   "S" Curve example.

Delphi Technique

The objective of the Delphi technique is to develop a consensus forecast of the future by asking experts, while at the same time eliminating the familiar problems of face-to-face communication. The technique algorithm is as follows:

1. Develop a questionnaire.
2. Select renowned subject matter experts.
3. Circulate the questionnaire and encourage exposition on opinions.
4. Analyze the results and structure them into quartiles.
5. Repeat step 3, but incorporate the opinions from step 3.
6. Repeat steps 4 and 5 until a consensus is reached.

This method gathers the opinions of the most qualified experts while eliminating the problems (badgering, shyness, group-think) of focus groups.

Scenarios

Scenarios are a structured way to define possible futures, understand the causation chain for each possible future, and develop options to deal with the uncertainties. Figure 3.29 illustrates the essential character of a scenario. The following definitions help explain Figure 3.29:

Start state. A summary of the current industry situation.

End state. The culmination of a set of events (causality chain). The state of

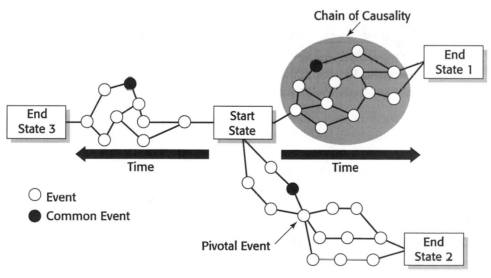

Figure 3.29 Scenario structure.

the industry is now different because the chain of events has altered the industry structure.

Event. Something that is controllable by people. We are not at the mercy of an uncontrollable future.

Causality chain. A set of interlocking events.

Pivotal event. An event that makes or breaks a scenario.

Common event. An event that is common to multiple scenarios.

A good scenario has the following attributes:

- It postulates plausible but divergent futures.
- The futures are deterministic; driven by controllable events.
- It captures strong biases and different points of view.
- It stimulates debate, perpetuates learning, questions long-held assumptions, and challenges embedded "mental models" of the industry.
- It includes, at minimum, three end states, including a "risk free" conventional wisdom end state.

Scenarios will necessarily overlap in their future description of the industry but should markedly differ in some dominant theme.

Scenarios provide fertile ground for insightful analysis. Alternatives could include the following:

- For a desired end state, what actions could be taken to make it happen?
- For an undesirable end state, what actions could be taken to prevent its occurrence?
- How you could position for common events?
- Should you do a complete assessment of each end state and compare required competencies, capabilities, etc.?
- Should you position for pivotal events?

Scenarios promote deep creative thinking, broad understanding of what drives an industry, development of horizontal thinkers as opposed to vertical thinkers, and preparation of a management team to recognize futures as they emerge (vigilance). As a consequence, scenarios stimulate development of strategic moves such as the following:

Hedge bets. Actions taken that prepare you for multiple futures.

Stagger. Development of strategic moves to which you can commit gradually.

Reserves. Plans to have resources in reserve to exploit the occurrence of a pivotal event.

Vigilance. Implementation of a set of watching systems to provide early warnings of emergence of a particular chain of events.

Given the dynamic nature of the IT industry, it is obvious that scenarios can be particularly powerful in developing the strategic thinking capabilities of a management team.

Management team discussions of scenarios will clearly improve the collective understanding of what the future may be like. It will also help develop more "renaissance" thinkers within the organization. To deal with change, you require horizontal thinkers who are able to understand a subject from a wide variety of perspectives. Scenarios liberate people from tunnel vision.

IT strategic planning impact: Forecasting techniques provide a robust set of analytical methods to sharpen the strategy team's view of the future. The key to properly using forecasting techniques is to constrain one's enthusiasm for and excitement about technological possibilities and test all forecasts against the caveats, which are listed at the beginning of this section. In analyzing forecasts, the IT strategist should be particularly vigilant in searching for technology discontinuities. It is difficult to surpass one's competitors when the *status quo* changes incrementally with everyone muddling along, more or less, at the same pace. Discontinuities, however, provide precious opportunities to improve one's advantage. In analyzing forecasts, one must always be asking: Does this fundamentally change how things are done and create a new basis for advantage?

Theory/Hypothesis

Purpose: Theory/hypothesis is a way of developing explanatory arguments by developing a general theory of events and then proving that theory by proving derivative hypotheses.

Description: In using this method, it is important, as it is in all strategy work, to argue logically. Logical reasoning permeates the entire strategy process, and any strategist must be cognizant of basic concepts of logic. The two basic forms of logical arguments are these:

Deductive argument. The relationship between the statements (premise) and the resulting conclusion is a logical necessity. If you grant the truth of the premise, you must accept the truth of the conclusion.

Inductive argument. The relationship between the statements (premise) and the resulting conclusion is not necessarily true. If you concede the truthfulness of the premise, the conclusion is highly likely, of extreme probability, but there is a "leap" to reach the conclusion.

Most strategy arguments are inductive; we are postulating future activities. Figure 3.30 illustrates the key building blocks of deductive or inductive arguments. The following definitions assist in understanding Figure 3.30:

Premise. A set of statements that are true or false.

Conclusion. The "therefore" from a true premise.

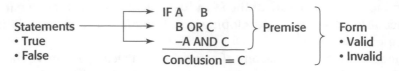

Figure 3.30 Argument structure.

Form. The structural relationships of the premise and the conclusion; the form may be valid or invalid.

Sound argument. The form of the argument is valid and the premise is true.

Cogent argument. A sound argument known to be sound.

Convincing argument. A cogent argument in which the truth of the conclusion is not known apart from the argument. The argument itself convinces us of the conclusion.

In proving hypotheses in support of a theory, we strive to develop convincing arguments.

Table 3.33 summarizes some of the key fallacies that people make in composing an argument. An argument is fallacious when there is something structurally wrong with it, which inherently prevents a rational person from accepting the argument. The fallacies illustrated in the table are only too common in the information technology literature, debate, and rhetoric. The criterion for truth and action should be reason as opposed to custom, tradition, time, feelings, hunch, revelation, majority rule, or political consensus.

Table 3.33 Fallacious Arguments

FALLACY CLASSIFICATION	FALLACY TYPE	EXPLANATION
Argument is fallacious even if form is valid	Suppressed evidence	The deliberate omission of known relevant evidence from the argument
	Doubtful evidence	The use of unsupported or questionable evidence to support and argument. This includes: a. Acceptance as evidence of a fact that is not known nor can be known b. Acceptance as evidence of a doubtful evaluation c. Acceptance of contradictory or inconsistent arguments
	False charge of inconsistency	An argument based on an invalid charge of inconsistency. Often exemplified by changes in position over time without regard to changing circumstances that justify change in position.

Table 3.33   (*continued*)

FALLACY CLASSIFICATION	FALLACY TYPE	EXPLANATION
Argument is fallacious because the form is invalid	Ad homonym	An attack on the arguer rather than the argument. This includes guilt by association.
	Two wrongs make a right	It's not wrong because the other side did it too.
	Strawperson	Attacking a pseudo position similar to but not the one that your opponent took.
	False dilemma	An improper reduction of the possible alternatives.
	Tokenism	Arguing an insufficient sample to prove the overall point.
	Begging the question	Arguing the conclusion to prove the conclusion.
	Improper appeal to authority	Appealing to an authority who is not an authority on the matter at hand.
	Provincialism	An unchallenged assumption that your way is correct.
	Irrelevant reason	Inclusion of evidence irrelevant to the conclusion.
	Ambiguity	Use of ambiguous terms to deliberately mislead.
	Slippery slope	Arguing that one step inevitably must lead to other steps without providing evidence.
	Hasty conclusion	Jumping to a conclusion on insufficient evidence.
	Questionable classification	Incorrectly classifying something and then proceeding erroneously based on that classification.
	Questionable cause	Establishing an invalid cause/effect relationship.
	Questionable analogy	Applying an analogy without establishing its likeness.
	Equivocation	The use of a term in more than one sense in an argument while the impression is given that it is being used to express one and the same meaning throughout the argument.

Table 3.33 *(continued)*

FALLACY CLASSIFICATION	FALLACY TYPE	EXPLANATION
Argument is fallacious because the form is invalid	Amphibology	The use of a statement that permits two interpretations.
	Composition	Asserting that which is true of a part is true of the composite.
	Division	Asserting that which is true of the composite is true of the part.
	Compound question	Combining several questions into one that places the opponent in a logical dilemma.
	Genetic error	Asserting something is false because of its origin.
	Contrary to fact conditional error	Altering historical evidence and then drawing conclusions.
	No true Scotsman	Denying the validity of a counter-example because it's a counter-example, i.e., declaring that contradictions are impossible.

The rules of admissible evidence are as follows:

- The evidence must be material, relevant, and probative.
- The evidence must be true.
- The evidence must be complete.
- The evidence must come from a qualified source.
- The evidence must be authentic.
- The evidence must be assembled into a valid argument form.
- The argument form must create a convincing argument.

No compromise of this is acceptable.

IT strategic planning impact: Understanding and applying the rules of logical reasoning is critical to the strategist from two perspectives:

- As the developer of arguments we must develop convincing arguments.
- As a listener to the arguments of others, we must insist that they provide convincing arguments and analyze them from a convincing argument perspective.

Because the long-term well being of the business hinges on the strategic decisions that are to be made, whim, prejudice, emotion, and "I want to" must be replaced by sound logic. It is worth noting that this entire book is one large inductive argument. The conclusion is that IT organizations must adopt strategic business planning methods, and the rest of the book provides the premise of the argument.

There remains, however, one problem: How is the dilemma of rational decision making and vision resolved? The acme of strategic success occurs when you foresee what has not yet occurred ("seize victory when there is no form"). The truly aware individual is one who knows what has not yet taken shape (see Appendix A, "Aphorisms of Strategy," under "Foresight" and "Vision" for quotes). It has been asserted that what will be believed and acted on should be provable or, at minimum, be provable to be highly probable. A belief or opinion for which a convincing argument cannot be provided should be discarded. But how then is it possible to suggest that we proceed based on unprovable foresight and expect acquisition of truth and success?

There is no dilemma. There is, however, an order. People are given different faculties in different degrees. Most are given the faculty of reason, and reason, the highly available ingredient, provides the normal method for developing strategy. Vision and foresight, however, are a faculty of a higher order and much rarer. Visionaries can provide an organization with simply extraordinary and unlimited possibilities. Of course, because foresight is less demonstrable, it is difficult to know whether you are being given advice from a "good witch" or a "bad witch." It is usually riskier to follow a visionary, and to follow one requires commitment and courage. This is not a contradiction. It is just that reason and foresight are different from one another, and this must be kept in mind when proceeding from either.

You ask, "What does the visionary see?" Imagine the progression of a business as an endless parade. The typical proletariat member of the organization stands at the parade barricade looking straight ahead at "what is" with minimal peripheral vision. The visionary perches on the top of the highest building. From this vantage point he or she can see all of what has come, what is, and what shall be. The choreography of business change is clearly displayed before his or her eyes. From the vantage point of foresight, the constraint of seeing the future is transcended. How different are the consequences of strategy based on what the visionary foresees versus what the barricade standee sees.

Strategy is to the strategist as clay is to the potter. How much greater is the result when the strategist can shape the strategy, the clay, from clearly seeing the formless. An organization that has visionary employees has a distinct and truly fortunate advantage. The perennial problem of believing and acting on their insights, however, remains irresolvable.

New Product Position

Purpose: A future product or service position is a series of interlocking matrices and graphs that collectively illustrate the anticipated position of a prospective product. This is the same concept as introduced before when "Product/Service Position" is analyzed, except here the concept is applied to products or services in development.

Description: Figure 3.31 provides a global relationship map for the set of graphs and matrices that collectively define the position of a prospective product or service. The graphs and matrices numbered 1 through 13 coincide with the identical graphs and matrices on Figure 3.20. Only the tense has to be changed. The four new matrices required for future product positioning (future product position, product development cost, probability of success, and first-year market share and growth) will now be explained in the order of development.

Future Product Position

Purpose: This matrix positions prospective products by the dimensions of technology cluster and type of market. This positioning illustrates how our technology set and target markets are changing, if at all.

Table 3.34 cell content: The content of a cell is a prospective product or service.

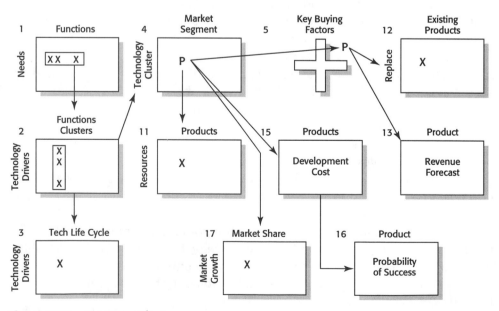

Figure 3.31   Future product map.

Table 3.34   Future Product Position

	INCREASING TECHNOLOGY NEWNESS (FROM LEAST TO GREATEST)		
	No Technological Change	**Improved Existing Technological Clusters**	**New Technology Clusters**
Increasing market newness (down) Existing markets	N/A	Reformulation	Replacement
Strengthen market	Remerchandising	Improved product	Product line extension
New market	New use	Market extension	Diversification

Product Development Cost

Purpose: This matrix illustrates the remaining development budget for each prospective product and the anticipated time until product announcement.

Table 3.35 cell content: The content of a cell is a prospective product or service.

Probability of Success

Purpose: This matrix illustrates the probability of success for the product. Together with the prior matrix, "Remaining Product Development Cost," and the following matrix, "First-Year Market Share/Growth," this matrix is used to assess risk.

Table 3.36 cell content: The content of a cell is a prospective product or service.

Table 3.35   Remaining Product Development Cost

	TIME REMAINING UNTIL PRODUCT ANNOUNCEMENT		
	Less than 6 months	**6 months–1 year**	**Greater than 1 year**
Remaining development budget $M $> 2M$			
$1M–2M$			
$< 1M$			

Table 3.36 Probability of Success

		PROBABILITY OF MARKET SUCCESS		
		Less than 50%	**50–75%**	**Greater than 75%**
Payoff	High			
	Medium			
	Low			

First-Year Market Share and Growth

Purpose: This matrix illustrates the marketplace projection for the product one year after its introduction.

Table 3.37 cell content: The content of a cell is a prospective product or service.

IT strategic planning impact: Map element 3, Table 3.26 in both Figures 3.20 and 3.31, bridges the product set "that is" with the product set "that will be." It is extremely powerful to place both maps on a wall and, probably for the first time, get a comprehensive picture of the evolution of the product line. With this global picture of the product set, decisions can be made about adding, changing, or deleting products. A final point: The power of the product maps is not the individual graphs or matrices but the complete picture of the state of a product or service that the set of graphs or matrices provides. A combined review of the current map with the future map amplifies this benefit.

Millennial Perspective

Because it has now been discussed both how to position current products and how to analyze future products, it is an ideal time to address an obvious question: What kinds of products and services will the IT organization have to sell in the new millennium to remain viable? Historically, the IT organization has sold the following:

Table 3.37 First-Year Market Share/Growth

		MARKET SHARE		
		High	**Medium**	**Low**
Market growth	High			
	Medium			
	Low			

- Computing resources (MIPS, storage, etc.)
- Business applications (life cycle development and maintenance services)

Growth for the IT organization will center around the following types of products and services:

- Professional services such as systems integration, business solutions consulting, business reengineering consulting, and project management
- Distributed processing platform and application production support services
- Information-sharing applications (global team and meeting support)
- Electronic commerce with customers and suppliers
- Support services for increasingly mobile and global computing
- Information brokering services
- Sales to customers outside the business to demonstrate competitiveness to those inside the business

The locus of products and services will shift from renting capacity on mainframes to selling solution-oriented services.

Additionally, services will have to be packaged to meet the fragmented needs of different customers. Rather than one size fits all, as illustrated in Figure 3.3, not a service, but a family of services built around one product theme will have to be provided. One should imagine that for a given service there would be, at minimum, a low-cost Spartan solution, a high-value solution, a high-end solution, and a customizable solution.

The successful IT organization of this decade will have to hit with power from both sides of the plate. It will have to be ambidextrous. On one hand, it will have to maintain, nourish, and extend the large embedded base of systems, which were built over the past 20 to 30 years. On the other hand, it will have to move aggressively to offering solutions for highly mobile and networked users deploying ever more application-specific information technologies as a result of reengineering. Such a situation is a challenge to manage, but it is to be expected during a paradigm shift.

Value Chain Analysis

Purpose: Value chain analysis is a method for classifying, analyzing, and understanding the translation of resources through processes into final products and services.[6] It is used as a mechanism to analyze how to improve cost structure (productivity) and value-added (product differentiation).

Description: Figure 3.32 provides two popular illustrations of the value chain concept. The basic notion is that one can trace a product or service as it

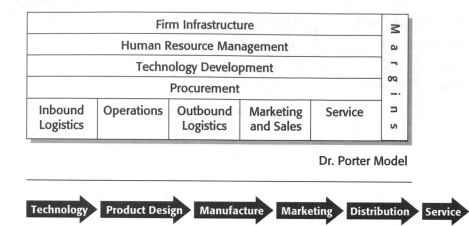

Dr. Porter Model

McKinsey Model

Figure 3.32   Value chain.

moves from your supplier's value chain to your value chain to your distributor's value chain to your customer's value chain. As it moves through the value chains, opportunities arise to improve productivity and value-added. Figure 3.33 illustrates the interrelationships of value chains.

Value chain analysis proceeds in the following two ways:

- Value chain analysis to improve cost (productivity)

    1. Disaggregate the chains into discrete activities.

    2. Establish relative weight of each activity as cost contributor.

    3. Identify for each activity the drivers (i.e., what drives costs, productivity, time, etc.).

    4. Identify links to previous and following value chains.

    5. Improve cost structure by redesign, reengineering, better linkage, outsourcing, etc.

- Value chain analysis to improve value-added (differentiation)

    1. Disaggregate the chains into discrete activities.

    2. Identify for each activity the drivers (i.e., what adds value at each step).

    3. Select the most advantageous drivers for the product.

    4. Link drivers to customer value chain to validate value-added.

    5. Invest in value-added drivers.

In analyzing value chains for productivity or value-added improvements, it is often advantageous to think in terms of a "perfect" value chain. How should my value chain be designed so it operates flawlessly?

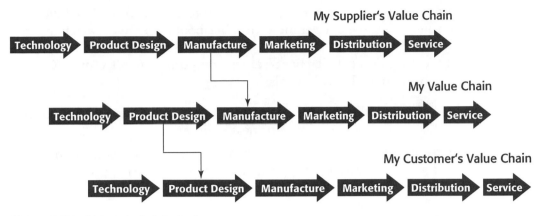

Figure 3.33 Value chain interlock.

A special form of value-chain analysis is called *bottleneck analysis* (see Figure 3.34). Bottleneck analysis suggests that it is profitable to trace the flow of products across the value chains and look for bottlenecks. You should then take actions to alleviate the bottlenecks. This method emphasizes speed as the focus of attention.

What are the major bottlenecks inhibiting the IT services value chain as we enter the new millennium? Three major bottlenecks to IT success are these:

Application development. The true value of IT is in its application, not in the raw resources. The rapid creation and amending of applications is a major bottleneck.

Configuration management. The migration to Internet/network computing puts the IT organization in the role of managing the integration of components from multiple vendors. The orderly evolution of the network components is a major bottleneck to successful network computing.

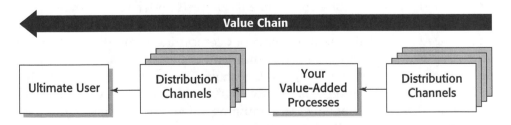

Trace the flow of a product from your suppliers to the ultimate user and look for "bottlenecks." Take strategic action to eliminate bottlenecks.

Figure 3.34 Bottleneck analysis.

Network computing operations, administration and maintenance (OA&M). The daily end-to-end operations (troubleshooting, help desk, repair, software distribution, node administration, backup and recovery, performance tuning, etc.) of client/server computing architectures. OA&M must be managed at two levels:

- Platform—the technology infrastructure that provides the operational environment for a business application

- Application—the business software that solves a specific transaction processing, decision support, or information-sharing problem for the user.

Table 3.38 identifies the primary functions that need to be performed in the Internet/network computing environment at both of these levels. Breaking these bottlenecks provides the basis for advantage.

IT strategic planning impact: Value chain analysis and bottleneck analysis provide structured ways in which to analyze the process flows of an organization for productivity improvement and value-added opportunities. The bottlenecks and value-added activities selected for attention must, of course, relate to a product need or requirement of direct importance to the customer. Specifically, they should be understood in the context of improving the results from the customer satisfaction measurement system (see Figure 3.24). Of particular concern to the IT strategist is how to apply IT throughout the value chain to accomplish these objectives.

In designing and analyzing value chains to support network computing environments, it will be important to focus on lateral ability rather than vertical specialization. Historically, value chain productivity has been optimized through decomposition and specialization. Capital is substituted for labor, and automation is applied to maximize component throughput. Because the notion of network computing is best encapsulated by the phrase "end-to-end," the horizontal capability of the IT organization to architect, design, and operate network computing environments will be critical. Especially until the real needs of network computing environments are well understood, it may prove advantageous to expedite the migration to network computing by assembling renaissance teams of staff to nurse network computing through the life cycle rather than initially attempting to automate and optimize. These teams of people with broad-based lateral capabilities should be supplemented by artificially intelligent "counselors and advisors" to assist them with detailed knowledge. The success of network computing value chains may well prove to be the ability to manage the horizontal complexity and not the vertical component optimization.

Table 3.38 OA&M Functions

OA&M LEVEL	FUNCTION	EXAMPLES
Application	Software release management	Distribution, installation, testing, change control, backout, intersite coordination
	Monitoring	Component connectivity, message movement, file transfer completion
	Performance management	Proactive prevention, trend analysis, tuning, bottleneck resolution, trending
	Change management	Application movement, topology management, directory maintenance
	Backup/restore	Full/incremental backup and restore, media management, off-site archival storage
	Database administration	Space management, permissions, restart, sizing
	Security administration	User-ID and password administration, incident tracking
	Help desk	User-query resolution
	Job management	Batch job startup, scheduling, monitoring, output distribution
Platform	Configuration management	Provisioning, system software distribution, installation, directory management, name management, change management
	Fault management	Help desk, trouble identification and tracking, tiered support, problem isolation, and resolution
	Performance management	Measurement, tracking, turning
	Security management	Access permissions, violation monitoring, permission levels
	Accounting	Billing identifiers, billing, asset utilization

Benchmarking

Purpose: Benchmarking is a process for measuring and comparing products and services, competencies, capabilities, and more against those recognized as best in class. Machiavelli summarized the essential motivation for benchmarking when he said:

*Men nearly always follow the tracks made by others and proceed in their affairs by imita-
tion, even though they cannot entirely keep to the tracks of others or emulate the prowess
of their models. So a prudent man must always follow in the footsteps of great men and
imitate those who have been outstanding. If his own prowess fails to compare with theirs,
at least it has an air of greatness about it.*[7]

Benchmarking permits you to profit from the experiences of many rather
than the more limited and expensive experiences of your own.

Description: There are three basic types of benchmarks:

- Analogous, used to compare specific processes, competencies, and more
  against industry leaders
- Competitive, used to compare oneself against specific competitors
- Strategic, used to understand the parameters of a major new initiative

The basic benchmarking process is a nine-step process as follows:

1. Define what you want to benchmark.
2. Define the purposes and objectives of the benchmark.
3. Define the subjects and metrics of comparison.
4. Define whom to benchmark against (see Table 3.38).
5. Develop the data collection method.
6. Execute the data collection.
7. Summarize the findings and results.
8. Define the gaps.
9. Perform a root cause analysis identifying the underlying reasons for the
   gaps.

The gaps provide ripe opportunity for drawing conclusions about both
what needs to be addressed and how to address it.

Table 3.39   Whom to Benchmark

PRODUCT/ SERVICES SIMILARITY	MARKET OVERLAP	
	Low	**High**
High	Parallel—second-best candidates	Clones—high candidates
Low	N/A (but what about their strategic intent?)	Potential—third-best candidates

Table 3.40   Benchmark Results

BENCHMARK AREA	BENCHMARK RESULTS			
	Noncompetitive	Very Competitive	Competitive	World Class
Core Competencies				
Capabilities				
Cost Structure				
Customer Satisfaction				
Supplier Relationships				

IT strategic planning impact: Benchmarking is an extremely powerful analysis tool because it replaces opinion and wishful thinking about the state of resources with concrete comparisons. The key areas for benchmarking are those strategic areas you have put under position management. By definition they are the most strategic dimensions of your business and therefore must be most successfully and aggressively managed. You may then determine, apart from your own internal (and biased) opinions, whether they are noncompetitive, competitive, very competitive, or world class in comparison to the competition (see Table 3.40).

Competitor Analysis

Purpose: Competitor analysis is the strategic analysis of a competitor so that you can take actions to foil their strategy.

What is valued is foiling the opponent's strategy, not pitched battle. A skillful strategist ruins plans, spoils relations, cuts off supplies, or blocks the way and hence can overcome people without fighting. Use strategy to thwart the opponents causing them to overcome themselves and destroy themselves. Overcome the opponent psychologically. Destroy their countries artfully, do not die in protracted warfare.

Sun Tzu, The Art of War

Description: To accomplish this, it is necessary to do a parallel strategic analysis of each competitor, a composite competitor, or a "perfect" competitor. Figure 3.35 illustrates the components of the strategic planning process that need to be executed for selected competitors. While this is difficult to do, there is a surprising wealth of public information available through financial

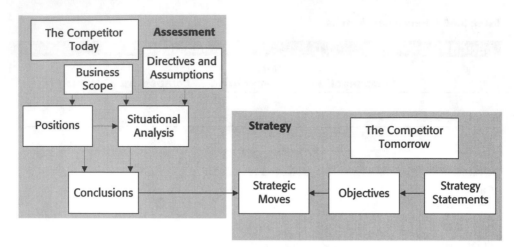

Figure 3.35   Understanding competitors strategically.

reports, market research reports, trade journals, and marketing literature. Some companies create "competition departments" whose objective is to create a staff that thinks and acts as the competitors would.

By understanding our competitors strategically, we can develop conclusions that can lead to elegant strategic moves to block them, change the rules of the game, disable alliances, date capabilities, and obsolete competencies. We design actions that increase our opponents' levels of friction and drag, making it ever harder for them to execute their strategy. In doing so, we create strategic paralysis and avoid pyrrhic victories that leave us an exhausted winner.

IT strategic planning impact: As explained previously, many companies are moving to a free-market economy for IT services. One can compete with the outsourcers, system integrators, or facilities managers by engaging in "warfare" or by heeding the admonition of Sun Tzu. The goal of competitive analysis in this case is to devise strategies that preempt an approach by a competitor or motivate them to abandon an attempt. A stubborn willingness has to be demonstrated to protect markets. Ways of doing this could include the following:

- First and foremost, demonstrating through benchmarking that you are, in fact, highly competitive.

- Leveraging advantages of being an internal supplier, i.e., concern for security, knowledge of applications, political connections, flexibility as opposed to commercial contractual obligations.

- Using alliances with friendly vendors to fill gaps in product line, i.e., if you are weak in business consulting, form an alliance with a consulting company that does only business consulting.

- Attacking your competitor where they will have to defend, i.e., case studies of failures, inexperienced staff, lack of industry knowledge. If possible, involve the highest levels of the competitor possible, draw out the decision-making process, create distractions, and keep raising the cost and time of getting the account.

Defense is normally the stronger partner of conflict. Change in this context raises fear, uncertainty, and doubt on the side of those who would outsource. All of this can be used to raise the perceived risk of such actions. One can defend first through merit and then by raising the ante so that the reward is not worth the risk or efforts (time or cost) to both the outsourcer and internal promoter.

The limited objective of the IT organization to maintain the *status quo* conveys advantages over the acquisitive intentions of the outsourcer.

What motivates competitors is profit . . . what restrains competitors is harm. . . . Wear enemies out by keeping them busy and not letting them rest . . . make them rush about trying to cover themselves, they will not have time to formulate plans. . . . To keep them from getting to you, attack where they will surely go to the rescue.

Sun Tzu, The Art of War

The strategy of defense is to first frustrate and then exhaust your adversary's commitment.

Pivot Position Analysis

Purpose: Pivot position analysis is a method of analyzing possible future positions to determine what positions will provide the organization with flexibility and maneuverability to deal with an unknowable future.

Description: A pivot position is a position that has the additional attribute of having to sit at a crossroads. As illustrated in Figure 3.36, a pivot position allows one to go in multiple directions. The classic definition of strategy places the strategist on the horns of a dilemma. Concurrently, strategy is to provide both focus and flexibility. Paradox often sits at the center of strategic problems and their resolution is a key aspect of strategic thinking. To resolve this dilemma, it is necessary to design both specific future positions to provide focus and pivot positions to provide flexibility. A pivot position is the same as a specific position except its definition would focus on the maneuverability attributes of its definition. Because the future specific position embraces the pivot position, if and when necessary, one can "back up" and set off in a new direction with minimum disruption.

In battle, confrontation is done directly, victory is gained by surprise.

Sun Tzu, The Art of War

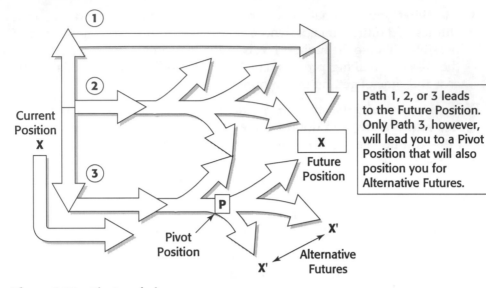

Figure 3.36   Pivot analysis.

Pivot positions are therefore required to deal with the fact that our desired and designed future is, at best, probabilistic. Time and circumstances will bring surprises. Competitors may surprise you, customers may surprise you, or you may wish to surprise others. Pivot positions allow for this flexibility and are mandated by the definition of strategy. A methodology for developing pivot positions would be as follows:

1. Using the scenario methodology previously presented, develop a set of information technology scenarios.

2. Using the scenario methodology previously presented, develop a set of customer futures scenarios. Customer needs and technology possibilities are the two primary drivers of future positions.

3. Create a scenarios matrix, Table 3.41, matricing the technology futures against the customer futures.

4. Select those strategic areas for which you desire to develop pivot positions. Typical candidates would be core competencies, capabilities, IT architecture, supplier relationships, and alliances.

5. For each selected area, test the continued viability of your current position for that area against the matrix cells. In which cells will your current position remain viable? This tells you the staying power of your current positions.

6. For each selected area, complete the matrix identifying what position is necessary to deal with that intersection of scenarios. Based on the posi-

Table 3.41 Scenario Matrix

CUSTOMER FUTURES	IT FUTURES			
	SCENARIO 1	SCENARIO 2	SCENARIO 3	SCENARIO N
Scenario 1				
Scenario 2				
Scenario 3				
Scenario N				

tions developed, lay them out into a combination of end states and enabling states (those positions that lead to an end state) analogous to Figure 3.36. If natural pivot positions do not emerge, design in a pivot position that leads to these end states.

As is the case with all positions, pivot positions must be designed to be extensible, that is, one must always be able to imagine that having achieved a position, an even better position is achievable.

IT strategic planning impact: It was previously asserted that one must decide which strategic areas will be put under position management. This notion has to be extended to a decision concerning which strategic areas will be placed under specific position management, pivot position management, neither, or both.

Summary

Situational analysis is the application of analytical methods for the purpose of developing insight and understanding about the state of the business. Situational analysis aids in effective and efficient data reduction. It assists in developing the agenda of what needs to be focused on in a given planning cycle. Without the use of the various analytical methods, the quantity and unstructured nature of the data about the business would prohibit meaningful analysis. Situational analysis is not a prescription for detached analysis, but a prescription for the use of structured inquiry tempered by sensitivity and intimate understanding of the business. It is a prescription for intense and focused strategic thinking about the business.

In this section, we have tried to cull the most advantageous methods from the wide assortment of techniques available. It is not at all improbable that although we have tried to present this information in a manner to minimize misunderstanding, it may nevertheless be understood to convey a meaning different from that which is intended. It is my view that these methods are equally important and of utility whether you engage in formal but expedited strategy formulation or engage in a more dynamic ad hoc method. In both cases, what is of prime importance is to have aids to focus the analysis of the information. This is exactly what situational analysis techniques provide.

Conclusions

Conclusions are explicit statements describing the state of the business. They are descriptive and demand exploitative or remedial actions. They are not an exhaustive "health check," and only conclusions requiring action need be itemized. Conclusions are the culmination of assessment and provide the focus of attention for the strategy step. Conclusions must be succinct and clear, and they must demand attention. They are the composite statement of what management must focus strategic attention on. A conclusion does the following:

1. Identifies which issues are vitally important

2. Identifies what drives each issue

3. Identifies the relationship of each issue to the whole

4. By absence, identifies which issues are not vitally important

It is in reaction to conclusions that creative and innovative strategy must be developed.

Table 3.42 illustrates the format of a conclusion. The elements are as follows:

- The conclusion is a succinct statement of the opportunity or problem uncovered.

- The description is a brief explanation of the conclusion.

- The etiology is an explanation of the root cause of the conclusion.

- Possible actions (strategic moves) is a speculative list of actions that could be taken to deal with the conclusion.

- Supporting evidence is detailed or summarized information from the positioning and situational analysis to support the validity of the conclusion. The evidence should provide a "convincing argument." The amount of evidence required is a function of the credibility of the creators of the conclusion and the controversy that the conclusion may invoke, i.e., how big a change would the conclusion imply and how politically upsetting would that be.

The description or etiology should identify the explanatory strategic framework, which governs the conclusion (that is, misalignment, five-force shift, value chain, etc.). By identifying the explanatory strategic framework, all the knowledge of the framework is associated with the conclusion.

Table 3.42   Conclusions

CONCLUSION ATTRIBUTE	DEFINITION
Conclusion	A short explicit statement that succinctly and clearly identifies a situation requiring strategic attention
Description	A one- to three-paragraph explanation of the conclusion
Etiology	An explanation of the root causes of the conclusion
Possible actions (strategic moves)	Examples of what actions may be taken to deal with the conclusion
Supporting evidence	Convincing arguments to support the conclusion

Summary

Assessment is the process of deciding what to focus attention on. Figure 3.37 illustrates the thrust of assessment, which is to perform a comprehensive review of the business from multiple dimensions in order to uncover gaps. Gaps may be gaps of performance and execution (cost, quality, logistics, cycle time, productivity, profitability) or gaps of opportunity (markets, customer satisfaction, growth, leverage, new products).

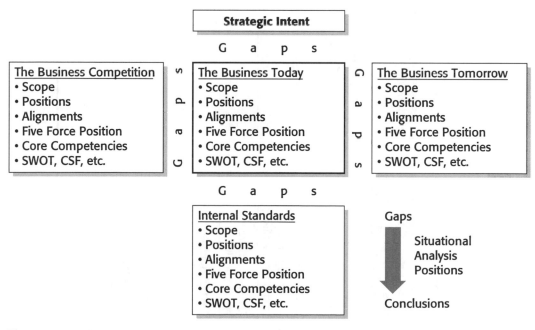

Figure 3.37   Assessment summary.

Table 3.43 IT Organization Economic System

KEY ECONOMY DESIGN QUESTIONS (EXAMPLES)	ECONOMIC SYSTEM BETWEEN IT ORGANIZATION AND OTHER BUSINESS ORGANIZATIONS				ECONOMIC SYSTEM WITHIN THE IT ORGANIZATION			
	Current State	Customer Desired	External Benchmark	IT Desired	Current State	External Benchmark	IT Desired
1. How is market demand governed?							
2. Are customers free to choose suppliers?							
3. Are suppliers free not to supply?							
4. Are technologies regulated?							
5. Who controls budgets?							
6. What is the relation-ship between sup-plier and customer—free market or monopoly?							

Gaps identify your Achilles heels and that of your competitors.

Attack what can be overcome, do not attack what cannot be overcome. . . . To advance irresistibly, push through their gaps. . . . So when the front is prepared, the rear is lacking, and when the rear is prepared the front is lacking. Preparedness on the left means lack on the right, preparedness on the right means lack on the left. Preparedness everywhere means lack everywhere. . . . Attack where there is no defense.

Sun Tzu, The Art of War

The gaps should not only identify the deltas between the current position and a desired one, but also explain the reasons for the difference. This provides initial hints for developing first-cut strategies. Table 3.43 illustrates how the gap perspective makes problems and opportunities visible. Gaps drive the identification of conclusions, which clamor for management attention and action.

While gap analysis drives the identification of conclusions, conclusions are often the synthesis of multiple individual analyses and therefore of complex origin. The corporate community's receptivity to the conclusion is enhanced by graphical presentation. As has been demonstrated throughout this section, diagrams, graphs, matrices, and so on are far superior tools for visualization and communication. Conclusions may be summarized using a *conclusion map* (see Figure 3.38). The conclusion map presents the primary logic chain that was followed to reach the conclusion and diagrams in the "Supporting Evidence" part of the conclusion (see Table 3.42). As shown by the legend of Figure 3.38, a piece of evidence leads to other pieces of evidence. The relationship between distinct items of evidence is indicated by a pointed arrow. A plus sign on the arrow indicates that the first piece of evidence had a "positive impact" in leading to the linked item. Conversely, a minus sign indicates that the first piece of evidence had a "negative influence" in leading to the linked item. The conclusion is stated in the octagon symbol. A conclusion map may be appended to each conclusion to enhance its validity, and it serves as an excellent means of presenting the conclusion to an audience. It is advisable to keep the maps straightforward, limit them to one page per conclusion, and not decompose them. The objective is to summarize the essence of the convincing argument as simply as possible. Obviously, at a summary or detail level, conclusion maps may be used as working documents to help develop as well as document the conclusions.

Assessment is based on understanding the current and projected future states of multiple strategic variables. When assessment is limited to only competition or only customers or only products, the seeds of future problems are sown. They are sown because misalignment is created and problems are not forestalled. A strategist must view the business as a polyphony, with each function performing its individual function in perfect harmony with all others.

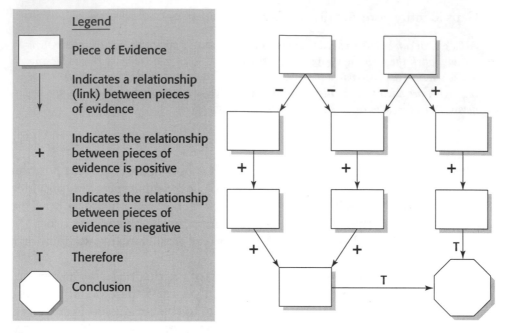

Figure 3.38 Conclusion map.

Notes

1. Based on the work of C. K. Prahaldad and G. Hamel.

2. *Top Management Strategy* by B. Tregoe and J. Zimmerman (New York: Simon & Schuster, 1980).

3. Based on the work of C. K. Prahaldad and G. Hamel.

4. *Competing on Capabilities* by G. Stalk, P. Evans, and L. Shulman (New York: The Free Press, 1994).

5. Based on the work of Dr. Michael Porter.

6. Northeast Consulting Resources, Inc.

7. *The Prince* by Machiavelli.

Strategy

The purpose of this chapter is to explain the strategy step of the strategic planning process. *Strategy* is the definition of both what is to be accomplished and the means of accomplishment. As the assessment step filters the environment to determine what to focus on, the strategy step sifts through the alternative objectives and actions to determine what is to be done. Figure 4.1 is an enlargement of the strategy step. It will be explained in the following manner:

Strategy statements. This section will explain the notion of strategy statements. In the assessment step, the current business scope and strategic positions are defined. In this step the broad statements of direction and desired outcome are identified. Strategy statements are supported by developing a future business scope and revised positions.

Objectives. This section explains the development of objectives. *Objectives* are specific, measurable results to be accomplished during this planning cycle.

Strategic moves. This section explains how to develop strategic moves. *Strategic moves* are coherent and purposeful actions taken to achieve an objective. They are the prescriptive actions that move the organization from its current positions to realizing its objectives and future business

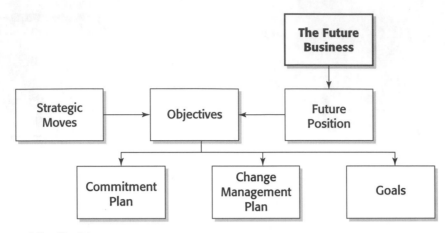

Figure 4.1 Strategy.

scope and strategic positions. The strategic moves make the strategy statements actionable.

Change management plan. This section explains the development of specific actions to deal with the problems of organizational change. Strategic actions are designed and intended to cause change and movement. Inevitably, resistance occurs within the organization due to multiple motivations. This section analyzes the cause of the resistance and actions to be taken to overcome change barriers.

Commitment plan. This section explains issues surrounding the development of a commitment plan. A *commitment plan* is a specific set of actions taken to establish the creditability of the overall plan. A strategic plan can succeed only with wide-ranging organizational commitment to its success.

When your strategy is deep and far-reaching, then what you gain by your calculations is much, so you can win before you even fight. When your strategic thinking is shallow and near-sighted, then what you gain by your calculations is little, so you lose before you do battle. Much strategy prevails over little strategy, so those with no strategy cannot but be defeated. Therefore it is said that victorious warriors win first and then go to war, while defeated warriors go to war first and then seek to win.

Sun Tzu, The Art of War

The strategy step identifies both what is to be accomplished and the means consistent with the business scope notion of strategic intent; the intent of the strategy step is to develop a strategy that is "deep and far-reaching."

Strategy Statements

Strategy statements are broad statements of direction and desired outcome. They have a dramatic impact on the future positioning of the organization and define the future ambition of our efforts. The components of a strategy statements are as follows:

- A title in the form of a sentence or phrase that succinctly documents the strategy statement
- The definition of the strategic area(s) or domain(s) that this strategy statement addresses
- A statement of the advantage that this strategy conveys to the business
- A paragraph description or elaboration of the strategy statement

The attributes of good strategy statements are as follows:

- They should be clear and unambiguous.
- They should be outcome-oriented.
- They should be directive.
- They should be rallying.
- They should be actionable.
- They should make a dramatic difference to the strategic position of the organization.
- They must help realize the new strategic intent.
- They should be worth a personal commitment.

The absolute maximum size of a strategy statement should be one page.

A sample strategy statement would be as follows:

Title: We will dramatically improve the utilization, integration, and adaptability of our IT assets through the implementation of an Enterprise IT Architecture.

Strategic Subject Area: IT Architecture

Advantage: Maneuverability

Description: In response to hyper-competition and the need of the business to become a digital enterprise, we will make major investments in creating and managing our IT assets through an Enterprise IT Architecture. The architecture will define the standards, models, and principles that will permit dispersed but integrated IT decision making. The availability of architecture blueprints and models will expedite the system life-cycle process and enable us to electronically bond with our business partners, supply chain, and customers.

Typical subject areas for strategy statements would include IT architecture, IT processes, IT governance, core competencies (skills), bill versus buy policies, vendor management and relationships, human resource policies, system development opportunities, organizational structure, client relationship management, and the design and functioning of the internal economy. Formulating strategy statements that make a difference is hard work. Strategy statements emerge from reaction to conclusions, strategic thinking, brainstorming and, in particular, modeling a future business scope and positions.

Future Business Scope and Positions

The future business scope and positions defines the desired future state of the business in terms of a new business scope and a new set of strategic positions. Developing a future business scope and positions can be invaluable as a method to stimulate the definition of dramatic strategy statements. It is this new business scope and set of positions that are to be achieved during the planning cycle. As illustrated in Figure 4.2, the intent is to move the business from its current scope and positions, which are documented in the assessment step (Chapter 3, "Assessment"), to a new scope and set of positions closer to the new strategic intent. We wish to transform the business from $P_{current \; business \; scope \; and \; positions}$ to $P_{future \; business \; scope \; and \; positions}$. The strategy statements define that movement.

The definition of the future business scope and positions requires the most intense strategic thinking on the part of the strategy team. This is the definition of what the business is to be; it may be incrementally different from the present, or it may be radically different. In either case, it is the "end zone" for the

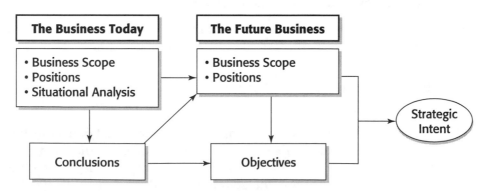

Figure 4.2 Future business scope and positions.

planning period and requires the most intense thinking. It is to this future that all strategic actions will be targeted; therefore it calls for careful definition and measured forethought.

Any change in the business scope will motivate realignment actions throughout the organization. Gaps between the current positions and desired future positions will require actions to close. The resulting strategy statements, future business scope and positions, coupled with the conclusions from the assessment step, make up the playing field for developing objectives and strategic moves for the planning cycle.

Two types of future positions must be defined: specific positions which provide focus for the organization, and pivot positions, which allow for flexibility in order to address any future surprises. There are five choices from which to select:

You cannot define any future positions. In this case, you have abandoned the responsibilities of leadership because you provide neither focus nor flexibility for the business.

You can define only specific future positions. In this case, you meet the responsibility of focus but neglect the equal responsibility of flexibility.

You can define only pivot positions. In this case, you meet the responsibility of flexibility but neglect the equally important responsibility of focus. Nevertheless, this may be prudent to do if you are one who believes setting fixed objectives is meaningless.

You can define both specific positions and pivot positions. In this case, you meet the classical definition of strategy.

You can mix and match, as appropriate, based on time and circumstances. This option may be best of all.

Your choice must balance the need to provide a clear target for the organization while permitting the organization to maneuver with minimal difficulty in the event of surprises.

The statement of positions and pivot positions can therefore be modulated and calibrated to be in conformity with the degree of stability or turbulence of the business environment. For highly turbulent times, pivot positions may be defined to posture for mobility in the face of certain uncertainty. In times of stability and predictability, fixed positions can be defined to provide a precise target for the business. As required, fixed positions only, pivot positions only, or both may be defined by the strategic area to be sensitive to the distinct condition of volatility of each area. In this manner, the future positions of the business may be defined in accord with the times and circumstances.

Objectives and Goals

Objectives define specific measurable states to be accomplished. A good objective is measurable, achievable, explicit, succinct and clear, dated, and consistent with all other objectives. Measurement may be defined in any of three modes:

Existence. Something that didn't exist now exists (or the converse),

Effectiveness. A quantifiable measure of satisfaction.

Efficiency. A quantifiable measure of productivity.

Objectives are realized incrementally in the form of serial goals, which are dated interim positions of accomplishment on the way to realization of the objective. Table 4.1 defines the format of an objective. The format of a goal is identical except a contingency plan is often not required.

Objectives are the enhanced definition of what must be accomplished to realize the strategy statements. Generally, there will be at least three objectives but no more than six per strategy statement. Strategy statements without objectives are too broad to provide specific directive action for execution.

Objective Setting

Objective setting is an art. As shown in Figure 4.3, objectives represent the resolution of conclusions and the realization of the desired future business state (strategy statements, business scope, and positions). While analytical techniques can provide assistance, especially in forecasting future financial and internal market-share objectives, objective setting is more characterized by vision, insight, and business feel and savvy than rigorous techniques. The question is, what must be done to realize the strategy statements?

As previously stated, good objectives are rigorously defined, explicit, dated, and measurable. Some theorists recommend an alternative called *regimen objec-*

Table 4.1   Objectives

OBJECTIVE ATTRIBUTE	DEFINITION
Objective	A precise and concise statement of the objective
Date	By when the objective is to be achieved
Measure	The measurement(s) to be used to assess whether the objective has been accomplished
Contingency plan	A plan to deal with a low-probability but high-risk event whose occurrence would jeopardize realizing the objective

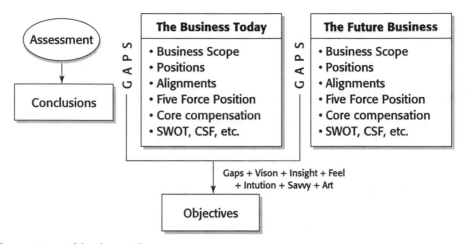

Figure 4.3   Objective setting.

tives. Regimen objectives focus on doing the right things; a healthy regimen will lead to success. Consequently, they focus less on objectives and more on strategic moves. Regimen objectives are an interesting but minority approach.

Objective Relationships

Objectives have important relationships with other strategic planning outputs, as shown in Figure 4.4:

- A conclusion is satisfied through the accomplishment of multiple objectives. Multiple objectives collectively satisfy a conclusion.
- A strategy statement will generate multiple objectives.
- Multiple strategic moves collectively enable the accomplishment of an objective. Multiple objectives are realized by each move.

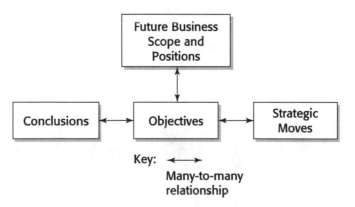

Figure 4.4   Objective relationships.

Objectives exist in a pivotal and complicated state of many-to-many relationships with the other strategic planning outputs of conclusions, strategic moves, and future business scope and positions.

Standing Objectives

Normally three standing objectives exist, that is, objectives that are always automatically defined. These objectives are as follows:

- Financial, which defines profitability, ROI, cash-flow, etc.
- Market share, which defines market share objectives for each internal market segment
- Customer satisfaction, which defines customer satisfaction objectives per product or product group

The logic of this is that continued success in these three critical areas is always mandatory to preempt IT business decay. At minimum, failure in these crucial areas leads to inadequate margins to fund reinvestment in new products, staff development, customer satisfaction, competencies, and capabilities. The consequence is a vicious downward cycle. Consequently, standing objectives represent the minimum set of objectives for the strategic plan.

Contingency Plan

A contingency plan is a plan to deal with a possible event that could prevent achieving an objective. Contingency plans cover high-risk but low-probability situations. By anticipating and planning for such events, responses may be designed that can contain the problem based on an identified trigger event.

Table 4.2 provides a decision aid to use in considering when a contingency plan is warranted. Contingency plan development consists of six steps:

1. Define the set of possible high-risk but low-probability situations for each objective.
2. Identify trigger mechanisms.

Table 4.2 Contingency Plans

	PROBABILITY OF OCCURRENCE	
RISK	**HIGH**	**LOW**
High	Include in strategic plan	Contingency plan
Low	Include in strategic plan	Deal with it when and if it occurs

3. Define consequences to objectives of each event.

4. Define responses. What actions would be taken and what alternative objectives would be set?

5. Test the plan (walk-through, simulation, devil's advocacy, expert opinion).

6. Interlock the plans.

Those who are good at getting rid of trouble are those who take care of it before it arises.

Sun Tzu, The Art of War

Contingency planning eliminates uncertainty, confusion, and delays in reacting to potentially catastrophic events and minimizing the damage. The contingency plan helps ensure that either the original objective is still obtainable or that a substitute but acceptable objective is realized.

Setting Goals

Goals are interim points of accomplishment on the path to achieving an objective. They share the same attributes as objectives in that they should be succinct, clear, measurable, and dated. As shown in Figure 4.5, goals may be developed by working backward from the objective and answering the question: Where must I be and when must I be there to achieve the objective by the stated date?

Summary

Leadership requires providing the organization with a clear definition of what is to be accomplished. How can alignment take place if the desired future state is fuzzy and ambiguous? Objectives coupled with the strategy statements, future business scope and positions define an unambiguous target for the

Figure 4.5   Setting goals.

organization. This is vitally important for an IT organization during such turbulent times.

Strategic Moves

Strategic moves are purposeful and coherent actions taken to achieve one or more objectives. Strategic moves are prescriptive; they identify exactly what is to be done. They are purposeful in that they directly act to achieve an objective. They are coherent in that there is synergy between them. They do not block, retard, or contradict each other; rather, they complement and support each other. Strategic moves identify what is to be done, but they do not tell how. As shown in Figure 4.4, a move may provide leverage by helping to realize multiple objectives.

There is a great deal of ambiguity with regard to the use and meaning of the word *strategy*. We use the word strategy to mean the second step of the strategic planning process, which embodies strategy statements, objectives, strategic moves, a change management plan, and a commitment plan. We use the label *strategic move* (used interchangeably with *strategic action* or *initiative*) to mean a specific action undertaken to achieve an objective. The word strategy is often used to mean strategic move, and sometimes in the same article, it is also used to mean both our meaning of strategy and strategic move based on usage context. As this can become very confusing, we use the phrase *strategic move* to denote specific strategic actions and the word *strategy* to denote the second step of the strategic planning process with all the components that it implies. Strategy is more than just actions. It is the robust definition of what is to be and how it is to be achieved.

Elements

Table 4.3 summarizes the format of a move. Each element is explained as follows:

Move. A brief, succinct, and clear statement of the action. A strategic move should contain an action verb and prescribe what is to be done.

Description. A brief elaboration of the strategic move. An important part of the design of a strategic move is *leverage*. Leverage is the amplifier, multiplier, and accelerator of the benefits of an action: leverage = (strategic move x multiplier x payoff). Typical multipliers are reusability, sharing, open accessibility, linkage, replicability, duplicability, layering, economies of scale, maneuverability, economies of scope, synergy, dispersion, cascading, and modularity. However beneficial a strategic move may be, it can be made an order of magnitude better by designing leverage into it. Leverage gives the strategic action "muscle."

The core competency framework presented in Chapter 3 is an excellent example of leverage. Multiple core competencies are combined into multiple core products, which serve multiple business units that contribute to multiple end products. Through this layering approach, core competencies are multiplied and reused to leverage their benefits.

Owner. The individual in the organization who is responsible for implementing the strategic move. Owners are individuals throughout the business; remember, strategic actions are horizontal in magnitude. There is only one owner per action, and that should be an individual, not an organization, so that accountability can be pinpointed.

Champion. The strategy team member charged with "championing" the move. Champions are alternatively referred to as managing partners, change managers, and executive sponsors. While the owner "owns" the direct problem of implementing the initiative, the champion has the ancillary responsibility of providing continual high-level support, counsel, and focus for the effort.

Rationale. Explains the business justification for the action: Exactly why should we take this action? Table 4.4 summarizes common approaches to justifying actions. Not surprisingly, many strategic moves are justified based on strategic importance, that is, in order to realize the strategy statements, this action is required. The other methods, particularly the economic justification set, are used by the implementation teams to choose how best to implement the action.

Priority. All strategic moves are, by definition, important. Priority should be understood as relative importance among the very important. A typical priority classification scheme would include labels of imperative, high, medium, and low.

Measurement. Defines by the criteria of existence, effectiveness, and efficiency the manner in which success will be measured.

Date. Defines the specific time by when the initiative is to be concluded.

Implementation program parameters (IPPs). Strategic moves define what is to be done but not how. IPP provide directions and boundaries of action for the implementation owner. IPPs are used to force alignment of actions and to explicitly state that not only does an action need to be done, but it needs to be done within certain constraints. Figure 4.6 illustrates this concept. It is interesting to observe that IPPs serve the same function, albeit at a lower strategy level, that directives and assumptions serve to the assessment step.

Figure 4.6 Implementation program parameters.

Strategic moves should be designed to encourage experimentation, trial and error, and continuous learning and adaptation in their implementation.

> *Test them to find out where they are sufficient and where they are lacking. Do something for or against them, making opponents turn their attention to it, so that you can find out their patterns of aggressive and defensive behavior.*

> *Sun Tzu,* The Art of War

No matter how carefully formulated the strategy is, it is still conjecture. Mixing in experimentation as an integral component first tempers and then guides our actions by the sobering effects of reality. Strategic moves, therefore, must also include sponsoring experiments, prototypes, trial and error, and more to provide proof-of-concept and generate convincing evidence to support a full commitment. In this way, endless cycles of experimentation and reason complement each other. The results from experiments provide evidence to evaluate whether full strategic commitment is warranted. Conversely, the actual results from monitoring strategic moves in progress provide feedback so moves can be accelerated, modified, or abandoned. In a sense, the sense of learning and adaptation, all moves are experiments, but experiments with widely varying degrees of expectations, maturity, and commitment.

Tactics

Strategic moves are executed through the development of *tactics.* Tactics are the detailed actions taken to implement the initiative. They are formulated by the implementation owner together with his or her project team. Tactics need to be responsive and sensitive to the evolving environmental situation.

Table 4.3 Strategic Moves

STRATEGIC MOVE ATTRIBUTE	DEFINITION
Move	A brief and clear statement of the action
Description	A few paragraphs of elaboration of the action
Owner	The individual in the organization responsible for making the action happen
Champion	The executive in the organization responsible for assisting the owner
Rationale	The business logic of the action
Priority	Relative importance of the action
Measurement	The way to measure that the action has been completed
Date	The date by which the action is to be concluded
Implementation program parameters	Rules, guidelines, boundaries, etc., that the implementation owner should follow in implementing the action

Adaptation means not clinging to fixed methods, but changing appropriately to events ... those who can face the unprepared with preparation are victorious. The ability to gain victory by changing and adapting to the opponent is called genius.

Sun Tzu, The Art of War

Table 4.4 Justification Methods

JUSTIFICATION METHODS	
Portfolio	**Analytic**
Views actions as contributing to building a balanced portfolio	Analytic techniques that balance risk against value
Economic	**Strategic**
Estimate cost savings and revenue growth and incorporate the time value of money **Examples:**	Justification based on meeting strategic requirements **Examples:**
1. Cash flow	1. Strategic intent
2. Discounted cash flow	2. Alignment
3. Net present value	3. SCA
4. Payback	4. Competitive parity
5. Accounting ROI	5. Maneuverability

Tactics provide the malleable part of the strategic plan to allow for adaptation to the constantly changing reality. Objectives define what is to be accomplished. Strategic moves define the ways. Tactics define the explicit "how," but do so in a flexible and dynamic manner in accord with events.

Formulation

The formulation of strategic actions is a difficult task. It is difficult because of the risk, uncertainty, and consequences of the actions. In addition to the ideas generated during the assessment step and the candidate actions proposed as part of the conclusions, there are six common approaches to developing moves. *Art* is clearly the dominant approach. Each is explained individually.

Formula

Formula methods represent codified experience, which has proved successful in the past. Table 4.5 and Table 4.6 are examples of this approach. The former defines actions in terms of the intersection of competitive position and market growth. The latter defines actions as a function of product life-cycle position. Strategic action equates to locating the position of a product on the respective matrices and executing the indicated actions.

While helpful as a starting point, these approaches are transparent, are easily decoded by competitors, and do not suggest novel or creative actions. Unfortunately, your competitors have access to the same formulas and may consequently anticipate your actions. Strategy is to be "deep and far-reaching," not ritualistic or fill-in-the-blanks.

Analytical Methods

Analytical methods are a set of frameworks, models, and analysis techniques that assist in formulating actions. They are similar in nature to those applied during the assessment step. Three representative methods are as follows:

Strategic thrust (Figure 4.7). The purpose of this method is to develop a repositioning goal for each product and define the means of attainment. The process is as follows:

- Position each product by the dimensions of competitive position and market share.
- Select a "strategic thrust" for the product (i.e., expansion, explosion, continued growth, slip, contraction, or consolidation).
- Define the actions needed to accomplish the thrust.

Strategic thrust is particularly powerful because of the way it can individually and collectively show the intended movement of the IT product portfolio.

Table 4.5 Competition/Market Growth

MARKET GROWTH	COMPETITIVE POSITION		
	Strong	**Medium**	**Weak**
High	**Protect** 1. Invest to grow at maximum rate 2. Maintain strengths 3. Expand business	**Invest to build** 1. Challenge for leadership 2. Build on strengths 3. Eliminate weaknesses 4. Expand business	**Build selectively** 1. Specialize around strengths 2. Build on strengths 3. Eliminate weaknesses 4. Expand business
Medium	**Build selectively** 1. Invest to grow at maximum rate 2. Maintain strength 3. Expand business	**Manage for earnings** 1. Protect 2. Focus on high-profitability segments 3. Low risk	**Limited expansion** 1. Low risk expansion 2. Minimize investment
Low	**Protect and refocus** 1. Manage for current earnings 2. Defend strengths 3. Milk product	**Manage for earnings** 1. Protect 2. Minimize investment 3. Milk product	**Divest** 1. Sell 2. Avoid investment

Market opportunity analysis. Market opportunity analysis is the use of a set of analytical and positioning methods to assess both the attractiveness of a market opportunity and the necessary actions that need to be taken in order to succeed. Typically included in a market opportunity analysis

Table 4.6 Product Life Cycle

STRATEGIC DIMENSION	PRODUCT LIFE-CYCLE STAGE			
	Introduction	**Growth**	**Maturity**	**Decline**
Overall thrust	Market establishment	Market penetration	Market defense	Milk
Customer	Innovative	Mass market	Mass market	Laggards
Channels	Few	Many	Many	Dwindling
Advertising	Awareness	Mass market benefits	Differentiation	Minimum
Price	High	Lower	Lowest	Rising
Configurations	Basic	Constant improvement	Sophisticated	Slow change

would be market segmentation, competitor analysis, SWOT analysis, critical success factors, core competencies, Five Force analysis, new product positioning, and market-entry analysis.

All these techniques have been explained except market-entry analysis, which is illustrated in Table 4.7. *Market-entry analysis* provides a structured framework to analyze the alternative paths of entering a market. Most of the market-entry alternatives require, in one form or another, the selection of a partner. In choosing the suitability of a partner, one must consider the following:

- What would be the form of the partnership governance?

- How will participation aid each partner in reaching its distinct strategic intents, future business scopes, future strategic positions, and objectives?

- What would be the shared objectives and strategic moves of the partnership?

- How would commitment be demonstrated?

- What leverage does each partner bring to the partnership?

- How do distinct competencies and capabilities provide superior value when joined?

- What will be learned from each other?

- How will the economy of the joint effort be designed?

- When the partnership expires, will there be a net gain or a net loss in terms of transfer of capabilities, competencies, and knowledge?

- Partnerships are very serious undertakings that require careful strategic forethought.

As the complexity of IT increases, IT organizations will increasingly need to enter into joint arrangements with other suppliers.

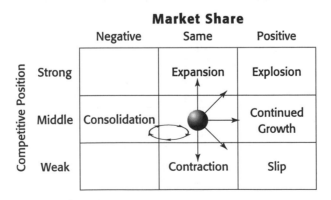

Figure 4.7 Strategic thrust.

Table 4.7   Market-Entry Analysis

MARKET ENTRY OPTIONS	CRITICAL SUCCESS FACTORS	RISKS	LEVERAGE	ADVANTAGES	DISADVANTAGES
Reseller					
Subcontractor					
Acquisition					
Strategic alliances					
Joint venture					
Start-up					
Existing product-line extension					
Franchise					

If you carry on alliances with strong countries, your enemies won't dare plot against you . . . Make informed alliances . . . compete for alliances . . . If you do not compete for alliances and helpers, then you will be isolated with little help.

Sun Tzu, The Art of War

Given the technology turbulence and the shift to a free-market economy for IT services in many corporations, strong and competent friends are to be welcomed.

Strategy coherence. *Strategy coherence* is an algorithm to force alignment. Its objective is to test the proposed moves set iteratively against each other and the business areas to discover additional actions that are required. Strategy coherence has four steps:

1. The complete list of actions, however generated, is assembled.

2. The actions are cross-checked for synergy. As a set, are they in alignment? If not, the actions are adjusted to force alignment. Recursively, this step is continued until alignment is achieved. Remember, when an action is adjusted it may cause new misalignment.

3. The aligned actions are tested and set against all the business areas. Because the actions will change the positions of the immediately impacted business areas, adjoining areas may also need modification. Again, when an action is adjusted or added, new misalignments may be inadvertently created.

4. Repeat the third step until perfect alignment is achieved.

This technique is time-consuming and meticulous, but it discovers missing actions during the strategy development phase rather then the implementation phase when shortcomings are more disruptive, embarrassing, and expensive to fix.

The rational for performing this technique is best understood by the analogy to chess. If you understand that a king may move one space in any direction, you know a little about the king and the moves of chess, but not very much. If you are told additionally that a king may not move into a check, you know more, but still very little. If you wish to truly understand the consequences of moving the king, then you must understand all the moves and rules of the game. You must see and understand the king's moves in the totality and context of the whole game. The same is true of strategic moves. If you truly wish to understand the consequences of a strategic move, it must be tested and understood in the totality of the strategic game board.

Principles. Principles are general rules or maxims that have repeatedly proven successful when followed. The most interesting set of principles for business strategy do not come from the field of business but from the sphere of military strategy. Because warfare is the primal metaphor used in describing business competition, this is not completely surprising. Some military strategic principles that have direct application to business strategy development are as follows:[1]

- Adjust your ends to your means.

- Keep your object in mind (focus).

- Choose the line of least expectation (surprise).

- Choose the line of least resistance—it is better to win through indirection than by direct confrontation.

- Choose a line of operation that offers alternative objectives (adaptability).

- Ensure that both dispositions are flexible and adaptable to circumstances (maneuverability).

- Do not throw your weight into a stroke while your opponent is on guard.

- Do not renew an attack along the same line or in the same form after it has once failed.

These principles provide a formula for developing moves that let you "thrive on chaos," but not in the popular meaning of the phrase. The popular meaning of the phrase suggests that one should accept and come to terms with the chaos of the business environment and prosper by living with it. The eight principles would suggest that a better definition for "thriving on chaos" would involve taming chaos, creating order, purpose, and intent for yourself while perpetuating and extending chaos for your opponents. With the popular definition of "thriving on chaos," it is not possible to build deep and far-reaching strategies because chaos invalidates any and all long-term plans. With the newer definition, not only can you build deep and far reaching strategies, but you can concurrently position yourself to win and your opponents to lose. The higher rung on the strategic ladder is mastery and exploitation of chaos rather than resignation to chaos and living by your wits.

Figure 4.8 illustrates how these principles are to be applied. The law (axiom) of military strategy is to apply "concentrated force against weakness." This is done as follows:

1. Develop a coherent set of strategic moves with two thrusts. Use the principles to guide the development of the actions.

2. The first thrust is to create enemy weakness. Through strategic actions, cause confusion, dislocation, paralysis, and fear in the enemy camp. Throw the opponent off balance.

3. Concurrently, take strategic action to strengthen and prepare yourself.

4. Exploit the strategic opportunity created by step 2. Take advantage of the opponent's dislocation and your own strength and "attack complete emptiness with complete fullness."

This model is very appropriate for understanding the true strategic significance of IT technology to the business. IT technology will achieve its

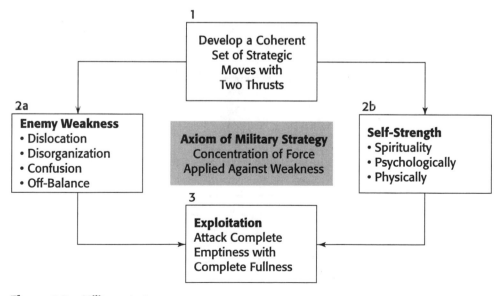

Figure 4.8 Military strategy.

optimum strategic value when the business can use it to create chosen dislocations in the marketplace and concurrently develop its own strength to exploit the consequences. Viewed in this way, IT is not just administrative and record-keeping systems; rather, IT is the cutting edge of business conflict, permitting the business management to choose the time, place, and terms of competitive engagement.

The use of this method to design strategic moves is richly illustrated by the use of what is called the *Kano Methodology*. If you will recall from the discussion on product positioning in Chapter 3, an integral component of a product map is the customer satisfaction measurement system. Following the Kano methodology, customer satisfaction drivers should be partitioned into three categories (see Figure 4.9).

Threshold attributes. Basic and important, but quickly reach a saturation point. Added investment after a point results in a decreasing marginal benefit.

Performance attributes. Very important; the more and better you do it, the more satisfied the customer. There is a linear effect between investment and customer satisfaction.

Excitement drivers. Extraordinary impact on customer satisfaction. The customer is satisfied far beyond expectations. There is a high leverage effect between added process investment and customer satisfaction.

The relationship between added process investment and customer satisfaction is illustrated by the three rectangles in Figure 4.9.

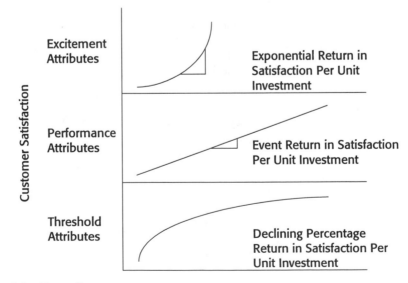

Figure 4.9 Kano diagram.

One would then manage the Kano attributes as follows:

1. Invest in threshold attributes only to the point of saturation and no more.

2. Invest in performance attributes until they decay into threshold attributes.

3. Invest heavily in excitement drivers. Invest in them to the point that you have them mastered. Then reposition them in customer perception as threshold attributes. As shown in Figure 4.10, you will then have a basic set of customer satisfiers, which you can fully meet that your competitors can't. By design, you will have created both a market dislocation and a large strategic distance between your ability to meet this basic customer requirement and that of your closest competitor.

By following the path of least expectation and least resistance, you concurrently create a difficulty for your competitors and a method of exploitation for yourself. There is no head-on competition; to the contrary, you win by creating a far superior position for yourself while creating an inferior position for the competitor. And, best of all, you vastly increase your customer's satisfaction in the process. Of course, this algorithm for dislocation and exploitation must be continuously reexecuted, or else a competitor will catch you, or worse, turn the tables and do it to you.

The Kano methodology is exactly what farsighted developers did in adopting prototyping as a superior requirements definition strategy.[2] Recognizing that simplicity, speed, and visuality of requirements definition combined to form an excitement attribute, they developed robust application prototyping

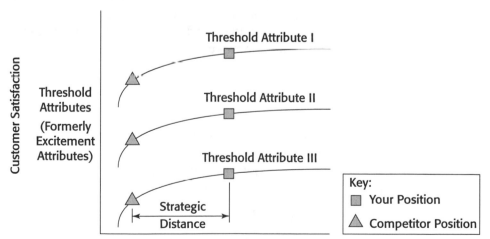

Figure 4.10   Excitement to threshold.

capabilities to replace incredibly slow and even more boring structured techniques. Users then flocked to those developers that could build requirements through prototyping. Developers who could do only rigorous prespecification methods were left behind with a large strategic distance to overcome.

> **Key findings.** *Key findings* are learned during the assessment step and are of particularly important value. Examples of key findings are Five Force drivers, capabilities, core competencies, SWOTs, critical success factors, bottlenecks, and value chain drivers (cost and value-added). Key findings-based formulation focuses on using the key findings as the basis for developing actions to achieve the objectives.

> **Art.** The book is called *The Art of War*, not *The Analytical Methods and Formulas of War*.

> *There are only five notes in the musical scale but the variations are so many that they all can't be heard. There are only five basic colors but the variations are so many, that they all can't be seen. There are only five basic flavors, but the varieties are so many that they can't all be tasted. There are only two basic charges in battle, the unorthodox surprise attack and the orthodox direct attack, but the variations of the orthodox and the unorthodox are endless. The unorthodox and the orthodox give rise to each other like a beginningless circle—who can exhaust them.*

> *Sun Tzu*, The Art of War

The heart of strategy is surprise: the sewing together of a unique set of actions, unanticipated and unsuspected by the opposition for *this* encounter.

The formulation of strategic actions remains an art. All of the other methods help, but deep and far-reaching actions are not the product of repetition. Instead, they spring from deep understanding of the situation. This is why strategy formulation is entrusted to the highest levels of the business. Through experience and demonstrated success, these individuals are best prepared to deal with the problem of developing a mixture of orthodox and unorthodox actions.

Organization Structure

Organization structure should follow strategy and should be crafted to facilitate the realization of the strategy. Reorganization alone is not strategy, and developing strategy with the constraint of a frozen organizational structure is not good strategy.

> *Structure depends on strategy. Forces are to be structured strategically based on what is advantageous.*

> *Sun Tzu*, The Art of War

Organizational Structure

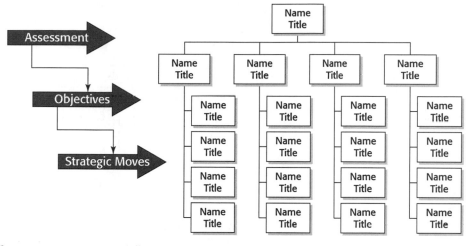

Figure 4.11   Structure follows strategy.

Organizational structure is a function of strategy; not the reverse. Figure 4.11 illustrates the relationship between structure and strategy.

IT organizational design, while always complex, is now even more challenging due to the unprecedented technology shifts we are experiencing. While organizational design must enable strategy, it must also take into account the pragmatic issues of culture, management style, and reward systems. While design is peculiar to each, a starting point does exist. Figure 4.12 provides a starting point for designing an IT organization to deal with the challenges of the new millenium. The primary functions are as follows:

Operations. Experts in running the IT services.

Technology support. Experts in selecting, supporting, and integrating IT technologies.

Architecture and standards. Development and consensus building for an IT architectural blueprint for the firm.

Product/service management. Overall product management responsible for all IT products and services.

Application development and systems integration. Experts in the design development and life-cycle evolution of complex business applications.

Account management and consulting. Responsible for account management and providing business solutions consulting.

Support services. Nondirect value chain functions such as finance and human resources.

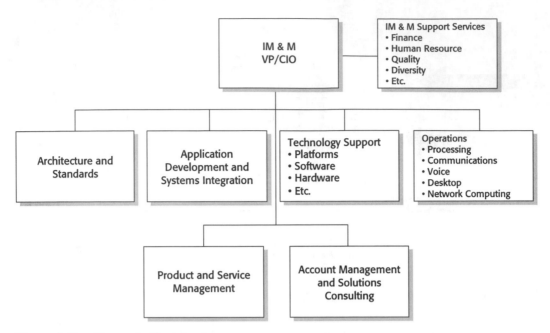

Figure 4.12 IT organization structure.

These seven functions would appear to be the building blocks for most IT organizations.

On top of this functional organization, an internal IT economy must be imposed to motivate desired behaviors and decision making. Given the shift to Internet computing (and its requirement for horizontal end-to-end solutions), the presence of growing competition to the internal IT organization, the importance of process to success (capabilities and value chain strategic frameworks), and the primacy of alignment, the following is suggested:

- Budget control should be given to the product management function.

- Product management should buy processes from process owners throughout the organization. Process owners, not functional managers, sit on the product teams.

- Process owners buy needed functions from the various functional organizations. The functional organization, analogous to object servers, advertise what services they can perform, and process owners string the services together to provide the end-to-end services needed to deliver the products.

Figure 4.13 illustrates this approach. Customers buy products. Product managers deliver products throughout their life cycle by contracting for horizontal process with internal process owners. Process owners subcontract with

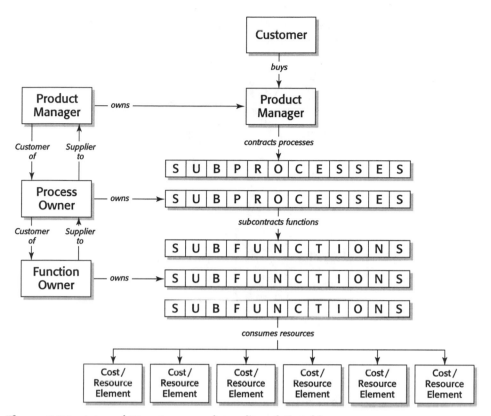

Figure 4.13   Internal IT customer and supplier relationship.

functional organizations to do required services. Functional organizations consume resources (expense elements) in delivering the services. This approach imposes a proper customer and supplier relationship within the IT organization, motivates desired cooperative behaviors, and forces alignment through the funding of horizontal capabilities as opposed to vertical functions. Product managers can measure (customer satisfaction measurements) and negotiate for required processes. Process owners can measure and negotiate for needed functions. Function owners compete for usage and focus on controlling expense. As a by-product of imposing this type of economy on the organization, the organization is well positioned to perform value chain anlaysis to improve productivity, time, or value-added. By organizing in this manner, product managers not only would fund research and development (R/D) for their products, but would also fund R/D for their processes; both product and process would be subject to continual improvement.

Figure 4.14 illustrates how this concept may be applied to developing new Internet environments. A core systems integration group of the technology support organization contracts to engineer a new network computing plat-

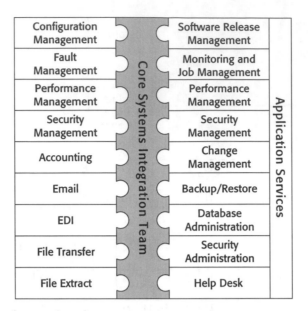

Core Systems Integration Team	Application Services
Configuration Management	Software Release Management
Fault Management	Monitoring and Job Management
Performance Management	Performance Management
Security Management	Security Management
Accounting	Change Management
Email	Backup/Restore
EDI	Database Administration
File Transfer	Security Administration
File Extract	Help Desk

Figure 4.14   Product engineering.

form. It then subcontracts to OA&M, the application support and application enabling specialist, to clip-on their respective pieces. This arrangement provides a proper customer and supplier relationship, encourages leverage, and ensures that complete solutions will be developed. Once completed, multiple business applications can then be built on top of this reusable platform. A federation of developers, traditional centralized IT, the users themselves, and consultants can all attack the bottleneck of application development by standing on the common shoulders of the engineered network environment.

Imposing a customer and supplier market economy on the IT organization represents "big change," and "big change" often requires radical restructuring. The largest IT suborganization (if not by headcount then by budget) is often the operations group. Understandably, they are often the most conservative; after all, they have to make it work everyday. For large IT shops, it may be prudent to break the operations organization into multiple internally competing "factories" that bid to win work. This drives competition to the largest expense item on many IT organization balance sheets, dismantles the operations hegemony, and encourages free-market entrepreneurship behaviors.

Figure 4.15 summarizes the economic problems of organization design. The organizational design must facilitate the efficient functioning of two economic systems, one between the IT organization and the other enterprise customers and one internal to the IT organization. Machiavelli (*The Prince*) coldly summed up the problem as follows:

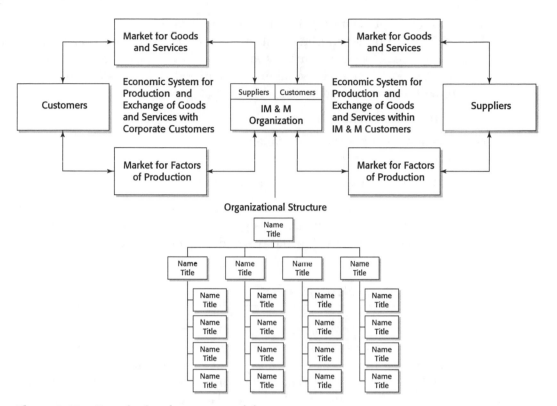

Figure 4.15 Organizational structure and the economy.

There is simply no comparison between a man who is armed (we read "armed" as budgetary control) and one who is not. It is unreasonable to expect the armed man should obey the one who is unarmed....This is how we can distinguish between innovators who stand alone and those who depend on others; that is between those who to achieve their purpose can force the issue and those who must use persuasion. In the second case, they always come to grief having achieved nothing. Whenever they depend on their own resources and can force the issue, then they are seldom endangered.

It is therefore impossible to properly do an organization design without proper consideration of how the economic system will provide gentle (and not so gentle) incentives to force alignment to serve the customer.

Summary

Strategic moves are the purposeful and coherent actions taken by the organization.

Go forth without having determined strategy and you will destroy yourself in battle.

Sun Tzu, The Art of War

The development of strategy is not an optional extra.

With this broad understanding of strategy now accrued, what constitutes a strategic action can be clearly understood. An action is strategic when its successful execution, alone or in collaboration with other actions (serially or in parallel), will do one or more of the following:

- Positively and materially alter one or more strategic positions
- Prevent a negative and material alteration in one or more strategic positions
- Support the realization of one or more strategy statements and objectives

We refer to the first item as an offensive action and to the second item as a defensive action. If a move, an action, a push, or an initiative can't do at least one of the above, it may of value and worth doing, but it is not strategic.

Change Management Plan

A *change management plan* is a subplan to infuse the strategic plan with premeditated actions to preempt resistance to change and enroll the organization in the change effort. Strategy is change—movement from the current set of (mis)aligned positions to a new set of positions. Many in the organization, for a wide variety of reasons, will resist. Resistance can be anticipated and planned for. The change management plan performs this function.

Frozen Mental Models

Table 4.8 uses the *root cause analytical method* to present an analysis of the causes of resistance. At the root of resistance is often a *frozen mental model*.[3] A mental model is a deeply held internal image of how the world works. It defines what is seen, how one sees, and how one comprehends and interprets what he or she she sees. It provides a very personal framework for coping and

Table 4.8 Why Resistance

Symptoms	Job status loss, loss of opportunity, limited mobility, loss of security, loss of relationships, loss of power, threat to skills, end of monopoly of knowledge or power, change of behavior and attitudes required, violation of implied covenant, likes the world as it is, devaluing of personal and career investment
Problem	Fear of change
Root cause	Frozen mental model

dealing with the complex world. Mental models become "frozen" when one fails to adapt the mental model to a changing environment; though the world around is changing, the individual persists in the old, comfortable, and complacent view in denial of the emerging new reality. One becomes hermetically sealed to new information.

Mental models are deeply embedded and reinforced in close-knit communities. They provide a familiar view of the world, "group think," which has been confirmed through shared experiences and successes. The underlying assumptions of how the world works are rarely stated or surfaced but shared by the community. Never subject to challenge or debate, the model freezes over time and automatically rejects new ideas that are considered threats rather than opportunities.

The genesis of many change problems is that a new idea is at variance with the "absolutely" correct mental model. Change threatens both the individual and community's mental model as they strive to reassert the "correct" view of the world. Given the tremendous personal investments and comfort it provides, individuals and organizations will fight hard and long to defend their mental model.

Change strategy must focus on altering mental models, the root causes of the resistance problem. To accomplish this, a change management plan must do the following:

- Take actions to explicitly surface the embedded models and externalize the deeply held but unstated assumptions about how the world works
- Demonstrate the forward invalidity of the assumptions
- Unfreeze the model; get the community to concede that their model could be dated (the use of scenario sessions is a beneficial technique to accomplish this)
- Provide convincing arguments that formulate a new mental model
- Assist the community in understanding their changed roles and value in the new mental model

It is not the intent to "refreeze" the organization in the new model. The staff must learn that especially in the IT field change will remain fluid. The enduring value of the staff members is in their professionalism, not their tactical expertise in a particular technology at a particular time. The creation of an adaptive organization that can gently switch mental models in accord with events has to be a linchpin of any IT strategy.

The problem of frozen mental models is a problem of insight or, more accurately, the absence of insight. *Insight* is the ability of an individual to fully comprehend the true cause, meaning, and implications of a situation. There are multiple levels of insight:

True insight. An understanding of the objective reality of a situation coupled with the motivation to take positive actions to master it.

Intellectual insight. An understanding and acceptance of the objective reality of the situation but an inability and unwillingness to take actions to master it.

Impaired insight. A diminished ability to understand (for whatever reason) the objective reality of the situation. There is a wide range of impairment states:

- Complete denial

- Slight awareness but strong denial

- Awareness, but rather than acceptance a state of anger and bargaining at the unjust situation

- Begrudging acceptance with no willingness to positively confront the situation

It is therefore the job of the change agent to move the organization from a state of impaired insight (a condition of being technologically comatose) to a state of true insight where positive actions can be taken to reverse the situation to everyone's advantage.

Methods for Dealing with Change

There exists a rich body of behavioral science literature that discusses ways to manage change. It is impossible to do justice to such a rich source of information in this book, and it is suggested that you research the topic. We would like, however, to present two examples. Table 4.9 is an example of generic guidance. It provides a variety of approaches based on the situational parameters. Except for "explicit coercion," they all attempt to weaken resistance before overcoming it. Direct assaults on ideas, which have substantial intellectual, emotional, and temporal investments, will almost always force increased resistance. It is much better to craft change methods around "indirection." When you can find allies among the impacted, divide and conquer. Package the change as natural evolution rather than revolution. Let people change at their own pace (see Figure 4.16). Find ways to appeal to their selfish interests to force alignment with your strategic interests.

It is unfortunate, but not unusual, that the decisive change move must be to create a pseudo-crisis to shock the organization out of complacency, smugness, arrogance, and misplaced confidence. Time decays the degrees of freedom for strategic action. If the partisanship of "what was" is so severe as to preempt any possibilities of anticipatory change, the creation of a spurious crisis can be used to stimulate action. If the organization will not be moved without acute

Table 4.9   Change Methods

APPROACH	USED WHEN	ADVANTAGES	DISADVANTAGES
Education and communication	Lack of information is cause of resistance	Supportative persuasion	Time-consuming
Participation and involvement	Empowerment is best method to gain buy-in	Enrolls organization	Time-consuming and risky
Facilitation and support	Organization suffers from morale decline	Deals with adjustment problems	Expensive
Manipulation	Time is of the essence	Quick	Staff reaction
Explicit coercion	Time is of the essence and you have the power	It works	Long-term consequences

pain, we will create artificial pain as preferable to real pain. A well-designed forged crisis is built on six variables:

Intensity. The depth of the crisis will be such that it penetrates defense mechanisms. It cannot be ignored.

Duration. The length of the crisis will be sufficient to force attention. The discomfort will be enduring.

Certainty. The problem will not go away. There will be no remission; it must be dealt with.

Immediacy. It will definitely happen soon. The days of judgment are at hand.

Shareability. The crisis affects everyone. There is no place to run; we're all in this boat together.

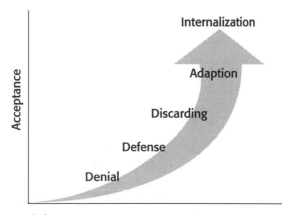

Figure 4.16   Stages of change.

Therapy. The proposed change, however distasteful it was before the forgery, offers an acceptable escape from the crisis.

Confront them with annihilation, and they will then survive; plunge them into a deadly situation, and they will then live. When people fall into danger, they are then able to strive for victory. . . . When they have fallen into dire straits, they obey completely.

Sun Tzu, The Art of War

Crisis elevates change from a matter of casual individual choice to a matter of urgent community necessity. Necessity is the prime mover of change.

A change agent must accept the axiom that it is possible to move a community from a state of hardened doubt and resistance to a state of new beliefs. A state of belief in the new order is the prerequisite for change. Belief is the pivot position for change. While creating forgeries has some ethical problems and a sham is normally not to be admired, it can pragmatically yield the desired result with minimal pain.

Figure 4.17 provides an example of a specific analytical method to be used to anticipate obstacles to each move and develop preempting strategies. *Barrier analysis* suggests that change agents will encounter three classifications of barriers:

General. Organizational history, culture, and style.

Role. Specific incumbent positions in the organization will object.

Individual. Specific individuals will object.

As shown in Figure 4.17, the approach is to matrix the objectives against anticipated barriers. Whenever there is an intersection, barrier reduction actions should be developed and added to the strategic plan. Typical barriers

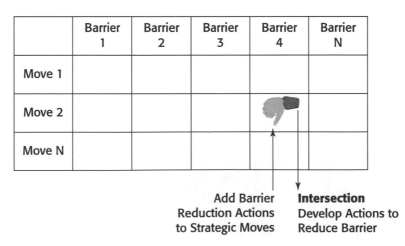

Figure 4.17   Barrier analysis.

are complacency, disbelief, fear of failure, expediency, culture, inertia, an "it works" attitude, partisan warfare, and a "kvetch" culture.

Those who face the unprepared with preparation are victorious.

Sun Tzu, The Art of War

Anticipating and preempting barriers is not easy, but it is better than facing them unprepared.

Organization Politics

By far, the most difficult barrier to overcome is organizational politics. A business organization, like any social community, naturally divides itself into political interest groups. These groups are defined by division of work, allocation of resources, shared mental models, aspirations, and training and skills. Change will revise the partitioning of status, power, opportunities and resources. Some political groups will perceive themselves as losers, and some will perceive a net gain. They all will be concerned about the threat of a change in the *status quo* and will prefer the known power equilibrium.

Political groups focus on the continued well-being of their constituency. They will not be amenable to change that hurts their group regardless of merit (who defines merit?). Preservation of group interests supersedes organizational interests. Political groups will therefore intensely lobby during the change debate. They will attempt to control the following:

- What can be debated
- How resources will be divided
- How much commitment will be devoted
- The legitimacy of the proposed change

Politics is a hard reality for the strategic change agent. Whatever its source of power, control of physical resources, control over or access to information, formal authority, reputation, charisma, or alliances, each political group will use their power to alter the strategy to their advantage.

Politics is not peripheral to the formulation of strategy; it is the threatening background against which all change plans and commitment plans must be designed. Veteran organizational politicians are not opposed to change because they object to creation; they are opposed because they know that with creation comes complementary destruction. The laws of conservation and experience have taught the savvy politician that the change agent is both a creator and, though not advertised as such, an annihilator. So the rule of behavior is simple: Better to protect and defend "what is" rather than be at the mercy of the change agent, or should we say the "annihilator."

Table 4.10 is a useful aid in dealing with organizational politics. Change can occur only if coalitions can be formed to bring adequate political power to permit mobilization of resources and commitment. The matrix should be used to identify each political group, its agenda, anticipated reaction, and what actions can be taken to improve its reaction. Examine each political group to see whose vanity will expand and whose will be reduced; who will grow in power and who will shrink in power; whose budget will escalate and whose will contract; whose security will be enhanced and whose will be jeopardized; whose mental model will be validated and whose will be rejected; whose counsel will be sought and whose ignored; whose fortune will rise and whose will fall; whose competitive position will be increased and whose will be reduced; whose glory will become known and whose will be negated. In this manner, you will be able to foresee who will tentatively be an ally of change and who will resist. The likelihood of success can thereby be judged in advance.

Politics is an extremely important but often overlooked reason for the development of convincing arguments. A truth, once established by proof, does not gain added certainty by the amount of consent by others, nor does it lose validity by the quantity of dissent. To overcome politics and the inertia to action it causes,

Table 4.10 Political Analysis

STRATEGIC MOVES	POLITICAL GROUPS (PG)			
	PG1 Basis of political agenda	PG2 Basis of political agenda	PG3 Basis of political agenda	PG4 basis of political agenda
Move 1	1. Reasons for support 2. Reasons for resistance 3. Actions to obtain support	1. Reasons for support 2. Reasons for resistance 3. Actions to obtain support	1. Reasons for support 2. Reasons for resistance 3. Actions to obtain support	1. Reasons for support 2. Reasons for resistance 3. Actions to obtain support
Move 2	1. Reasons for support 2. Reasons for resistance 3. Actions to obtain support	1. Reasons for support 2. Reasons for resistance 3. Actions to obtain support	1. Reasons for support 2. Reasons for resistance 3. Actions to obtain support	1. Reasons for support 2. Reasons for resistance 3. Actions to obtain support
Move N	1. Reasons for support 2. Reasons for resistance 3. Actions to obtain support	1. Reasons for support 2. Reasons for resistance 3. Actions to obtain support	1. Reasons for support 2. Reasons for resistance 3. Actions to obtain support	1. Reasons for support 2. Reasons for resistance 3. Actions to obtain support

persuasive arguments that transcend the ability of the factions to resist must be developed. It is kinder to overwhelm them with the need for change when change can still be managed in a prevenient manner than to debate until a point of crisis change is reached and everyone, finally but too late, appreciates the need.

Heritage

A barrier, second only to organizational politics, is the monopolistic mind-set and behaviors of the IT staff. Game theorists have developed a diagramming technique called a "payoff matrix" to illustrate the risk and reward payoffs for alternative actions and consequences. Table 4.11 shows a payoff matrix for introducing new technology in an organization that has prospered under little competition and control of all (almost all) IT resources. The columns depict behaviors, the rows depict possible consequences, and the cells depict the payoff (reward) for each intersection.

The individual game players, having been raised in a culture that does not reward risk, quickly conclude the following:

- There is little to gain and much to lose through entrepreneurship.
- A "minimax" (minimize the maximum possible loss) strategy, while not exciting, results in a satisfactory payoff.

Game players will consequently almost always choose slow and conservative introduction as the optimum behavior. Although this worked while the IT organization had a hegemony over IT resources, as more and more companies move to a free-market system, this risk and reward system is incompatible with being a viable competitor.

The change agent is thus confronted with a compound barrier:

- The agent must deal with a technology revolution that is obsoleting the competencies of the IT staff, a staff whose frozen mental model doesn't believe it.
- The change agent must deal with an embedded behavioral system that rewards noncompetitive behaviors.

Nobody said it would be easy.

Table 4.11 Payoff Matrix

POSSIBLE CONSEQUENCES	NEW TECHNOLOGY INTRODUCTION STYLE	
	Slow/conservative	**Entrepreneurship**
No problems	+10	+10
Problems	-10	-100

Other Barriers

There are two other barriers to success that deserve special attention; they are the overwhelming desire of management to simplify and the problem of "worthiness."

Simplification. While understandable, the desire to simplify is often taken to extremes. Some have suggested that had Einstein worked for corporate America, his famous formula, $E = MC^2$, would have been repackaged as $E = M + C$ because addition is so much simpler for everyone to understand than are multiplication and exponentiation. This is an exaggeration, but it does make the point. Concepts, actions, and consequences should be simplified only to the point where the essence is not compromised. If one is going to engage in sophisticated strategy, a community level of understanding must be achieved above the lowest common denominator.

The demand to simplify strategy so that it is understandable by all, without any instruction in its fundamentals, trivializes it. Few would be expected to sysgen an operating system, repair a corrupted database, or interpret a memory dump without proper training, apprenticeship, tutoring, and graduated experience. Distinct ideas, perspectives, and skills surround strategy, just like any other discipline. Shouldn't the process that commands all the other processes insist on excellence?

. . . The universe cannot be understood unless one first learns to comprehend the language of mathematics, and its characters are triangles, circles, and other geometric figures without which it is not humanly possible to understand a single word of it.

Galileo, The Assayer

The universe is written in the dialect of mathematics. Strategy, likewise, has its own distinct dialect that must be comprehended to effectively develop, communicate, and execute strategic programs.

Worthiness. To develop strategies that are deep and far-reaching, the management community must be worthy—that is, they must be literate in the ways of strategy. A management team uneducated in strategic planning will block initiatives because they don't understand the underlying frameworks that rationalize the actions. The community must raise themselves to be worthy of more than tactical muddling through, which always equates to taking too long and costing too much. The benefits of strategic planning are commensurate with, and proportional to, the state of preparation. Preparation effects a positive change in the ability of the management team to participate in and understand the consequences of the strategy process. Any benefits to be accrued through strategic planning are therefore contingent on the management team's achieving the requisite state of literacy, preparation, and worthiness.

To achieve mastery of a discipline, preparation is either required or it is not. If it is not required and one engages in preparation, then one wastes time and effort; the activity of preparation is superfluous. It is superfluous because no benefit is derived from its execution. If it is required and one does not engage in it, then one commits a hoax. A hoax is committed because one proceeds with the persona of knowledge and skill while, in reality, one does not even have the ability of a novice. Strategy belongs to the class of disciplines that require preparation.

Change Plan Structure

A change plan consists of *change objectives*, which define what is to be accomplished, and *change moves*, which define the actions to be taken to achieve the change objectives. Table 4.12 and Table 4.13 summarize the elements that compose each.

Table 4.12 Change Objectives

CHANGE OBJECTIVE ATTRIBUTE	DEFINITION
Objective	A precise and concise statement of the objective
Date	By when the objective is to be achieved
Measure	The measurement(s) to be used to assess whether the objective has been accomplished

Table 4.13 Change Moves

CHANGE MOVE ATTRIBUTE	DEFINITION
Move	A brief and clear statement of the action
Description	A few paragraphs of elaboration of the action
Owner	The individual in the organization responsible for making the action happen
Champion	The executive in the organization responsible for assisting the owner
Priority	Relative importance of the action
Measurement	The way to measure that the action has been completed
Date	The date by which the action is to be concluded
Implementation program parameters	Rules, guidelines, and boundaries that the implementation owner should follow in implementing the action

Summary

Machiavelli (*The Prince*) understood best the challenge of being a change agent:

> *It should be borne in mind that there is nothing more difficult to handle nor more doubtful of success, and more dangerous to carry through than initiating change. The innovator makes enemies of all those who prospered under the old order, and only lukewarm support is forthcoming from those who would prosper under the new. Their support is lukewarm partly from fear of their adversaries, who have the existing laws on their side, and partly because men are generally incredulous, never really trusting new things unless they have tested them by experience. In consequence, those who oppose the changes attack vigorously and the defense made by the others is only lukewarm.*

Jack Welch, the CEO of General Electric, provides the circa-1990s version of Machiavelli's insight in his book when he says:

> *Change has no constituency. People like the* status quo. *They like the way it was.*

Nothing is harder than being a change agent. The only thing harder than getting a person with a frozen mental model to accept a new idea is to get him or her to give up the old idea. Every change agent shares the moment of horrific realization when he or she knows what needs to be done but nobody cares. Imagine the ambivalent organization, hesitant and resistant, approaching the edge of a monstrously deep and wide canyon. Across the precipice is the objective, the desired future state of the organization. Imagine then, beyond the obstacles of frozen mental models, beyond the obstacles of organizational politics, beyond the obstacles of simplicity and unworthiness, beyond the obstacles of disincentive payoff matrices, and beyond the obstacles of delusional self-satisfaction rests a frail bridge that crosses the abyss, the bridge of change, and you are its sole guardian. Nothing is harder.

Commitment Plan

A *commitment plan* is a specific set of actions taken to establish creditability. A commitment plan is a set of actions designed to alter the beliefs, actions, and behaviors of others to motivate desired behaviors. You will wish to devise a commitment plan that will push the organization to voluntarily and enthusiastically reposition itself in harmony with the strategic plan.

It is unfortunate, but the reality is that many management teams have little credibility with the mass of workers. Each year, new programs are announced with tremendous fanfare, and each year they die a slow death. The staff, understandingly jaded and cynical, reacts with a predictable maxim: "This too shall pass." They suspect that management believes deeply in little and is committed to less. Because of this and the reality that little is accomplished without the endorsement and efforts of all the people, the inclusion of a commitment plan to provide and sustain credibility in an expedient world is a necessary part of the plan to ease the implementation effort. The commitment plan explains how, both symbolically and substantively, management will convince the corporate community that objectives will be pursued to realization—that this time there will be staying power.

The method for developing a powerful commitment plan was explained in the essay, "Commitment in Information Technology Strategy" in Chapter 2, "Managing IT for Competitive Advantage," and will not be repeated here. It is strongly suggested that you do not leave commitment to chance and that you carefully design building and sustaining commitment into your plans. Strategists who do not get commitment will see their strategies go nowhere.

Summary

Strategy is the most intellectually stimulating part of the strategic development process. With few formal methods of assistance, you are confronted with the crafting of strategy statements, future positions, objectives, and moves. Because it is not easy, when it is well done it offers the basis for building advantage. Because "much strategy prevails over little strategy," the strategically focused organization is well rewarded. How else should we expect it to be?

Figure 4.18 provides a summary "big picture" of the strategy step. It should be understood as follows:

- The assessment step culminates with the generation of a set of conclusions that itemize strategic imperatives for management attention.

- A desired future state is defined for the business. It brings the business closer to its strategic intent.

- Strategy statements and objectives are defined; they explicitly list what is to be accomplished.

- Strategic moves are defined that itemize the ways to achieve the objectives.

- The strategic moves are executed in the next step of the planning process, execution.

The change management plan and the commitment plan posture the strategy for success.

The strategy step, as we have presented it, is in the form of a process model. Consequently, the outputs are organized by process type—that is, all the positions, then all the objectives, and finally all the strategic moves. Some would prefer a functional presentation by strategic area. In this case, you would just

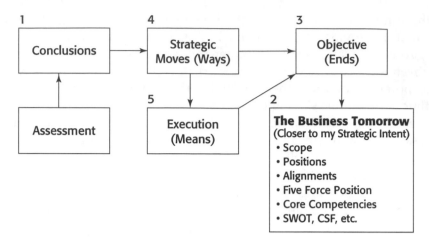

Figure 4.18   Strategy summary.

sort the positions, objectives, and strategic moves and arrange them by strategic area: (market position, market objectives, market strategic moves), (human resource position, human resource objectives, human resource strategic moves), and (core competency position, core competency objectives, core competency strategic moves).

Now, a business must choose either to stay at rest or to move. If it chooses to stay at rest and its trading partners continue to evolve, then it will become increasingly irrelevant. *Hibernation* is a strategy of planned decline through complacency. If it chooses to move, then there are four alternatives:

- It can define its strategic moves but not its objectives. In this case, anyone's and everyone's objectives are equal, and the strategy is purposeless.

- It can define its objectives but not its strategic moves. In this case, it leaves realization to the chance congruence of each organizational entity, and the strategy is futile.

- It can define neither its objectives nor its strategic moves. In this case, it abrogates its responsibility of leadership, participates in a hoax, and leaves the strategy to divine providence.

- It can define both its objectives and its strategic moves. In this case it provides strategic leadership.

Movement requires a first mover, and the first mover is strategy.

Objectives and strategic moves, however, are not alone sufficient. A strategist must overcome the challenges of lack of commitment and resistance to change. Like Odysseus in Homer's *Odyssey*, who had to navigate between the twofold horrors of Scylla and Charybdis, the strategy must navigate between failure because of lack of commitment and failure because of resistance to change. A whole strategy must include a change management plan and a commitment plan.

The question is asked: Is there the notion of a perfect strategy? If your strategic plan can command fortune rather than making you the victim of times and circumstances, then your strategy is perfect. What could be a greater accomplishment than being immune to misfortune and being assured that you can avert ruin.

Those who believe in a rational approach to strategy formulation do not believe that repeated successes are due to good fortune, the roll of the dice, Faustian pacts with the devil, magical incantations, prayer, or wishful thinking. Success is the consequence of strategy, which makes the success of execution inescapable and anticlimactic. Success is the consequence of creating a perfect score for the corporate orchestra to play—each note perfect unto itself and in perfect harmony with all others. In summary:

> *The successes of the IT organization may only be as grand as the foundation of strategy on which they are built. Strategy may be of two kinds; it may be shallow and nearsighted, or it may be deep and far-reaching. When it is shallow and nearsighted, all successes are temporary and isolated. This is because the foundation has been mixed with strategy that is weak and hollow. The foundation inevitably cracks and buckles under the load. When the strategy is deep and far-reaching, then successes compound and support each other. This is because the foundation has been mixed with strategy that is holistic and has the strength to support the business. The foundation easily holds the load. The priority of IT management is therefore obvious. The first priority of management is the mastery, internalization, and application of strategy, and then, and only then, the mastery and exploitation of IT technology. This is the only path to building, sustaining, and compounding competitive advantage through IT. There is no other path.*

Such is the primary and enduring relationship between strategy and IT.

Notes

1. *Strategy* by B. H. Liddell-Hart (Meridian Books, 1991).

2. *Application Prototyping: A Requirements Definition Strategy for the 80s* by Bernard Boar (New York: John Wiley & Sons, Inc., 1984).

3. *The Fifth Decipline* by P. Senge (Doubleday, 1994).

CHAPTER 5

Execution

The purpose of this chapter is to explain the execution step of the strategic planning process. *Execution* is the act of putting the plan into motion. Strategies are operationalized through implementation programs under the leadership of a strategy owner and the sponsorship of a strategy champion. Figure 5.1 is an enlargement of the execution step. Execution confronts the strategy owners and champions with a wide assortment of problems, including the following:

- Inadequate project management skills
- Discovery of unforeseen problems
- Lack of organizational commitment
- Lack of executive leadership
- Churning strategy
- Resistance to change
- Demands for immediate results
- Cost containment efforts

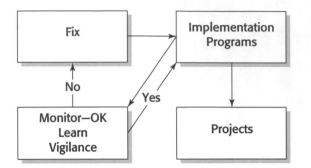

Figure 5.1   The execution step puts the plan into motion.

Execution can be anticipated to be extremely difficult, or it can be approached as a creative opportunity to imagineer, improvise, experiment, and prototype to discover the best way to accomplish strategic moves.

Execution Success

The success of the execution step must be positioned prior to beginning it.

A victorious army first wins and then seeks battle, a defeated army first battles and then seeks victory.

Sun Tzu, The Art of War

Success is designed and prepared for by the following:

- A thoughtful commitment plan
- A fully developed change management plan
- The selection of able strategy owners and champions
- The design of a human resource architecture that stimulates desired behaviors
- Wide strategy development participation (covered in Chapter 7, "Administration")
- Project management training and support
- A professional strategic planning process that earns the organization's respect
- A strategic intent worthy of extended individual effort, excitement, and commitment
- A "deep and far-reaching strategy" that captures the imagination of the staff

- The design of an internal IT economy that motivates desired behaviors and decision making
- A well-designed customer satisfaction measurement system

Without such preparations, it is not surprising that the execution step can turn into a nightmare. Remember the admonition of Machiavelli, "There is nothing more difficult or doubtful of success." The depth and breadth of preparation performed in the prior steps determine the success of the execution step.

Implementation Programs and Projects

Implementation programs are the master projects to implement the strategy. Implementation owners develop tactical projects to operationalize the moves within the boundaries defined by the implementation program parameters. Each program is divided into manageable subprojects. Projects strive to achieve goals. Implementation programs and projects are done using the tools of professional project management for which there exists an abundant and rich literature.

As would be expected, everyone is anxious for rapid results. When actions are independent, a matrix such as the one shown in the top part of Figure 5.2 can be used to order projects. For interdependent actions (the most common type), PERT charts such as the example at the bottom of Figure 5.2 must be used to evaluate dependencies for ordering.

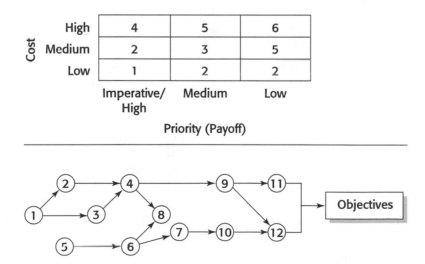

Figure 5.2 Implementation.

Although implementation programs are divided between owners and champions and partitioned into projects, the implementation should be conceptualized as one unified grand project. Collaboration, interproject coordination, and cooperation are required for the collective success of the individual efforts.

Execution is often cited as the most difficult step of the strategy process. Failures of strategy are routinely attributed to poor project management. I do not share this view. Undoubtedly the mechanics of project management can be poorly executed, but the ability of the project managers to execute implementation programs is preordained during the strategy step by the design of the internal IT economy, the design of the human resource architecture, the assignment of owners and champions, the customer satisfaction measurement system, the commitment plan, and the change management plan. The etiology of execution failure is most often due to failures in the strategic plan, not to incompetent project management. The six items create an implementation environment on which change agents can effect change. Given what has been learned about frozen mental models, organizational politics, management fickleness, and payoff matrices, assigning the success—or failure—of execution to the discipline of project management is faulty.

Strategy execution is won or lost based on the depth, insight, and foresight of the strategic plan, not the procedures of project management. The success of execution can be foretold at the completion of the strategy step. Project management inadequacies are relatively easy to correct. It is the prepositioning for success that is the challenge.

Monitoring, Learning, and Vigilance

Monitoring is the periodic formal review of the projects to assess progress. Actions as well as tactics must be revised, adapted, and tuned based on real-world experience. One can only be endlessly amused at the all-too-human but vain efforts of bowlers to redirect their bowling balls once they have been thrown. As the ball rolls down the alley, the bowler jumps up and down and pushes the air in front of his or her face with his or her hands in a futile attempt to redirect the ball's projection. Fortunately, this is not the case with the monitoring of implementation programs. By careful and regular review, purposeful actions can be taken to meaningfully redirect the course of our strategies to be in accord with evolving times and circumstances. Monitoring, however, must go beyond conventional project management reviews. We are equally concerned with learning and vigilance.

By *learning* we mean actively seeking lessons from the practical experiences and incorporating those lessons into processes and programs. The day-to-day experiences of the project teams are some of the best sources for gaining insight into how to improve the strategy process. Learning answers the question, "What can be done in the assessment and strategy steps of the process to improve and simplify the execution step next time?"

Vigilance is continual proactive scanning of the environment for events that may require a real-time strategic assessment and response. The strategic planning model presented is a "calendar model." Unfortunately, the world does not always choose to evolve in synchronization with a given planning schedule. One must be vigilant to recognize unforeseen events that may change plans. The process that deals with unanticipated events of a strategic nature is referred to as *Dynamics Issues Management*.

The need for vigilance raises an important question: Is the calendar model a valid approach, or must strategy development be continuous (dynamic and real-time)? A response to this is as follows:

- Strategy is by definition forward-looking.

- Strategy, by definition, deals with the mega-issues. Mega-issues are long-term issues.

- Strategists must anticipate.

- Strategic implementation programs may take years to realize. Sustainable competitive advantage, new organizational cultures, world-class capabilities, and new core competencies are not developed overnight.

- Large organizations cannot change fundamental directions every day and overnight. The massive logistical issues make it impossible.

- If all strategy is dynamic, the organization will quickly learn the game and wait for the next change.

- Given the time to develop, productize, and diffuse new technologies, overall direction should be reasonably foreseeable. What state-of-the-art or state-of-the-market technology, now available, was not observable on the horizon five years ago? What technology, which will be available five years from now, is not currently being speculated about or in development or productization at some research lab or product house? Products are not created by spontaneous combustion.

- If it is necessary to continually change course, either one needs new strategists or the situation is so chaotic (in turbulent transition) that one must proceed tactically without strategy.

- Tactics, the heart of the implementation programs, provide an adaptable and fluid vehicle to deal with environmental changes.

- Pivot positions infuse the strategy with flexibility.

- A primary objective of strategy should be to develop a highly adaptive and maneuverable business so that the day-to-day business processes can maintain a strategic fit with the environment.

Consider what the notion of "real-time strategy" really means. A *real-time system* typically consists of two components: a regulatory (controlling) component, which monitors and controls, and a regulated (controlled) component, which is monitored and controlled. Either periodically or when driven by events, the regulatory component evaluates the situation and sends corrective and adaptive instructions to the regulated component. The regulated component adjusts its state accordingly, and the cycle continues indefinitely.

Strategy, as has been defined (strategy statements, objectives, strategic moves, change management plan, and commitment plan), is the corporate regulatory agent. The business is the regulated component. Now, if the analogy is followed, real-time strategy would require that as the strategy is event-driven reformulated, the business, the regulated component, could respond to a continual stream of strategic change messages—a stream of messages dictating major redirections. Is this doable or desirable? Is this not both practically

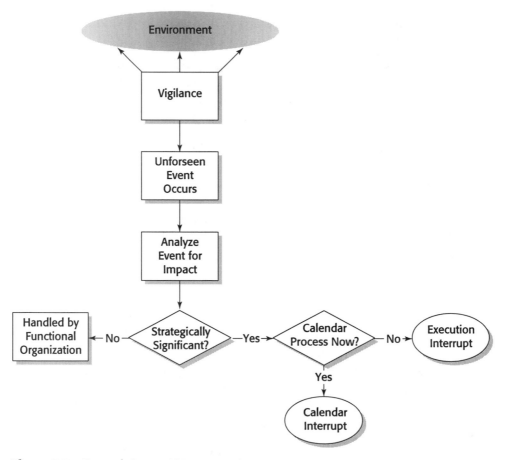

Figure 5.3   Dynamic Issues Management.

impossible and definitionally incorrect? Strategy is supposed to be "deep and far-reaching," not "shallow and nearsighted." It is therefore asserted that the calendar model as a strategy anchor is valid, but unanticipated events of significance do occur, and they must be dealt with.

An unforeseen event of strategic import is an event that was not anticipated, was grossly incorrectly anticipated, or was anticipated and will not occur. Also, a change may occur in the directives and assumptions received or in the business scope *and* the event is of strategic significance. To be of strategic significance, the event alone or in collaboration with other events must have the potential to materially alter a strategic position. These events are discovered through vigilance.

The process used to manage unforeseen strategic events is called *Dynamic Issues Management*. Figure 5.3 is an umbrella illustration of the process. Nonstrategic events are directed to the appropriate functional organization for action. The method of handling strategic events is determined by whether one is in the strategic planning stage (calendar interrupt) or the execution stage (execution interrupt).

A calendar interrupt occurs when an unforeseen event happens during the current assessment or strategy step of the process (see Figure 5.4). Because this type of interrupt occurs during plan development, it can be handled fairly smoothly, as illustrated in Figure 5.4. An execution interrupt occurs when an unforeseen event happens during the execution step (see Figure 5.5). If the interrupt does not alter the plan or if handling it can wait, the event is incor-

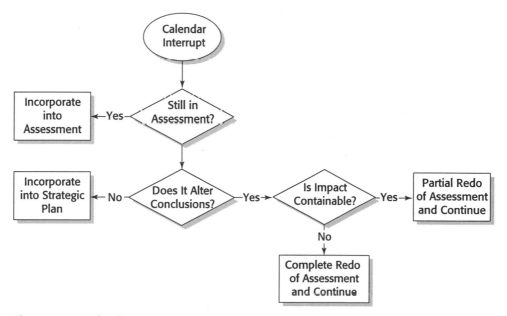

Figure 5.4   Calendar Interrupt.

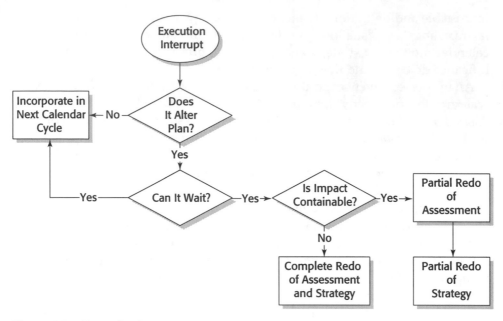

Figure 5.5 Execution Interrupt.

porated into the next planning cycle. Otherwise, a partial or, in rare cases, a complete redo of the strategic plan is dictated.

When Dynamics Issues Management is included as part of the strategic planning process, a balance is achieved in the need for dealing with both strategy anchoring and environmental dynamics. The notion of a purely real-time strategy would whipsaw any large business. Conversely, you cannot stop the world until the time is convenient for your next planning cycle. The calendar process provides the necessary baseline of strategy. The dynamic process allows for incorporating new information when it appears. Together all the strategic planning needs are met. While dynamic issues have to be dealt with expeditiously, they must also be analyzed within the context of the whole business system for impact, and response actions must be disciplined or else latent disorder will be created.

Summary

Execution is strategy in motion—the directed mobilization of resources toward a defined end. Through the use of Dynamic Issues Management, execution adapts the strategy to unforeseen strategic events. Tactics handle day-to-day melding of the implementation programs with the ever-shifting environment. Figure 5.6 summarizes the essence of the execution step. Execu-

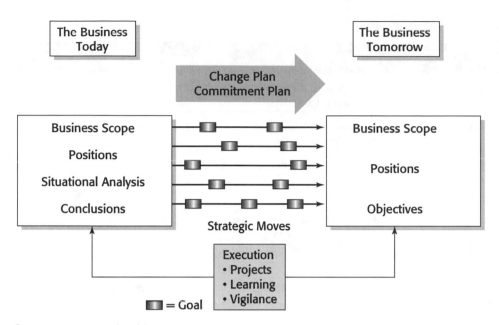

Figure 5.6 Execution is movement.

tion is the project management, monitoring, and vigilance required to move a business from the business of today to the business of tomorrow. Strategic moves are executed in parallel to achieve multiple objectives. On the path to reaching the objectives, strategic moves achieve serial goals. Execution is the process of organizational transformation—the transformation of the future business from a state of potentiality to a state of actuality.

Project management is the primary tactical tool of execution. The strategic component of execution occurs in the prior strategy step. Implementation managers dispersed throughout the organization do not have the ability of a fairy tale Rumplestilskin to weave gold out of straw; they cannot unilaterally overcome deeply embedded organization infrastructure obstacles. Eliminating such obstacles is the responsibility of the strategy team by virtue of the change plan, commitment plan, customer satisfaction measurement system, economy design, human resource architecture design, and assignment of "move" owners and champions. Table 5.1 summarizes why these items are so cardinal to positioning for execution success. An implementation phrase characterized by implementation owners thrashing wildly about in a tar pit of problems is most often a sign of poorly developed strategy, not poor project management. It is a sign that all efforts to implement it will be in vain.

The design of the internal economy, the measurement system, and the human resource architecture are critically important to encouraging cooperation because, unlike most other things, they are not easily ignored. The reac-

Table 5.1   Execution Enablers

EXECUTION ENABLER	WHY CARDINAL	PENALTY FOR ABSENCE
Change plan	Anticipate and minimize resistance to change	Overt and covert resistance to change
Commitment plan	Demonstrate management commitment to strategy	Collective attitude that "this too shall pass"
Customer satisfaction measurement system	People pay attention to what they are measured on	Measurement system that is not linked to meeting customer satisfiers—gross misalignment
Economy design	Economic system pushes feel of competition throughout organization and prompts competitive reactions	Monopolist behaviors
Human resource architecture	Convert values into desired behaviors	Misalignment of behaviors with strategy
Selection of "move" owners and champions	Both symbolic and substantive message of importance of strategy	Both symbolic and substantive message of unimportance of strategy

tion of obstructionists is often benign neglect; they do not directly challenge the strategy, they just simply ignore it, hoping it will wither away. It is much more difficult to ignore a new zero-based budgeting system where product teams, at a level of detail they select, negotiate budgets. It is difficult to ignore customer satisfaction measurements that are used to monitor your processes. It is difficult to ignore new salary and bonus systems that are directly linked to budgetary goals and customer satisfaction measurements. If you are really committed to change, you must use as the spearhead those things that get and keep everyone's attention. Usually, those things have a strong and personal financial attribute.

In considering the character of execution, one should always remember the following three points:

- Project management, the management process of strategy implementation, is a strategic core competency. It is the tool for the coherent management of movement, learning, vigilance, and adaptation.
- Execution is an integral component of strategic planning. It is a nondivisible part of the strategic planning triad of assessment, strategy, and execution. Assessment is the antecedent of strategy, strategy is the antecedent of execution, and execution is the antecedent of assessment.

The essence of something includes those properties of it that cannot be removed without its losing its identity. All three—assessment, strategy, and execution—compose the essence of strategic planning and must be understood as a unity of one. It is therefore meaningless to discuss strategic planning without the intention of execution, and it is impossible to execute strategy without its being preceded (whether formally or informally) by assessment and strategy design.

It is not uncommon to attend strategic planning seminars and hear speakers talk about the new millennium being "the era of transition from planning to execution." What are they babbling about?

Some rulers are fond of words but do not transfer them into deeds.

Sun Tzu, The Art of War

Up until now, could management engage in magical thinking, believing that simply writing down strategies equated to making them happen? Conversely, do actions now arise spontaneously without forethought? The only rational approach to strategic planning is to consider the three steps as sharing a unity, which demands that each be executed in return. Each step has been and always will be necessary because the three steps share the same essence.

- Execution is "the battle." As taught by Sun Tzu, it is won or lost before the actual engagement, based on how deep and far-reaching your strategy is.

Such is the nature of execution.

CHAPTER 6

Quality Control

The purpose of this chapter is to provide a robust set of tools that can be used to improve the quality of the assessment and strategy steps of the strategic planning process. Quality is not appended at the end of the process as an afterthought, nor does a separate group do it. Quality control is interleaved throughout the process and is as important a responsibility for the strategy team as all other activities.

Infusing quality into the planning process will be explained from three perspectives:

Logical relationship checks. This section explains a set of checks that can be applied to ensure the logical consistency of the plan.

Completeness checks. This section explains a set of checks that can be applied to ensure that the strategy is comprehensive.

Correctness checks. This section explains a set of techniques that can be used to evaluate the value and validity of the strategy.

Together, the three types of checks provide a system for evaluating the strategy. The logical checks ensure that the logical flow of the strategy is correct (that is, it is a valid format). The completeness checks ensure that "all the bases" have been covered. The correctness checks answer the bottom line question: Is it good strategy?

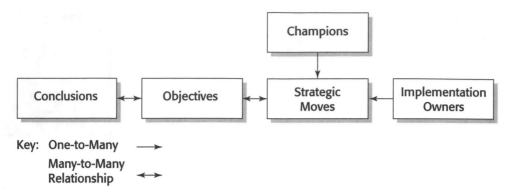

Key: One-to-Many $\longrightarrow$
Many-to-Many
Relationship $\longleftrightarrow$

Figure 6.1   Logical relationship checks.

Logical Relationship Checks

Logical relationship checks provide a way to trace the forward and backward logical flow of the strategic move. These checks answer the question: Is the strategy structurally sound? Figure 6.1 provides the overall framework for tracing logical validity. It may be understood as follows:

- A conclusion is addressed through multiple objectives. An objective meets the needs of multiple conclusions.
- An objective is realized through multiple strategic moves. A strategic move enables the realization of multiple objectives.
- A strategic move has one and only one owner. An owner may own multiple strategic moves.
- A strategic move has one and only one champion. A champion may champion multiple strategic moves.

Figure 6.2 illustrates a forward and backward trace.
The logic may be traced forward as follows:

1. Conclusion "a" is addressed by objectives "b" and "c."
2. Objective "b" is realized through strategic moves "d" and "e."
3. Objective "c" is realized through strategic moves "e" and "f."
4. Strategic move "d" is owned by owner "g" and championed by champion "h."
5. Strategic move "e" is owned by owner "i" and championed by champion "j."
6. Strategic move "f" is owned by owner "g" and championed by champion "j."

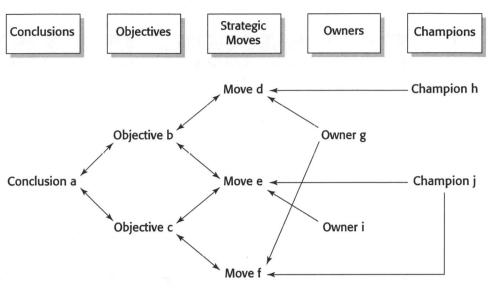

Figure 6.2 Logical relationship example.

A partial backward trace would be as follows:

1. Champion "j" champions strategic move "f," which is owned by owner "g."

2. Strategic move "f" is used to realize objective "c."

3. Objective "c" addresses the problems identified in conclusion "a."

The analysis of the relationships is managed through four matrices as follows: conclusion/objective check, objectives/strategic move check, owner/strategic move check, and champion/strategic moves check.

Conclusion/Objective Check

Conclusions are matrixed against strategy statements. In Table 6.1 an "x" in a cell indicates that the strategy statement address the requirements of the conclusion. All strategy statements must support at least one conclusion. This check may be performed once strategy statements have been formulated

Objectives/Strategic Move Check

Objectives are matrixed against strategic moves. In Table 6.2 an "x" in a cell indicates that the selected objective is realized through the corresponding strategic move. All objectives must have at least one enabling strategic move. This check may be performed once strategic moves have been formulated.

Table 6.1 Conclusion/Objective Check

OBJECTIVES	CONCLUSIONS				
	Conclusion 1	Conclusion 2	Conclusion 3	Conclusion 4	Conclusion N
Strategy Statement 1					
Strategy Statement 2					
Strategy Statement 3					
Strategy Statement 4					
Strategy Statement n					

Owner/strategic moves check owners are matrixed against strategic moves. In Table 6.3 an "x" in a cell indicates that the designated owner owns the corresponding strategic move. Each strategic move must have one and only one owner. This check may be done once strategic moves have been formulated. This check may also be used to provide an owner's view of the strategic moves, which will assist in assessing whether ownership is balanced and if it has been properly assigned.

Table 6.2 Objectives/Strategic Move Check

OBJECTIVES	STRATEGIC MOVES				
	Strategic Move 1	Strategic Move 2	Strategic Move 3	Strategic Move 4	Strategic Move N
Objective 1					
Objective 2					
Objective 3					
Objective 4					
Objective N					

Table 6.3   Owner/Strategic Move Check

OWNERS	STRATEGIC MOVES				
	Strategic Move 1	**Strategic Move 2**	**Strategic Move 3**	**Strategic Move 4**	**Strategic Move N**
Owner 1					
Owner 2					
Owner 3					
Owner 4					
Owner N					

Champion/strategic moves check champions are matrixed against strategic moves. In Table 6.4 an "x" in a cell indicates that the designated champion supports the corresponding strategic move. Each strategic move must have one and only one champion. This check may be done once strategic moves have been formulated. This check may also be used to provide a champion view of the strategic moves that will assist in assessing whether championship is balanced and if it has been properly assigned.

Though not illustrated, checks similar to those shown in Tables 6.2, 6.3, and 6.4 may be done to ensure the logical correctness of both the commitment plan and the change management plan.

Logical checks confirm validity of a strategic move structure, but they do not ensure that a strategic move is complete or correct. For these items, other checks are required.

Table 6.4   Champion/Strategic Move Check

CHAMPIONS	STRATEGIC MOVES				
	Strategic Move 1	**Strategic Move 2**	**Strategic Move 3**	**Strategic Move 4**	**Strategic Move N**
Champion 1					
Champion 2					
Champion 3					
Champion 4					
Champion N					

Completeness Checks

Completeness checks are used to test the plan for completeness; *complete* means that all areas of importance have been considered. This is accomplished through a series of analytical techniques as follows: strategic areas check, business P's check, 7 "S" check, strategic intent check, time-line check, directives/assumptions check, and key findings check.

Strategic Areas Check

The business areas of strategic import are matrixed against the strategy statements. In Table 6.5 an "x" in a cell indicates that the strategy statement relates to the corresponding strategic area. Strategic areas with no checks should be reviewed. This check may be performed once objectives have been formulated.

Business P's Check

The business P's are the heart of a marketing mix. The traditional P's are these:

Product. The product or service offered.

Price. The amount of money customers have to pay to obtain the product.

Place. The activities that make the product available to the marketplace.

Promotion. The activities that communicate the merits of the product to the marketplace.

Table 6.5 Strategic Areas Check

OBJECTIVES	STRATEGIC AREAS				
	Markets	**Competition**	**Structure**	**Competencies**	**Etc.**
Strategy Statement 1					
Strategy Statement 2					
Strategy Statement 3					
Strategy Statement 4					
Strategy Statement n					

Table 6.6 Business P's Check

BUSINESS P'S	STRATEGIC MOVES				
	Strategic Move 1	**Strategic Move 2**	**Strategic Move 3**	**Strategic Move 4**	**Strategic Move N**
Product					
Promotion					
Place					
Price					
People					
Process					

Because the business P's summarize critical elements of market success, we check the plan to ensure that they are covered. We extend the traditional business P's with two new P's equally important to market success:

People. The human resource policies to promote a winning team.

Process. The business processes that enable servicing the customer.

The business P's are matrixed against the strategic moves. In Table 6.6 an "x" in a cell indicates that the strategic move affects the related business P. Business P's for which no strategic moves exist should be investigated. This check may be done once strategic moves have been formulated.

7 "S" Check

The 7 "S" model asserts that strategic alignment means developing a strategic fit between strategy and structure, style, systems, staff, skills, and shared values. The 7 "S" model provides a check for alignment. As shown in Table 6.7, the strategic moves are matrixed with the 7 "S." In Table 6.7 an "x" in a cell indicates that the strategic move affects that corresponding "S." The resulting matrix should be analyzed from the 7 "S" perspective. Are all the 7 "S" covered? Are they still in alignment? This check may be done once strategic moves have been formulated.

Strategic Intent (Vision) Check

Strategy statements are matrixed against the strategic intent. In Table 6.8 the intersection is populated with an explanation of how the strategy statement contributes to realization of the strategic intent. Strategy statements that don't contribute to this end should be carefully reviewed.

Table 6.7   7 "S" Check

7 "S"	STRATEGIC MOVES				
	Strategic Move 1	**Strategic Move 2**	**Strategic Move 3**	**Strategic Move 4**	**Strategic Move N**
Structure					
Style					
Systems					
Staff					
Skills					
Shared Values					

Time-Line Check

Completion dates for objectives, goals, and strategic moves are plotted on a shared time-line, shown in Figure 6.3. Are the completion dates doable? Do they distribute across the planning horizon? This check may be done once strategic moves have been formulated.

Directives/Assumptions Check

Directives and assumptions provided by the higher-level organizational authority are matrixed with the strategic moves. In Table 6.9 an "x" in a cell indicates that the strategic move *violates* the directive.

Table 6.8   Strategic Intent Check

STRATEGY STATEMENT	STRATEGIC INTENT
Strategy Statement 1	
Strategy Statement 2	
Strategy Statement 3	
Strategy Statement 4	
Strategy Statement n	

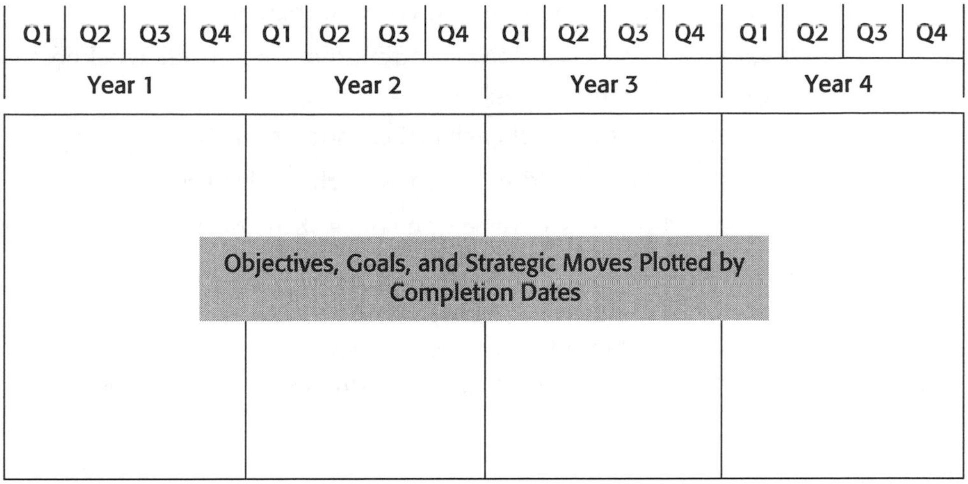

Q1	Q2	Q3	Q4	Q1	Q2	Q3	Q4	Q1	Q2	Q3	Q4	Q1	Q2	Q3	Q4
Year 1				Year 2				Year 3				Year 4			

Objectives, Goals, and Strategic Moves Plotted by Completion Dates

Figure 6.3 Time-line check.

Key Findings Check

As previously explained, key findings are information such as core competencies, critical success factors, Five Force drivers, and capabilities. These are items of strategic importance to success. One must ask questions such as these:

- Have we taken actions to build SCA?
- Have we taken actions to reposition the Five Force drivers more favorably?
- Have we taken actions to nourish our strategic capabilities?

Table 6.9 Directives/Assumptions Check

DIRECTIVES/ ASSUMPTIONS D/A	STRATEGIC MOVES				
	Strategic Move 1	**Strategic Move 2**	**Strategic Move 3**	**Strategic Move 4**	**Strategic Move N**
D/A 1					
D/A 2					
D/A 3					
D/A 4					
D/A 5					
D/A N					

- Have we taken actions to nourish our core competencies?
- Have we taken actions to exploit our strengths, correct our weaknesses, deflect threats, and exploit opportunities?
- Have we taken actions to meet each critical success factor?
- Have we taken actions to address our value-chain drivers?
- If not, why not? This check may be done once strategic moves have been formulated.

Completeness checks are beneficial because they view the strategic moves through multiple lenses. They identify possible shortcomings or incompleteness, which may be visible only when viewed from a sectarian perspective.

Correctness Checks

Correctness checks are used as a means to assess the absolute value of the strategy. While logical checks ensure that the format of the strategy is valid and the completeness checks ensure that the strategy is comprehensive, correctness checks address this bottom-line question: Is this a good strategy for the business? If you achieve it, do you realize a noble cause or have you engaged in a community delusion, and will you find yourself irrelevant to customers? Five approaches to be used in assessing correctness are as follows: devil's advocacy, expert review, external perspectives check, simulations, and valuation check.

Devil's Advocacy

Devil's advocacy is a method wherein a distinct and separate team is formed to critique the strategy aggressively. This devil's advocacy team has the mission to question all aspects of the plan and *propose alternatives*. Devil's advocacy results in heated debates and may get out of hand if people-sensitivity issues are not well managed. Nevertheless, many of the stakeholders may review the strategy only superficially (time constraints, immediate crises, etc.). A focused devil's advocacy team may discover errors that can be corrected prior to execution. Devil's advocacy may be done at the completion of assessment or the strategy step.

Expert Review

Expert review is the hiring of independent and outside experts to review the strategy and planning process. This technique works best when a long-term relationship has been established with the expert so that he or she has extensive familiarity with your business. To be both effective and efficient in reviewing the strategy the expert should have these characteristics:

- Be familiar with your business
- Be familiar with the IT industry
- Be familiar with your customers
- Be familiar with your competitors
- Have entry and access to industry benchmarking

When used, expert review is often done in the form of a panel of at least three experts. Of particular importance are the review of the commitment plan and the change management plan. A strategy is of little value unless it can be successfully implemented. The change management plan and the commitment plan are critical enablers to successful execution. This technique may be applied at the completion of the assessment or the strategy steps.

External Perspectives Check

The purpose of an *external perspectives check* is to test the strategy from the perspectives of key external constituencies. Typical external perspectives would include questions such as these:

- Would stockholders want to own a company with this strategy?
- Will competitors be afraid of a company with this strategy?
- Will employees be excited by a company with this strategy?
- Will your customers find a compelling reason to do business with a company with this strategy?
- Will other companies wish to form alliances with a company with this strategy?
- Will suppliers want to develop preferred cooperation relationships with a company with this strategy?

For each of these questions, a convincing argument in the affirmative should be developed. If such an argument cannot be developed, the strategy's shortcomings need to be corrected.

Simulations

Simulations are computerized executions, or simulations, of the strategy. By building a software business model, the strategy may be "tested." This approach permits trial-and-error practice, what-if analysis, and learning—when it is still easy and painless to learn and improve. A good simulation has the following attributes:

- It is played by decision-makers.
- It is built on a realistic model of how the competitive market operates.
- It includes "game theory" algorithms to develop player moves.
- It includes strategy frameworks to help analyze actions.
- It includes a competitor team in role.
- It mimics real-world options.
- It has a rigorously defined set of measurable outputs by which to judge results.

Simulation playing offers the following benefits:

- Iterative learning
- Trial-and-error improvement of strategy
- Understanding of the dynamic interplay of strategies
- Improved tuning of strategies
- All the benefits of prototyping
- Team building

Along with scenarios, simulation is one of the best ways to prepare the management team for vigilance.

Be prepared and you will be lucky.

Sun Tzu, The Art of War

Simulations are one of the few methods available that let you test the strategy for correctness by executing it without the possibilities of harm but with the possibilities of great improvement.

Valuation Check

Financial performance remains the premier measure of business success. It is therefore mandatory that financial performance be one of the key measures of strategy correctness. A strategy cannot be correct if it does not meet the financial goals of the business. Consistent with whatever measures (payback, ROI, net present value, cash flow, shareholder value, IT as percent of sales) are used to evaluate IT performance, the strategy should be evaluated financially to see that it meets or, better yet, exceeds whatever financial hurdles have been established. Market success as measured by financial success is the reward for an excellent strategy. It is through financial measures that the clinical outcome of efforts is assessed.

A caveat is required. While financial valuation is important, strategic actions remain difficult to quantify. There is a continuing debate in the strategic planning community on how best to determine the financial value of a strategic plan. A common-sense way to address this problem is to make a simple value assessment. Given your current business scope and set of strategic positions, are you sure that if you invest in this strategy to achieve the proposed business scope and positions that you will get your money's worth? Will you receive value for your investment? Will you have nourished and created a set of sustainable competitive advantages that will generate the accident of success? Isn't this the central question?

Conclusion

These five techniques provide assistance in judging the correctness of the strategy. Perhaps one more that should be added is extensive draft read-outs throughout the organization. By engaging in extensive communications with staff members and their wide range of views, improvements can be made and buy-in can be promoted concurrently.

Summary

Being involved in an industry that has enjoyed such continual growth and technological innovation, many members of the IT community forget that the IT industry is littered with business failures. Many seemingly successful companies have enjoyed, in retrospect, only temporary success. Unable to change with the times, their success was passing. Their failures were failures of strategy.

Table 6.10 summarizes the techniques explained in this chapter. Sixteen methods are available to test the strategy for quality. It is strongly recom-

Table 6.10 Quality Methods

QUALITY METHODS		APPLICABLE STRATEGIC PLANNING STEP	
Classification	**Technique**	**Assessment**	**Strategy**
Logical relationship checks	Conclusion/strategy statement check		X
	Objectives/strategic moves check		X
	Owner/strategic moves check		X
	Champion/strategic moves check		X
Completeness checks	Strategic areas check		X

(continues)

Table 6.10   *(continued)*

QUALITY METHODS		APPLICABLE STRATEGIC PLANNING STEP	
Classification	**Technique**	**Assessment**	**Strategy**
	Business P's check		X
	7 "S" check		X
	Strategic intent check		X
	Time-line check		X
	Directives/assumptions check		X
	Key findings check		X
Correctness checks	Devil's advocacy	X	X
	Expert review	X	X
	External perspectives check		X
	Simulations		X
	Valuation check		X

mended that they be used to ensure the quality of the strategy. A strategy without quality is useless. If you are not willing to invest in quality, you are not prepared to invest in strategic planning.

> *So it is said that good warriors take their stand on ground where they cannot lose. Ground where one cannot lose means invincible strategy that makes it impossible for opponents to defeat you.*
>
> *Sun Tzu,* The Art of War

An "invincible strategy" is a strategy infused with quality.

CHAPTER 7

Administration

The purpose of this chapter is to understand the issues involved in administering the strategic planning process. Strategic planning is a process. One can argue that it is the most important capability of an organization because it provides the direction and context for all other IT business activities. It therefore must be implemented and managed with concern for quality, speed, participation, and clarity.

Strategic Planning Method Critique

The strategic planning method, which has been explained, is not without its critics. The "totality" of the approach subjects it to criticisms of being bureaucratic and painstakingly slow, preventing "learning by doing," promoting a bias for thinking rather than a bias for action, not being action-oriented, and, perhaps worst of all, it is fatally flawed because it is fundamentally based on attempting to plan for an uncertain future with reasonable certainty.

Alternative methods of strategy development are proposed that emphasize hustle, accelerated decision making, a "do something and do it quickly" attitude, attack each and every opportunity, strategy in real time, and act-do-learn-refine. The alternative approaches are action-oriented and are based on two premises:

- The future is not foreseeable.
- The only way to learn is to do.

While these arguments are attractive and appealing, the defense of the presented method is based on the view that the IT business is one system and that strategy must operate comprehensively at the system level or dysfunction will be inevitable. A business provides only a superficial delusion of consisting of parts; it has a clearly knit unity. Just as one cannot touch any part of a bowl of Jell-O without the whole thing quivering, one cannot change parts of a business without the other parts being affected. The challenges of obtaining and maintaining commitment, achieving alignment, developing core competencies, capabilities, and sustainable competitive advantages, and stimulating winning behaviors are long-term endeavors. These arguments also miss an important point. The most critical benefit of strategic planning is not the plan but the process of focused thinking about the organization. By learning the planning methods and becoming strategy literate, the management team internalizes strategy and acts strategically on a daily basis. While strategic planning does not itself qualify as the basis of competitive advantage, its consequences do.

It is an interesting paradox that the impeccable logic of the strategic planning process, the rule of reason, also serves as the basis for its most severe criticism, most clearly stated: What benefit is derived from investing in time-consuming perfect logic when dealing with an ever faster-changing and unknowable future? This argument also misses the point. It is not the case that rationalist-based strategic planning is perfect; it's just that it's the best of the available alternatives. While the "ready-aim-fire," "hustle," and "empowerment" promoters provide appealing arguments, after the rhetoric ends there is little substance on which to build. How do they suggest that you create competitive advantage, core competencies, and leverage? They don't provide any prescription; somehow they are just supposed to occur. It is not the case that rationalist-based strategic planning should be embraced because of its state of perfection; it should be embraced because of its relative superiority.

Sun Tzu (*The Art of War*), while encouraging speed, adaptation, and surprise, envisioned them occurring within the context of an overall-guiding plan:

> *If you have no ulterior scheme and no forethought, but just rely on your individual bravery, flippantly taking opponents lightly and giving no consideration to the situation, you will surely be taken prisoner.*

Ad hoc actions without forethought, design, and an integrative purpose are nonsense.

The core problem with the nonrationalist school of strategy is that beneath its superficial appeal as a strategy of action, it is, correctly understood, a philosophy of hopelessness and impotency. The days of decision are at hand, and you must surface your *weltanschaug:* What is your outlook, your worldview of strategy? Do you believe that "their victories were not flukes," or do you believe that "their victories were flukes"? Do you embrace the Nietzschean philosophy that "He who considers more deeply knows that, whatever his acts and judgments may be, he is always wrong," or do you believe positive change can be a consequence of premeditated planning? This is the pivotal question.

In reality, the conflict is often artificial; the disagreement is one of degree of formality. Even the most ardent proponent of hustle must, even if only done dynamically in his or her cerebellum, perform a situation analysis, reach a conclusion, decide on an objective, and define actions. His or her actions do not arise spontaneously out of nothing as did the universe in Genesis. This person also must get resources allocated (commitment) and overcome obstacles (change management). Whether one believes in rigorous formal strategy formulation or ad hoc dynamic formulation, the methods described in this book are of equal utility. What varies is the degree of formality, documentation, research, and reflection.

Nevertheless, the critique further emphasizes the need to implement strategic planning in a world-class manner. This is not easily done. Barriers include the following:

- Translating analysis into succinct and precise conclusions, objectives, and moves
- Organizational skepticism of a process that is future-oriented
- Organizational preoccupation with tactical survival
- Cultural defense of "what is" currently being done
- Lack of competency in strategic planning methods at all levels of the organization
- A culture that equates strategy to IT strategy only
- Politics, politics, and more politics of implementing a new process

To minimize the pain, here are some guidelines for designing the strategy process.

The Players

Figure 7.1 illustrates the major participants in the strategy process. The executive strategy team, lead by the CIO, is responsible for developing the strategy. Successful strategists think holistically and abstractly, accept ambiguity, work well with models, think in metaphors, are open-minded, unbiased, humble, research-oriented, curious, and worried. They are worried because they

Figure 7.1   The players.

understand the ephemeral nature of success and the need to constantly change.

If you can always remember danger when you are secure and remember chaos in times of order, watch out for danger and chaos while they are still formless and prevent them before they happen, this is best of all.

Sun Tzu, The Art of War

Strategists, unlike most, understand that the time to plan for major innovations is at the high points of success when time and resources are abundant—not at the point of crisis when time and options are limited.

The strategist understands that the prosperity and bounty that the organization enjoys is under constant attack. The jungle always stands ready to reclaim civilization. The strategist is never content with "what is." "What is" is the legacy of those who have come before, and it must be continually refreshed to remain vital. The bounty and prosperity of "what is" buys but fleeting time against fortune. The strategist is never self-satisfied. While accountants count revenue, programmers count function points, marketers count accounts, and operations count outages, strategists count advantages.

A team of "Art of War" strategists has three attributes:

1. They create unique analytical frameworks to understand the current situation.

2. Members have internalized strategy—their thoughts, actions, and perspectives are strategy-centric.

3. Members have achieved a strategy state of being—strategy is not super-imposed on them; they emanate strategy.

They achieve a state of heightened involvement with the business wherein their personal destiny and the fate of the business are intertwined.

In *The Divine Comedy*, Dante explains that the Inferno, Purgatory (Hell), and Paradise (Heaven) are not geographical places to which the immortal soul migrates after earthly death. Instead, they are "the state" of the soul after death. The soul does not go to its afterlife; it becomes, takes on the condition of its afterlife. This must also be the notion of strategic thinking: a notion of unity. Strategic thinking is not something appended or super-added to the strategist's intellect; it is the condition of the intellect.

The distinction between strategic thinking and a strategic plan is therefore evident. Strategic thinking is the real-time analysis, understanding, and reaction to events through dynamic mental invocation of strategic frameworks. All is seen, understood, interpreted, and reacted to through strategic frameworks. A strategic plan is a point-in-time summary, a bookmark, of strategic thought. Because strategic understanding is continual, a strategic plan as a reflection of strategic thought is always subject to revision based on events.

> *The multitudes know when you win but they do not know the basis. Everyone knows the form by which I am victorious, but no one knows the form by which I ensure victory. The science of ensuring victory is a mysterious secret. Victory is not repetitious, but adapts its form endlessly.*

> *Sun Tzu,* The Art of War

Other Players

The support team provides the support function to the strategy team. They are responsible for managing the process, maintaining the process documentation, providing expertise in methods, preparing strawpersons and drafts for strategy team review, coordinating meetings and read-outs, conducting quality control, coordinating education, and guiding and facilitating debate. A competent support team is a critical success factor for the process.

Stakeholders represent key middle- and lower-level members of the organization hierarchy who provide input and advice and are the primary implementers of the strategy. Stakeholder buy-in is critical to success. One cannot expect middle and lower management to implement what they have had absolutely no say in and do not understand.

Data Collection

Strategic planning is a data-intensive activity. Processes must be developed to provide recurrent data that provides intimate knowledge of the actual situation. For each business area of interest, a data collection process (see Figure 7.2) must be designed and implemented that identifies the following:

- Exactly what data is required
- Who owns the data
- The frequency of collection
- The format of collection

Data collection must occur on a scheduled basis. Obviously, without quality data, the entire planning process is compromised.

The methods of data collection used should encourage direct participation by as many people as possible. Focus groups, informal discussions, presentations, and open e-mail can be used effectively to gather information as well as formal and scheduled processes. While broad participation should be encouraged and all ideas entertained, all ideas should be incorporated into the planning only in proportion to their wisdom. Some people reason fallaciously that "because all people are equal in some things," that all "people are equal in all things." This is the fallacy of composition (see Table 3.31). When personal opinion is equated *a priori* to reason and vision based on a fallacious view of

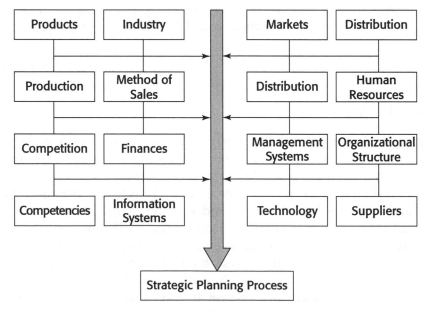

Figure 7.2   Data collection.

organizational democracy, pseudo-equality dilutes reason and vision and yields mediocrity.

What is of interest to our research is not what anyone thinks—opinions are of minimum strategic value—it is what someone knows. The ante to participate in the strategy debate is reason (convincing arguments) and vision (insight or imagination). If we abrogate insistence on basing debate on intellectual faculties (reason and vision), then equal consideration must be given to revelation, superstition, provincialism, or any other irrational criteria. Perhaps then we should add a seance to the planning process and improve the perfection of our efforts by conjuring up Sun Tzu and Machiavelli (how wonderful!) as our advisors. We could also burn at the stake as heretics any witches or warlocks who disagree with our findings—how convenient and permanent a method for forcing alignment. One can quickly see where admittance of irrationality leads.

Calendar of Events

The strategy process is best managed and communicated by publishing a master calendar of events. More detailed schedules of events may also be published to amplify the details for the items on the master schedule. Figure 7.3 illustrates a running 12-month calendar that is published monthly. Key items on the calendar are as follows:

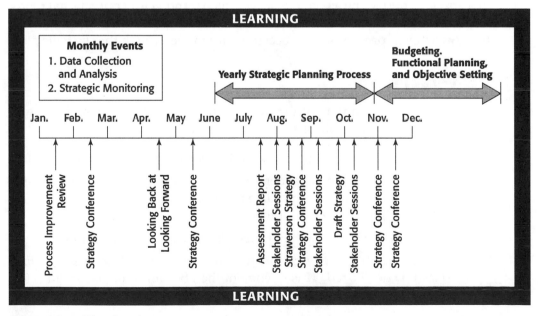

Figure 7.3 Calendar of events.

Mid-June through October. The yearly strategic planning steps of assessment and strategy are performed.

Mid-January. A process improvement review is held to review the previous year's activities and propose improvements in the overall strategic planning process.

Quarterly. A strategy conference is held where action owners present plans and progress.

Mid-April. A "Looking Back at Looking Forward" conference is held to review the accuracy of historical forecasts and assess ways to improve forecasting.

Monthly. Data is collected and strategy is monitored.

The entire strategy process takes place against a background of continuous learning, both formal and informal, to support the maintenance of fresh, open, and fluid mental models in accord with the times and circumstances.

Extendibility and Process Linkage

The proposed strategic planning process is highly modular with well-defined interfaces (conclusions, positions, business scope) The process can therefore be easily extended to interlock multiple strategy processes. While being extensible, the process must also be designed to feed and direct downstream dependent processes. Strategy should direct organizational objective setting, capital investments, budgeting, customer service plans, and yearly operational plans. Feedback loops and monitoring processes must be developed to ensure that the downstream processes are proceeding in symmetry with the strategic plan.

Deliverables

There are four key outputs of the assessment and strategy steps of strategic planning. These outputs are as follows (see Table 7.1).

- The *assessment report* is generated at the conclusion of the assessment step.
- A *strawperson strategy* is generated as the initial output of the strategy step. Its purpose is to accumulate the ideas to date into a structured format to facilitate plan development.
- A *draft strategy* is a complete strategy being circulated for comment.
- After the draft strategy comments are collected and analyzed, a *final strategy* is developed. This document then becomes the basis and reference for all downstream planning activities.

Execution outputs consist of normal project management reports.

Table Z1 Deliverables

DELIVERABLE STEP	ASSESSMENT REPORT	STRAWPERSON STRATEGY	DRAFT STRATEGY	FINAL STRATEGY
Deliverables				
Business scope	Current	Future	Future	Future
Strategic positions	Current	Future	Future	Future
Conclusions	Complete set			
Strategy statements		Complete set	Complete set	Complete set
Objectives		Complete set	Complete set	Complete set
Strategic moves		Complete set	Complete set	Complete set
Logical quality control checks		x	x	
Commitment plan			Complete set	Complete set
Change management plan			Complete set	Complete set
Completeness quality control check			Complete set	
Strategy valuation statement			x	x

IT and Strategic Planning

Strategic planning is a process that lends itself to improvement through the intelligent use of IT. IT support can vastly improve the quality, efficiency, effectiveness, and timeliness of the effort. Table 7.2 provides a taxonomy for business applications. Strategic planning would fall into the "about the business" class of applications. Table 7.3 summarizes the types of IT technology that are most opportunistic to deploy in support of strategy work.

Implementing a strategic planning process within an IT organization is a four-step process consisting of these steps (outlined in Table 7.3):

1. **Assessment.** Understanding how strategic plans are currently formulated and executed. What is the process used, who participates, and what analytical methods are favored? Does a business scope exist? Are there managed positions? What types of execution monitoring and vigilance are used? At the completion of this step, the analyst should have a complete answer to the question: "What are they doing and how are they doing it?"

2. **Design.** The design of a customized strategic planning process to meet the needs of this IT organization. Research must be done to determine how the process described in this book is to be modified to meet the particular culture and style of your organization. Gap analysis can then be done to understand the chasm between where the organization is currently and where it should be in the future. At the completion of this, the analyst should have a model of the three-step strategic planning process that the organization will adopt and the necessary steps to transition it there from its current processes.

3. **Preparation.** Doing the necessary one-time "startup" activities of education, data collection processes, initial business scope definition, consultant briefings, initial positioning, and kickoff strategy studies to enable

Table 7.2 Application Classification

BUSINESS PRACTICES							
THE BUSINESS APPLICATIONS				**ABOUT THE BUSINESS APPLICATIONS**			
Online Transaction on Processing (OLTP)	Operational Support Systems (OSS)	Business Process Automation (BPA)	Time-shared	Modeling	Information retrieval	Ad hoc reporting	Decision support
Transaction processing				Information sharing			

Table 7.3 IT and Strategic Planning

IT TECHNOLOGY	STRATEGIC PLANNING APPLICATION
Word processing software	Preparation of documentation
Project management software	1. Management of strategic planning process 2. Evaluation of strategic plan
Presentation graphics	Presentations
E-mail	Announcements, communications, meeting notices, reminders, distribution, solicitations, etc.
Imaging	Collection of information about external business environment (market forecasts, articles, financial statements, etc.)
Groupware	Collaboration, information sharing
Video conferencing	Meeting facilitation
Financial and simulation software	Forecasting, modeling, and spreadsheets
Internet	Communication and document sharing and exchange
Artificial intelligence	Rule-based models
Database access (remote terminal emulation access)	1. Industry newsletters 2. Library access 3. Competitor and financial databases 4. Clipping services 5. Internal databases
Strategic planning application software	Process automation through software products that have packaged the various strategic planning models

an orderly first execution of the strategic planning process. At the completion of this step, the organization is postured to execute the new strategic planning process.

4. **Execution.** Execution of the new strategic planning process of assessment, strategy, and execution per your design and preparation.

As has been strongly suggested before, the biggest hurdles in implementing change will be resistance to change and a shortage of commitment. It is therefore incumbent for the successful strategic planning process implementer to carefully include in his or her design a well-thought-out change plan and commitment plan to support his or her efforts. Strategic business planning is a radical departure from the way in which most IT organizations have traditionally planned. One must anticipate frozen mental models, overt resistance, and passive resistance. Be of strong courage and always remember, "It is best to win without fighting." Use indirect means to facilitate change and acceptance.

In priming the management team for the strategic planning process, it is essential to impress on them the importance of what they have chosen to undertake. The desired end state of strategy, deep and far-reaching strategies that position you for assured success, cannot be achieved without proper preparation, process, and commitment. If you do not master strategy but pretend to manage through strategy, you create a fraud. A charlatan, you will create problems even greater than those from which you had hoped to escape. Your actions will be in vain. The choice of mastery is the only valid alternative.

Communication

The strategy team cannot be omnipresent. Omnipresence is an impossibility; absence of it is therefore not a fault, but the cause for the requirement of a communication plan. The strategic plan is not a secret. While certain details of it may be restrictive, the strategy cannot serve as the context for push-down empowered decision making if it is known to only a select few. The empowered masses can either become the "aimless empowered" who, without guidance, do their best and accidentally align in actions, or they can be the "focus empowered" who share a common strategic agenda. Should they wander about in awe of a great but hidden purpose without fathoming it? What advantage is accrued by a stealth strategy?

Administration is responsible for developing a communication program that ensures the strategy is communicated throughout the organization in detail appropriate for each job function. What is not known nor understood cannot be implemented. Because you want the strategy implemented, you must ensure wide pollination of the strategy message.

Fundamental to successful communication is the concept of *procedural justice*. Procedural justice is the extent to which the dynamics of a process are judged to be fair by those who have to implement the actions and, even more importantly, by those who are affected by the actions. Procedural justice involves taking communication actions to engage, explain, and clarify expectations. It invokes feelings of respect, participation, and fairness. Extensive research indicates that change goes much more smoothly and there is enhanced voluntary cooperation and spontaneous initiative when procedural justice is included in the communication plan. For maximum benefit, it must be applied throughout the entire strategic planning process.

Summary

Strategic business planning is the highest level of decision making for the business. It provides direction, focus, and purpose as a business continually strives to move closer to its strategic intent. Because it is such a crucial business process, the administration of the effort is important to overall business success.

Successful implementation of strategic business planning hinges on the following critical success factors:

Education. The affected community must be educated in the process, strategic planning methods, and roles and responsibilities.

Stakeholder commitment. The strategy team must be committed to strategic business planning as the vehicle of strategic business management.

Linkage. Downstream processes must be linked with and measured by their support and execution of the strategic plan.

Competency. The support team must be competent in the strategic planning process and methods to develop organizational respect and credibility.

IT. The use of IT to infuse the process with quality, speed, effectiveness, and efficiency.

Learning system. The design of both a formal and informal learning system to continually challenge and update the mental models of the strategy team.

These items must be done to ensure success.

CHAPTER

8

Epilogue

Unfortunately, business schools do not routinely graduate the greatest entrepreneurs; neither do the most pious monasteries regularly serve as the spiritual birthplace for saints. Likewise, neither this book nor any other can instantly provide sufficient tutoring and insight to transform you into a "great IT strategist." It would have been very satisfying to commence this paragraph with the phrase "Now that we are learned strategists," but such is simply not the case. At best, we are aware of the possibilities, we understand the approaches, and we are energized to increase our proficiencies.

We are aware that the future can be planned for, influenced, and shaped. It is understood that there exists a rich and robust set of frameworks, models, and analytical tools through which we can discover and develop the possibilities. We are energized to master the merging of strategic planning and IT through doing. We have a new clarity of the importance and purpose of IT, and we fully appreciate that its contributions are too critical to be left to the novice prowess of those who can't understand and those who won't understand what lies before us, however unclear.

The therapy prescribed in this book, the marriage of strategic planning methods and IT, is cause for optimism. IT is not some exotic and unique business resource. The rich techniques of strategic management can be applied to use it effectively and efficiently. Some, however, are not optimistic. They believe that the root problems with IT lie not in the arena of strategy but in the immaturity of IT. They believe both IT as an engineering discipline and the level of hardware, software, and communications sophistication are simply too immature to serve as the foundations of business advantage. I believe that they are wrong. They are wrong because the fundamental problem is not one of immature technology but one of the absence of strategy.

On reflection, the strategy problem is not so much that the IT community continues to be a poor strategist, but that it never was required to bother with strategic thinking. The first 30 years of commercial IT supported monopoly hegemony over centralized and mystique-oriented IT technologies. What was required was functional expertise, efficient operations of expensive MIPS, storage and memory to maximize utilization of resources, nursing the IT mystique of being "special and different (sorcerers)," and showing up. All of that is now in massive transition. We are subject to competition, the internal business and IT economy requires us to be market-oriented, the new and emerging technologies of IT both obsolete our skills and move IT technology away from the data center, and users have an ever-growing understanding of IT; the sorcerer's apprentices are becoming quite capable themselves. In the absence of continued good fortune, like all others subject to the stress of competition, we must adopt and proceed with strategy as our guide. We must learn to observe, think, interpret, analyze, plan, and act strategically.

The need for strategic planning thus originates in the dynamics of three variables: *change, uncertainty*, and *complexity*. If change was minimal, the future was highly predictable, and the complexity level of IT technology was declining, then strategic planning would not be necessary. Conversely, when change is rampant, uncertainty is prevalent, and complexity is growing exponentially, strategic planning is required to provide direction, guidance, and flexibility to the organization. It is this latter situation that confronts the IT organization of today.

But where are we to focus our attention? Given limited time and resources, should we focus on capabilities? Or should it be core competencies? Or perhaps commitment or maybe the human resource architecture? What should be the soul of strategy? The answer is obvious; it must be all of them. While different strategic frameworks take on temporary preeminence at a particular time in accord with events, strategy is the discipline of aligning the whole toward a unified purpose. Neglect creates dysfunction.

When you can attack anywhere and defend everywhere, then your strategy is complete.

Sun Tzu, The Art of War

Time and circumstances have not abridged, abrogated, or nullified this requirement; the heart of strategy is completeness. "But we can't, we have neither the time, resources, nor concentration to create such an exhaustive strategic plan; it is too great a burden," you protest. You are in error and still do not grasp the deeper truth. It is just the opposite. It is when you manage the business in a day-to-day tactical manner that you carry the burden of Atlas. When you manage the business strategically, the burden lifts and you can ascend to ever greater accomplishments. As your strategic prowess grows and matures in completeness, winning becomes ever easier, yielding more time and energy to even greater stratagems. This is the promise of strategy.

So what have you learned; what is strategy? Strategy is choice: making choices in the present to position for the future. Strategy is change: moving the organization from where it is to where it needs to be. Strategy is leadership, and leadership is strategy.

> *The lives of the people and the order of the nation are in the charge of the generals. When their assistance is complete, the country is strong. When their assistance is defective, the country is weak.*
>
> *Sun Tzu*, The Art of War

Strategy is foresight: the deep intellectual challenge of trying to see and understand when the future is still "formless," communicating that foresight, and mobilizing the organization to act. Strategy is a process in motion, unending and never complete, constantly adapting to be in accord with events. Strategy is holistic understanding of all the functions of the business—including all, neglecting none. Strategy is alignment: creating a shared competitive agenda and preempting misalignment. Strategy is leverage, multiplying and amplifying each benefit. Strategy is an art, assembling a plan from a puzzle of missing and irregular pieces. Strategy is commitment, perseverance in the face of obstacles and hurdles. Strategy is qualitative over quantitative; all can add and subtract, but few can see before existence. Strategy is the means of *fairly* creating and maintaining an *unfair* marketplace advantage. Strategy is the Quixote quest to command (or at least bend) fortune rather than be a timeless victim of it. Strategy is learning: maintaining a fluid mental model in accord with ever-changing times and circumstances. Strategy is seeding many experiments now to cull the best ideas for commitment later. Strategy is confronting the hard issues of change; the problem of leadership is not acknowledging the need for change, the challenge of leadership is choosing, from the endless permutations, when to change, how to change, and most importantly, what to change to. Strategy is following reason (and vision) to wherever they lead: incremental change for times of stability and radical change for times of discontinuity. Strategy is preparing yourself to win the endless race, the race between the organization's speed of adaptability and the swiftness of change in the marketplace.

While strategy is all these things, these definitions are incomplete. Strategy transcends them all. Perhaps Sun Tzu (*The Art of War*) best captures the true meaning of strategy:

> *Strategy is important to the nation—it is the ground of death and life, the path of survival and destruction, so it is imperative to examine it. There is a way of survival, which helps and strengthens you; there is a way of destruction, which pushes you into oblivion.*

Such is the essence of strategy.

Aphorisms of Strategy

The teachings of Sun Tzu and Machiavelli provide an enduring set of fundamental principles of strategy. These teachings provide a broad schema of strategy on which one can build specific strategies consistent with the times. A philosophy of strategy would be more akin to theology than the traditions of science. It is for this reason that the insights of the greatest strategists maintain their integrity, constancy, and relevancy over time. While adhering to these teachings does not guarantee success, violating them almost certainly ensures failure. When the advice of a current pundit or guru contradicts these maxims, one should proceed with caution. The continuing validity of these insights has been demonstrated over 2000 and 500 years, respectively. While the details of implementation have changed radically, the generic principles have remained remarkably constant. Sun Tzu and Machiavelli have stood the test of time. Most of the advice and counsel given by modern day pundits is forgotten by the end of the seminar coffee break. This may be exaggerated, but only slightly so. Those who give advice that violates the teachings of these masters indict and convict themselves of being false prophets by their own words.

The majority of aspiring strategists would be much better off studying the teachings of Sun Tzu and Machiavelli than most teachers of business or IT strategy. The teachings of Sun Tzu and Machiavelli provide a holistic mental framework from which to master and manage the strategy problem. Their teachings provide a deep and far-reaching philosophy of strategy. Relatively, most contemporary strategists are but temporaries who provide partial insights and procedural mechanics. Time will demonstrate whether they provide persistent value. There is more to be learned in the classics section of the library than the business section.

As we enter the 21st century, information technology will assume a position of preeminence among the engineering sciences. It will assume such a position because the vast majority of worldwide commerce and personal communications and entertainment will be information technology-centric. As stated before, information technology success will first demand success as a strategist. Information technology success will be an accident of your strategic wisdom. One day you should expect to find in the classics section of your library a volume entitled *Philosophia Strategiea (A Philosophy of Strategy)*. On that day, strategy will take its rightful place among the philosophical issues of life. In the interim, we proceed with the best advice available, the superb and timeless advice of Sun Tzu and Machiavelli.

Advantage

Struggle means struggle for advantage; those who get the advantage are victorious.
. . . It is best to win without fighting.

Alignment

Those whose upper and lower ranks have the same desire are victorious. . . . Those skilled in strategy achieve cooperation in a group so that directing the group is like directing a single individual with no other choice. . . . Employ the entire force like employing a single individual.
Strategy is a problem of coordination, not of masses.

Alliances

If you carry on alliances with strong countries, your enemies won't dare plot against you. . . . Make informed alliances . . . compete for alliances. . . . If you do not compete for alliances and helpers, then you will be isolated with little help.

Assessment

Compare the strength of the enemy with your own and you will know whether there is sufficiency or lacking. After that, you can assess the advisory of attack or defense.

The one with many strategic factors in his favor wins, the one with few strategic factors in his favor loses. . . . Observing the matter in this way, I can foresee who will win and who will lose.

If you know others and know yourself, you will not be imperiled in a hundred battles; if you do not know others but know yourself, you will win one and lose one; if you do not know others and do not know yourself, you will be imperiled in every single battle.

The considerations of the intelligent always include both harm and benefit. As they consider benefit, their work can expand; as they consider harm their troubles can be resolved.

Attack what can be overcome, do not attack what cannot be overcome. . . . To advance irresistibly, push through their gaps. . . . So when the front is prepared, the rear is lacking, and when the rear is prepared the front is lacking. Preparedness on the left means lack on the right, preparedness on the right means lack on the left. Preparedness everywhere means lack everywhere. . . . Attack where there is no defense.

Benchmarking

Men nearly always follow the tracks made by others and proceed in their affairs by imitation, even though they cannot entirely keep to the tracks of others or emulate the prowess of their models. So a prudent man must always follow in the footsteps of great men and imitate those who have been outstanding. If his own prowess fails to compare with theirs, at least it has an air of greatness about it.

Change

It should be borne in mind that there is nothing more difficult to handle nor more doubtful of success, and more dangerous to carry through than initiating change. The innovator makes enemies of all those who prospered under the old order, and only lukewarm support is forthcoming from those who would prosper under the new. Their support is lukewarm partly from fear of their adversaries, who have the existing laws on their side, and partly because men are generally incredulous, never really trusting new things unless they have tested them by experience. In consequence, those who oppose the changes attack vigorously and the defense made by the others is only lukewarm.

Time sweeps everything along and can bring good as well as evil, evil as well as good.

Confront them with annihilation, and they will then survive; plunge them into a deadly situation, and they will then live. When people fall into danger, they are then able to strive for victory. . . . When they have fallen into dire straits, they obey completely.

Commitment

When an army goes forth and crosses a border, it should burn its boats and bridges to show the populace that it has no intent of looking back.

Competition

What causes opponents to come of their own accord is the prospect of gain. What discourages opponents from coming is the prospect of harm.

So the rule is not to count on opponents not coming, but to rely on having ways of dealing with them; not to count on opponents not attacking, but to rely on having what can't be attacked.

What motivates competitors is profit . . . what restrains competitors is harm. . . . Wear enemies out by keeping them busy and not letting them rest . . . make them rush about trying to cover themselves, they will not have time to formulate plans. . . . To keep them from getting to you, attack where they will surely go to the rescue.

Execution

Some rulers are fond of words but do not transfer them into deeds.

. . . One must never allow disorder to continue so as to escape a war. Anyhow, one does not escape; the war is merely postponed to one's disadvantage.

Foresight

What the aware individual knows has not yet taken shape. If you see the subtle and notice the hidden when there is no form, this is really good. What everyone knows is not called wisdom. A leader of wisdom and ability lays deep plans for what others do not figure on.

The multitudes know when you win, but they do not know the basis. Everyone knows the form by which I am victorious, but no one knows the form by which I ensure victory. The science of ensuring victory is a mysterious secret. Victory is not repetitious, but adapts its form endlessly.

A general must see alone and know alone, meaning that he must see what others do not see and know what others do not know. Seeing what others do not see is called brilliance, knowing what others do not know is called genius.

If you can always remember danger when you are secure and remember chaos in times of order, watch out for danger and chaos while they are still formless and prevent them before they happen, this is best of all.

All wise rulers must cope not only with present troubles but also with ones likely to arise in the future and assiduously forestall them. When trouble is sensed well in advance it can easily be remedied; if you wait for it to show itself any medicine will be too late because the disease will have become incurable. . . . Disorders can be quickly healed if they are seen well in advance (and only a prudent ruler has such foresight); when, for lack of a diagnosis, they are allowed to grow in such a way that everyone can recognize them, remedies are too late.

Leadership

The lives of the people and the order of the nation are in the charge of the generals. . . . When their assistance is complete, the country is strong. When their assistance is defective, the country is weak.

Act when it is beneficial, desist if it is not. Anger can revert to joy, wrath can revert to delight; but a nation destroyed cannot be restored to existence, and the dead cannot be restored to life. Therefore an enlightened government is careful about this. This is the way to secure the nation.

Learning

Test them to find out where they are sufficient and where they are lacking. Do something for or against them, making opponents turn their attention to it, so that you can find out their patterns of aggressive and defensive behavior.

Maneuverability

Adaptation means not clinging to fixed methods, but changing appropriately to events . . . those who can face the unprepared with preparation are victorious. The ability to gain victory by changing and adapting to the opponent is called genius.

Some win through speed. . . . Use swiftness to wear them out. . . . Get the upper hand through extraordinary swiftness . . . be as fast as the lightning that flickers before you can blink your eyes.

Market Research

What enables an intelligent leader to overcome others and achieve extraordinary accomplishments is foreknowledge. All matters require foreknowledge.

Organization Design

Structure depends on strategy. Forces are to be structured strategically based on what is advantageous.

There is simply no comparison between a man who is armed and one who is not. It is unreasonable to expect the armed man should obey the one who is unarmed. . . . This is how we can distinguish between innovators who stand alone and those who depend on others; that is between those who to achieve their purpose can force the issue and those who must use persuasion. In the second case, they always come to grief having achieved nothing. Whenever they depend on their own resources and can force the issue, then they are seldom endangered.

Outsourcing

. . . The arms on which a prince bases the defense of his state are either his own, or mercenary or auxiliary. Mercenaries and auxiliaries are useless and dangerous. If a prince bases the defense of his state on mercenaries, he will never achieve stability or security . . . the reason for this is that there is no loyalty or inducement to keep them on the field apart from the little they are paid and that is not enough to make them want to die for you . . . I conclude, therefore, that unless it commands its own arms, no principality is secure, rather it is dependent on fortune since there is no valor and no loyalty to defend it when adversity comes.

Planning

In ancient times, skillful warriors first made themselves invincible.
    It is easy to take over from those who do not plan ahead.
    Those who are good at getting rid of trouble are those who take care of it before it arises.
    Those who face the unprepared with preparation are victorious.
    . . . A victorious army first wins and then seeks battle, a defeated army first battles and then seeks victory.
    Be prepared and you will be lucky.
    If you have no ulterior scheme and no forethought, but just rely on your individual bravery, flippantly taking opponents lightly and giving no consideration to the situation, you will surely be taken prisoner.

Positioning

In ancient times, those known as good warriors prevailed when it was easy to prevail. Their victories are not flukes. Their victories are not flukes because they position themselves where they will surely win, prevailing over those who have already lost.

Quality

So it is said that good warriors take their stand on ground where they cannot lose. Ground where one cannot lose means invincible strategy that makes it impossible for opponents to defeat you.

Strategist

They do not wander when they move. They act in accord with events. Their actions and inactions are matters of strategy.

Strategy

There are only five notes in the musical scale but the variations are so many that they all can't be heard. There are only five basic colors but their variations are so many, that they all can't be seen. There are only five basic flavors, but the varieties are so many that they can't all be tasted. There are only two basic charges in battle, the unorthodox surprise attack and the orthodox direct attack, but the variations of the orthodox and the unorthodox are endless. The unorthodox and the orthodox give raise to each other like a beginningless circle—who can exhaust them.

Go forth without having determined strategy and you will destroy yourself in battle.

When your strategy is deep and far-reaching, then what you gain by your calculations is much, so you can win before you even fight. When your strategic thinking is shallow and nearsighted, then what you gain by your calculations is little, so you lose before you do battle. Much strategy prevails over little strategy, so those with no strategy cannot but be defeated. Therefore it is said that victorious warriors win first and then go to war, while defeated warriors go to war first and then seek to win.

Strategy is important to the nation—it is the ground of death and life, the path of survival and destruction, so it is imperative to examine it. There is a way of survival, which helps and strengthens you; there is a way of destruction, which pushes you into oblivion.

Success

Some princes flourish one day and come to grief the next without appearing to have changed in character or in any way. This I believe arises because those princes who are utterly dependent on fortune come to grief when their fortune changes. I also believe that those who adapt their policy to the times prosper and, that those whose policies clash with the times do not. This explains why prosperity is ephemeral. . . . If time and circumstances change, he will be ruined if he does not change his policy. If he changed his character to the times and circumstances, then his fortune would not change.

Surprise

In battle, confrontation is done directly, victory is gained by surprise.

Vision

What everyone knows is what has already happened. What everyone knows is not called wisdom. What the aware individual knows is what has not yet taken shape; what has not yet occurred. If you see the subtle and notice the hidden so as to seize victory when there is no form, this is really good.

The frustrating challenge confronting all of us who seek strategic wisdom is that there is a chronic surplus of Salieris and an ever-acute shortage of Mozarts. Salieri was a highly successful and celebrated court composer in the time of Mozart. While honored and acclaimed in his day, time judged him mediocre and sentenced him to obscurity. Mozart, his antagonist, was controversial but brilliant, and time promoted him to the status of musical genius. Salieri was but a run-of-the-mill composer who offered fleeting value while Mozart, less honored in his day, offered persistent value. I am fearful that many who present themselves as oracles of strategic advice are but modern day Salieris. Few have known strategy as deeply and in the manner as have Sun Tzu and Machiavelli, the Mozarts of strategic thinking. All strategic wisdom starts with them.

APPENDIX

B

Glossary

7 "S" model An analytical model that views strategy as a strategic fit between the strategy and structure, style, systems, staff, skills, and shared values.

Alignment Coordination, collaboration, and perseverance toward a shared set of objectives.

Argument An inductive or deductive method of reasoning.

Assessment The activity of developing a clear and thorough understanding of the business situation from both an internal and external perspective.

Benchmarking Measuring and comparing against the recognized best.

Bottleneck analysis The analysis of value chains for bottlenecks.

Business model Answers to the basic questions of what a business will sell, how it will relate to its customers, and how it will make money.

Business P's Product, position, promotion, price, people, and process.

Business scope Defines the essential characteristics of a business.

Capabilities The business practices and processes that deliver value and satisfaction to the customer.

Champion The executive responsible for assisting an owner.

Change management plan Planned actions to preempt resistance to change.

Commitment plan A set of actions taken to establish credibility.

Competitor analysis Strategic analysis of a competitor.

Conclusions Explicit statements describing the state of the business.

Contingency plan A plan to deal with a low-probability event whose occurrence would prevent achieving an objective.

Core competency The collective learning of the organization.

Critical success factors Specific competencies, capabilities, processes, etc., that an organization must do well to succeed.

Delphi technique A process to develop a consensus forecast about the future.

Devil's advocacy A quality control method where a subteam critiques the strategy.

Directives and assumptions Givens that govern the strategic planning decision making.

Driving force Primary determiner of products and services and markets.

Dynamic Issues Management Process used to mange unforeseen events of strategic importance.

Economy The processes used to govern the production and exchange of goods and services.

Emergent strategy Realized strategies that were not intended. They emerged from the dynamics of the situation.

Execution Putting the strategic plan into motion.

Expert review A quality control method where external experts review the strategy.

Five Forces A framework that asserts that the competitive position of an industry can be understood by the relationships between five forces of supplier power, buyer power, threat of entry, substitute products, and rivalry.

Fortune Serendipity or good luck.

Fragmentation The partitioning of a marketplace into groups of customers with extremely distinct needs.

Frozen mental models A view of the world that is not subject to change.

Gap analysis The difference between a current state or position and a desired state or position.

Goal An interim objective.

Human resource architecture A framework for translating values into behaviors.

Implementation program parameters Rules, guidelines, etc. that are to be followed in implementing a strategic move.

Implementation programs and projects Specific projects to execute the strategy.

Information form, function, and movement A way of understanding IT as the relationships between information form (sound, data, image and text), information functions (presentation, processing, storage, transport and OAM), and information movement (people to people, people to machines, and machines to machines).

Intended strategy The explicit product of the strategic planning process.

Kano Methodology A methodology for causing marketplace dislocations by mastering excitement customer satisfaction attributes and driving them to threshold attributes.

Key findings Knowledge learned during the assessment step of particular value.

Kondratiev waves A theory developed by Dr. N. Kondratiev that asserted that productivity in Western societies was fueled by a dominant era technology.

Learning Continued improvement of process by feedback from actual experiences.

Leverage The multiplication of the benefit of a strategic move.

Market leader The manner in which a business follows or leads its customers.

Market opportunity analysis The use of a set of analytical methods to determine the attractiveness of a market opportunity.

Matrix analysis Analyzing through matrices the intersection of two strategic business areas.

Mental model How both an individual and an organization view and understand the world.

Mission The purpose of the business.

Monitoring Periodic review of implementation programs for corrective actions.

Objectives Specific measurable and dated states to be achieved.

Owner The person responsible for making a strategic move happen.

Payoff matrix A diagramming technique to illustrate the "payoff" for different actions.

Pivot position A position from which many alternative actions may be taken.

Politics The divisions of an organization into special-interest groups.

Position An illustration of a strategic area along one or more strategic dimensions.

Product map A set of graphs and matrices that together illustrate the position of a product.

Rationalist school of strategy Strategy is the product of rational, purposeful, conscious, and deliberate acts.

Reach/range/maneuverability architecture The IT architecture of the business that permits anyone, anywhere, at anytime to access (reach) any shareable information object (range) or service.

Realized strategy Those intended and emergent strategies that worked in practice.

Reengineering Radical redesign of business processes with the employment of IT.

Root cause analysis Decomposition of a problem into the segments of symptoms, problem, and etiology.

"S" curves A life-cycle growth and decline pattern common among technologies.

Scenarios The definition of possible futures.

Segmentation Partitioning a market based on common needs.

Simulations Computerized simulations of a strategy to test it.

Situational analysis The collection and analysis of information about the business for the purpose of developing conclusions about the state of the business.

Strategic alignment A state of coordination, perseverance, coordination of effort, and commitment.

Strategic business unit A collection of related businesses with a distinct mission, a market, a set of competitors, a set of products, profit and loss responsibility, and a dedicated management team.

Strategic intent Long-term ambition of the business.

Strategic move An action to achieve an objective.

Strategic planning A plan to provide direction, concentration of effort, consistency of purpose, and flexibility as a business moves to continually improve its competitive position.

Strategic thinking Dynamically analyzing and understanding events in terms of strategic frameworks.

Strategic thrust A repositioning goal for a product.

Strategy (a.k.a. strategic plan) Identifying the desired future state of the business in terms of a business scope and future positions, objectives, strategic moves, a commitment plan, and a change management plan.

Strategy coherence A method to force alignment across strategic moves.

Strategy statement A concise and directive statement of strategic direction.

Structure follows strategy Organizational design follows the definition of a strategy and enables that strategy.

Sustainable competitive advantage The distinct asset, skill, capability, resource, process, etc. that creates a capability gap between the company and its competitors.

SWOT analysis (strength, weakness, opportunity, threat) Analysis of the business from the perspectives of strengths, weaknesses, opportunities, and threats.

Tactics Detailed actions taken to implement a strategic move.

Theory/hypothesis A theory is a systematically related set of statements, including some law-like generalizations that both explain and predict phenomena. A hypothesis is a predictive assumption derived from a theory which is testable for validity.

Unrealized strategy Intended strategies that fail.

Value chain analysis A method for understanding the translation of resources through processes into final products.

Values What the business believes in.

Vigilance Continual proactive scanning of the environment for events requiring strategic responses.

Vision A guiding theme that articulates the nature of the business and its intent for the future.

Customer Satisfaction Measurements

In the competitive business environment in which more and more internal IT organizations will find themselves, customer satisfaction is one of the most important, if not the most important, dimension of strategic success. Table C.1 provides an example of the types of measures that need to be implemented. A level of measurement granularity must be selected. For example, for production transaction processing systems, performance measurement may be done by transaction within time of day (peak/nonpeak) or within time of month (critical/noncritical). These measures must then be linked to the Kano Methodology to direct investment. Table C.2 provides a more detailed expansion of customer service measurements for fault management.

Table C.1 Strawperson Customer Satisfaction Measurements

CUSTOMER VIEW OF PRODUCT	INTERNAL PROCESS VIEW OF PRODUCT		
Customer satisfier	Satisfier driver (product attributes)	Value chain process	Correlated measurements
Quality	Availability	Fault management	1. (Total, average, median) number of outages per unit of time 2. Mean time to repair by problem severity level 3. Mean time between failures 4. (Total, average, median) time unavailable per unit of time
	Performance	Service delivery	1. (Average, median, 90% <, 95% <) interactive response time (end to end, internal host) 2. Percent of batch jobs completed on time 3. Percent of input and output delivered on time
Price	Cost	Asset management	1. By asset category, percent utilized 2. By asset category, percent utilized and billable 3. By asset category, forecast to actual
		Vendor management	1. Percent of key vendors with best price agreements 2. Percent of key vendors delivering components ready to integrate
		Cost management	1. Value chain function cost per billable unit 2. Value chain function head count per billable unit
Pre-sales service	Order management	Product provisioning	1. Percent of orders completed on time 2. Percent of orders backlogged 3. Percent of orders revised
Post-sales service	Billing accuracy	Billing	1. Percent of debit/credit corrections 2. Percent of customers notified of billing errors 3. Percent of billing inquiries closed with one call 4. Percent of billing entries late billed

Table C.2 Detailed Fault Management Matrices

Domain: All Systems Images
Time Period: All Scheduled Hours
Period: Calendar Month

MEASUREMENT TYPE	MEASURE	DEVELOPMENT AND TEST ENVIRONMENTS				PRODUCTION ENVIRONMENTS							
		Prime shift		All scheduled hours		Prime shift				All scheduled hours			
						Critical monthly processing periods		All periods		Critical monthly processing periods		All periods	
		Result	Target	Result	Target	Result	Target	Result	Target	Result	Target	Result	Target
System time between failures	Mean												
	50%<												
	80%<												
	95%<												
	100%<												
System time to repair	Mean												
	50%<												
	80%<												
	95%<												
	100%<												
System outages	Number												

329

Index